O

PRISON LIFE AND REFLECTIONS;

OR,

A NARRATIVE

OF THE

ARREST, TRIAL, CONVICTION, IMPRISONMENT, TREATMENT, OBSERVA-
TIONS, REFLECTIONS, AND DELIVERANCE

OF

WORK, BURR, AND THOMPSON,

WHO SUFFERED AN

UNJUST AND CRUEL IMPRISONMENT IN MISSOURI PENITENTIARY,

FOR

ATTEMPTING TO AID SOME SLAVES TO LIBERTY.

THREE PARTS IN ONE VOLUME.

BY GEORGE THOMPSON,

ONE OF THE PRISONERS.

HARTFORD:
PUBLISHED BY A. WORK.
1855.

THE INTERIOR OF THE JAIL IN PALMYRA, MISSOURI.

WE were confined in this place eleven weeks, previous to our being taken to the Penitentary at Jefferson City. SEE PAGE 18.

PREFACE.

READER, do you know the heart of a *prisoner?* Are you a friend of *convicts?* If not, you may not be much interested in the following pages—for they tell you much about the inside of a prison, and its suffering inmates. They are not confined entirely to the strict history of Alanson Work, James E. Burr, and George Thompson—they tell you much about other prisoners—much about the officers—something about the Governors, and Legislators, and Ministers of a slave State —they tell you a little about the poor slave—the spirit of slaveholders—the influence and effects of slavery, and numerous incidents, with brief reflections on various subjects.

You will not charge me with telling something about somebody of whom I know nothing—or with attempting to describe imaginary scenes—or telling of something that occurred, nobody knows where—for " I speak that I do know, and testify that I have seen," heard, and experienced. The book is principally a compilation from our prison writings—mostly from my own, as the greater part of that which came from the pens of my " companions in tribulation," has been lost, or I was not able to obtain it.

However, as we all lived together, I was constituted, by mutual consent, the scribe or secretary.

In my journal, I recorded for all. When we came into our cell at night, if either had seen or heard anything during the day, that was of interest, he made it known, and it was recorded by the secretary. Of the writings which are lost, the most valuable are their letters, which were written from time to time, and would give a better idea of their individual feelings, than I can in my own language—yet our feelings were so similar, and so nearly in unison did our hearts beat, that the reader must feel when reading mine, that he is in . them reading the feelings of the other two brethren.

I have been obliged to omit and pass by much that I desired to insert. Much of my journal—many letters, and various incidents, have been excluded.

The reader need not expect connexion of subjects, or beauty of style, or elegance of language, or logical reasoning. I have mentioned things generally as they occurred, in their order, without regard to connexion. In some places, I have classified things of the same kind. The style, and language, are the spontaneous overflowings of my soul—in words which most readily presented themselves to my mind. And I have endeavored to present everything in its proper, natural light. The whole has been written in great haste, amid cares and anxieties.

When speaking of other prisoners, I have withheld all names, for reasons I need not mention. When speaking of officers, I have given names. And I think no one can charge me with partiality—I have endeavored to give both sides. When they acted like men, I have said so—when they played the part of brutes, or demons, I have mentioned it. If they were kind, I have given them credit—if cruel, it is charged against them. If they complain of any one, they must complain of themselves—if Missourians are disgraced, or condemned, they themselves have done it. I have recorded *facts*.

If they are enraged, because the world has looked in upon their abominations, let the thought that God will expose them to the *universe*, compose their troubled consciences. If they are vexed with themselves, because they have so long harbored an enemy in their midst, let me say to them, as they said to us—"Just mind *your own business*, next time, and let other people alone." They must have been fools indeed, to suppose they could press a viper to their bosom without being wounded—or tread on coals, without being burned—or that they could lay open their hearts before a "*dyed-in-the-wool abolitionist*," and not expect that it would be laid before the world—or that an opossum is dead, merely because he does not kick, and squall, when beaten by his enemy.

If the reader is not a Christian, he will here see the excellence and importance of that religion, which will support and cheer its possessor in all possible conditions in life. And oh! that he may be influenced to choose a friend, who will never forsake—a guide who will never mistake.

If he *is* a Christian, I trust he will, in the following pages, learn the secret of having the mind kept in "perfect peace," though billows dash, and tempests roar—of being filled with a "joy unspeakable, and full of glory," though surrounded by a darkness as dense as Egyptian—and of "rejoicing in the Lord *alway*," though he "die daily"—namely, *trusting in God, rationally, sincerely, implicitly*, and *continually*.

The book has not been written to make money, nor to get a name—but to *do good*. I felt it to be my duty to write such a book, long before I left my cell—and *there* the most of it was written.

I have endeavored to exhibit our own feelings—as also those

of our enemies. I have tried to exhibit the circumstances, and influences, by which we were surrounded, that the grace of God might the more be magnified, in our preservation from the jaws of destruction—in our deliverance from the oppressor's power.

Reader, you will here see the faithfulness of God to his promises—you will see the unfaithfulness of man. You will get a glimpse at the sufferings of a portion of your fellow creatures, of whom, perhaps you never thought much, and if by reading this book, you shall be induced to "*remember them in bonds as bound with them,*" I shall not have spent my time in vain.

Part first, includes an account of the time we were in the County Jail, trial, sentence, &c.

Part second, comprises about sixteen and a half months, under the government of John Gordon and William Burch.

Part third, embraces the remainder of our history, under James Brown, Capt. Richmond, Blaine, and Co., &c.

That every one who reads the following pages, may be stimulated to labor more zealously for suffering humanity, is the desire and prayer of

THE AUTHOR.

Oberlin, April 9, 1847.

NOTE.—The First Edition having met with so speedy a sale, and the testimony of those who have read it, being so uniform, that it has been a great blessing to their souls,—another Edition is sent forth to the world, which I desire to leave as a token of my *love to the Slave,* and the cause of SUFFERING HUMANITY, while I go far hence to labor, and die, for the degraded of other lands.

GEORGE THOMPSON.

Oberlin, December 10th, 1847.

CONTENTS

PART FIRST.

CHAPTER I.

CHAPTER II.

CHAPTER III. *V·· ·c̸ //. 26·27· 28*

CHAPTER IV.

CHAPTER V.

CHAPTER VI.

Verse 11 96

PART SECOND.

CHAPTER I.

CHAPTER II. Verse 1/ 122-123

Verse ff. 142-143

CHAPTER III.

Verse f. 149-1

152-153

Verse 4;   319
               326
               323
               347
               3-5
            360-361
            375

PART THIRD.

CHAPTER VII.

CHAPTER VIII.

CHAPTER IX.

CHAPTER X.

CHAPTER XI.

CHAPTER XII.

PRISON LIFE AND REFLECTIONS.

PART FIRST.

CHAPTER I.

MOTIVES, ARREST, IMPRISONMENT, ETC.

THE subjects of this narrative are ALANSON WORK, JAMES E. BURR, and GEORGE THOMPSON. The former was a man about forty years old—having a wife and four children—he was living at the Mission Institute, for the sake of educating his children, and training them up for usefulness. The other two persons were young men studying for the ministry.

The Mission Institute being situated near the Missis-sippi River, and just across the River from a Slave State (Missouri), we could, as it were, hear the crack of the overseer's whip—the shrieks and groans of those who were suffering its cruel inflictions. Their earnest cries for help—their sighs for deliverance—their importunate entreaties, as they rehearsed to us their tales of woe, reached our ears, and our hearts melted with pity, while the resolution was formed to respond to their call; and if need be, risk our own liberty and lives to effect their rescue.

Inasmuch as we desired mercy from the "God of heaven," should we at any time, be brought into trouble, we did not dare to shut our eyes, nor our ears, nor our hearts, nor to restrain our hands from delivering them out of their troubles—remembering, "Whoso stoppeth his ears at the cry of the *poor*, he also shall cry himself, and *shall not be heard*." We knew if we were in their condition, we should feel very thankful to any one who would render us the desired assistance ; and then calling to mind the gospel rule, " As ye would that men should do to you, do ye even so unto them," we felt impelled to lend a helping hand. Likewise the command to love our neighbor as ourselves, impressed upon us the same obligation—so that we made up our minds, with earnest prayer for divine guidance, and anxious consultation, in view of these and many other principles and commands, to make the attempt—to " rid them out of the hand of the oppressor."

About the first of July, 1841, James, with another brother, made a tour of mercy into Missouri, which resulted in an agreement with two slaves, to meet them at a certain point on the river, on a certain evening, to assist them across the river, on their way to freedom. On the day appointed, we went, arriving at the place about the middle of the afternoon. Alanson and James went into the country to view and reconnoitre, while I remained in the skiff to fish, and await their return. While thus alone my prayer was, " O Lord, I beseech thee, send us *good speed* this day." And we now feel that the prayer was abundantly answered—though in a very different way from what we expected. We desired the liberation of the slaves. God knew how to bring it about, better than we did. We longed to be instrumental in doing something for our brethren in bonds. God granted us our hearts' desire. And a happy day for the slaves of Missouri was it, when we were taken captive, bound, and incarcerated in their midst. This was placing the light just were it was most needed—in the dense darkness—and where it made visible the abominations that prevailed. Blessed be God ! After dark, a number of slaves came to Alanson and James, in the prairie, and pretended they were going with them. They had proceeded but a short distance, when on a sudden, the slaveholders arose out of the grass, with their rifles, and took them prisoners—placing the muzzle of their guns to their breasts, and threatening, " I will shoot him any how,"— but the mercy of the Lord prevailed. They were bound.

and taken to a house, where they were kept, while the blood-hounds came in hot pursuit of me. I was in the skiff. At first three or four slaves came, and approaching the bank very cautiously, one asked, " Are you a *friend?*" I replied, " I am." I had talked with them but a short time, when suddenly I heard another kind of a salutation, " Come out of that, or I'll blow you through !" I looked up, and two guns were pointed at me from the bank. I was obedient to my new commanders—dropped my fishing pole, and marched up to them, in secret ejaculations committing myself to God, to do with me as He saw best. Though the thing was so perfectly unlooked for, and unthought of, the Lord stood by me, saying, "*fear not*, I am with thee"—and my mind was calm—my soul composed—and my faith unwavering, that all was right and for the best. Of what was before me, I could form no conception, but felt that infinite wisdom and goodness would lead me. Sudden death seemed quite probable, amid their numerous threats to shoot me ; " but none of these things moved me, neither counted I my life dear unto myself, so that I might finish my course with joy" in the holy cause of suffering humanity. To die for the slave I felt willing, if this was the thing needed—the Lord being Judge.

I was bound, and marched barefoot, over hubs, roots, and stones. Host after host came with all speed to meet us, and " the earth rang again" with their fiendish yells. It seemed almost as if the infernal regions had been uncapped, and had vomited forth their legions to hail our approach, as if some long dreaded monster had been captured. But oh ! how sweet it was to feel that they could not go beyond what my Father should kindly and wisely permit. This kept me in peace.

After they had eaten supper, they marched us some miles through the woods to another house. They made the slaves lead us by a rope, and sing " corn songs."* It seemed as if the very forests themselves were moved at the bursts of such unearthly sounds—and if there

* See page 18, for explanation.

were any wild beasts in the region, they must have fled
for their lives, to their caverns, or dens, or more distant
forests.   When we came to the house, we were marched
round it time and again ; and when we halted in front
of the piazza, the old grand-father and mother, and children—old and young, male and female, came out in
their night dresses to gaze upon the wonderful monsters.
The old grandfather, tottering just on the verge of the
grave, gave a little vent to his boiling soul, in the ex-
clamation—" Ah ! you gallows-looking devils !"   After
their curiosity was somewhat gratified, we laid us down
upon a feather bed, on the floor—all tied together—and
slept sweetly till morning.   We awoke refreshed and
strengthened to endure the reproaches and sufferings
which were before us, with patience, fortitude, and I
trust submission.   That morning a man came in to see
us, who asked many questions, and made threats of
shooting us on the spot.   He was a professor of religion
—seemed very much excited, and had hard struggles to
keep from drawing his pistols on us, but " the good hand
of our God upon us," saved us from his burning fury.

At the breakfast table, we asked a blessing on our
food, while the landlady and others stood by.   She
seemed almost horror struck, that such wretches as we
should *pray !*—for she looked upon us as *monsters of
iniquity*.   The poor woman seemed to have some idea
of the numerical strength of the Abolitionists—for said
she, " They are as thick down there in the bottoms, as
maggots in a dead horse, watching for slaves."   And so
terrified was she at the thought, that she had not been
able to sleep soundly for two weeks !   Poor woman !
Who can help *pitying* one who is obliged to live in
such constant fear ?

After breakfast, a crowd gathered round, who questioned us in many things, and gave vent to their raging
bosoms, in sneers and reproaches.   We were then tied
together, and led by the slaves (to mortify us) five miles,
to Palmyra.   The city was moved at our approach, many
saying, " Who are these ?"   " Well, you've made a fine
haul," &c.   In the court house, we had a mock trial

before a magistrate and were "thrust into prison," to await the sitting of the court, two and a half months from that time. After they had left us, we knelt down, and committed ourselves to God, imploring his guidance and protection, feeling that He had wise purposes to accomplish by this unintelligible dispensation.

The following from Alanson to a brother in Quincy, will give further particulars.

♦ LETTER.

DEAR BROTHER:—I am a *prisoner* in a land, where to tell a man, made in the image of his Maker, that he has a right to *freedom,* is a crime of the deepest dye. James and I walked four or five miles back into the country. The first human being that we saw, was a woman and her son hoeing tobacco. James spoke to her, and I walked on. He found that she wanted to be free, and agreed to help her. We next came to a house ; James went in, and learned from a slave (the whites being absent), that the slaves he had seen before, were in the field alone. We went to them, it being now sunset. We asked them if they were going—they told us they were, and that one, living a mile from them, where they had some clothes to get, was going with them, and that they would come three hours after dark. We were seen by white men while with the slaves. After dark, we came and waited, anxiously listening for the signal. After some time we heard a distant whistle, and by answering repeatedly, soon came to five slaves—three or four miles from the river, on a bottom prairie. After salutations and professions, we started in a foot path for the river, rejoicing in the prospect of helping the oppressed to liberty and happiness—when, suddenly three men arose from the high grass. The slaves having betrayed us, now seized us, bound our hands, and marched us back in triumph to the first house. A company then started, and after two hours, returned with Brother George,—the slaves singing and shouting—making a song for the occasion. We were soon put on the march for the residence of one of the party, two or three miles distant—each of us being led by a slave—others following, weaving the past and present circumstances, with our future prospects, into a song, which they made to echo through the woods, to the great satisfaction of their masters and friends, who were on horseback. When we arrived at the house, we were marched around, and stared at as little less than Infernals. The language used, I will not attempt to describe. The next morning we were tied together, and taken on foot to Palmyra—being led by slaves, and escorted by fifteen horsemen. We were taken to the court house, a warrant issued against us—witnesses examined, and we committed, for *stealing slaves* (!) We were not permitted to speak for ourselves, but were taken to Jail, and the doors closed upon us. Under these trying circumstances we looked up to Him, who came to preach "deliverance to the captives, and the opening of prison doors to them that are bound," and found the promise of God precious to our souls.

Soon after dark, the Sheriff, Jailer, and others came in, and made us fast to a chain fifteen or sixteen feet long. One end of the chain was made fast to the wall. Near the other end, an iron was put through a link and riveted around my ankle. Brother Burr was placed about two feet from me, and George about two feet farther.

To his wife, Alanson wrote :

" MY DEAR WIFE :—I write from Palmyra Jail. The wall is about four feet thick, made of two thicknesses of hewed logs with one foot of stone between them, and the outside brick. We feel that God is here. Send to us if you can. We have asked for a Bible, a Hymn Book, and paper. They reply, 'yes,' but do not. (Nearly a week elapsed, before we could get a Bible from any of them—at length an impenitent Lawyer brought us his.) Our enemies rejoice over us. Pray that we may be Christ-like. Be not troubled : the Lord will provide, and protect. Myself and companions sit on the floor. We have three or four (very poor) blankets for a bed. Our food is corn bread and bacon, which we eat with our fingers; but we have meat to eat which they know not of—'*a contented mind* is a continual feast.' I am not anxious about myself, but feel that 'tribulation will work patience.' I feel that if you will trust in God, He will make 'all things work together for your good'—and this affliction prove a blessing to you, and give an impulse to the cause of truth and mercy. We know not our destiny, but fear the worst, and trust we shall be prepared for it."

On the same piece of paper I wrote : " Dear Brother Hunter, if we could see you and Mr. Warren, we should like it. It is evident they are determined to send us to Jefferson. Two men were sworn who testified falsely. Can you come? We rejoice in our chains. May the Lord direct."

On the same I wrote to the church of which we were members.

" Brethren and Sisters, you may think we repent the step we have taken. *Not at all.* We feel that we are in chains for *Jesus' sake.* The 2d, 3d, and 4th chapters of 1 *Peter* are very precious to us, as also the whole 'Letter of our Father.' We feel that *good* will result from our being here—that our Master knows best what kind of a school we need. We can now sympathize with the slave as never before. We know how the chain feels. But our trials are light, compared with his. Pray for us. Our only hope is in God. Pray in faith— God will hear.

" Yours in bonds,
" GEORGE."

About the same time (July 15), I wrote to M. C., " I am now separated from you very unexpectedly—but however the case may turn, I know the ' Judge of all the earth will do right'—and that ' all things shall work together for good to them who love God.' You may think that I am unhappy. *By no means.* I am happy in my Savior."

July 19. I wrote to the same :—" It seems very strange for me to date a letter to you from *Prison.* Yet so it is. Did you ever imagine such a thing? I had thought of trials and persecutions when we should be far among the heathen, and had imagined the thing possible, that I might be cast into prison in Illinois, ' for conscience toward God,' but such a circumstance as this I now realize, I had not thought much about. Yet be assured, I am happy in my Savior. I have an unshaken confidence that this shall turn out for my good, for yours, and for the good of Christ's cause. With this confidence can I be troubled or uneasy? ' Be careful for nothing ; but in everything, by prayer and supplication with thanksgiving, let your requests be made known unto God, and the peace of God, which passeth all understanding, shall keep your hearts and minds, through Christ Jesus.'—*Phil.* iv. 6, 7. This is very sweet. My Bible is more than ever precious. Pray for my mother, that this may be sanctified to her present and eternal good. Try and make the same profitable improvement of it yourself. Don't be over-anxious. Roll the care upon Jesus, and there let us leave it. Exercise an unwavering confidence in his providence. Our kind Father has wise reasons for putting me here ; and ' what thou knowest not now thou shalt know hereafter.' We should be willing to be in just that school that He sees we need. I hope I am willing. Pray that I may learn thoroughly and faithfully the lesson He intends I shall learn. When I have learned my lesson well, then I know He will take me out. And should I desire to leave school before I get my lesson? Oh no. I do desire that discipline and instruction which will best qualify me for the greatest usefulness.

" Yours, in chains and gospel bonds,
" George."

CHAPTER II.

EXTRACTS FROM ALANSON'S JOURNAL.

JULY 14-17. Visited often by the sheriff and many others, but still without the means of communicating with our friends. Had many anxious thoughts about my family, from whom I can hear nothing.

18. *Sunday.* Our prison was the " house of God and the gate of heaven" to our souls. In the forenoon George talked to our companions (two colored and one white man) about the prodigal son. In the afternoon he spoke on the Judgment day. Jesus was with us, and fed us with the bread of heaven. To me it was the most precious Sabbath I have enjoyed for many months.

19. Feel willing to go to the penitentiary or wherever the Lord wills. This afternoon Esq. Warren and Brother Hunter came in to see us. (The first we had seen or heard of any of our friends since leaving home.) We were happy before, but our happiness was increased on seeing them, and learning the sympathy in our behalf.

The goodness of God and the kindness of friends broke my heart. We received books and paper. (We had received from the jailer in the forenoon one sheet of paper for us all, on which I was writing a joint letter to the Church, which was, at the time, published extensively—but now I have it not. This letter the jailer gave to Brother H., without showing it to the sheriff; but its being published, and the consequent excitement being so great, we could not, after that, get any more letters to or from our friends through the sheriff.) After consultation they went out to see what could be done for us. In the evening we attended prayers as usual. As we closed, C. I. (the free black), of his own accord, broke out in prayer.

20. Have been here a week to-day. Brother H. and

Esq. W. came in, consulted about employing other counsel, and, much to our comfort, brought us a table and chairs. Had with them a precious season of prayer.

21. No visitors to-day. The horse-thief is an unpleasant companion. The truth does not reach his heart. I find the night season the most precious to my soul. When all are still, I have sweet communion with Him who heareth the sighing of the prisoner.

22. Found great satisfaction in reading the lives of Bunyan and other men, who suffered for well-doing.

23. Feel the want of exercise and pure air. The horse-thief held a conversation with a stranger outside, the most abominable and profane, which makes it very unpleasant. O! "gather not my soul with sinners, nor my life with bloody men."

25. *Sabbath.* Brother George described heaven and hell, and pressed on our impenitent companions the question, whether they would leave their sins and go to heaven, or have them and go to hell.

26. The Lord hears prayer; blessed be his name. My chain feels light this morning. O! let me not trust in man. Last evening being monthly concert for the oppressed, we remembered those in bonds, as *bound with* them. After lying down to rest, and while thinking of those bound in more galling chains than ours, we overheard a conversation, by which we learned that six slaves had crossed the Mississippi, the night before, and that some persons were preparing to go to the river to intercept other fugitives. Gladly will I wear this chain till it galls my ankle to the bone, if thereby the slave may go free. (We all felt so and rejoiced.)

27. We are not disturbed with company. Spend our time in reading, writing, meditation, and prayer.

28. Health good. Peace of conscience and the presence of my Savior. Our prison is a pleasant place, although we are surrounded by that which is filthy and abominable.

31. Have seen none of our friends to-day, as we expected. Our companions now stand talking with some

children in the street. The conversation is the most
filthy imaginable. Slavery seems to have corrupted the
very buds of society. It would be pleasant to be alone
This evening we prayed that if we could do John (the
horse-thief) no good, we might be rid of his company.
Just after, the jailer came in and said that the sheriff
was going to take him away in the morning.

Aug. 1. *Sabbath.* When the officers came in for
John, numbers came in to gape upon us. They staid
some time, and we were obliged to hear their revilings,
oaths, and filthy conversation. When they were gone,
we hoped to have a still, pleasant, and profitable Sabbath. We were disappointed. The room overhead was
occupied, most of the day, by a vile woman, and two
more than vile would-be gentlemen; yet the Lord was
our " sun and shield." George spoke on *Ps.* lxxxiv.
The tabernacle of God appears more lovely, because we
cannot enter therein. In the afternoon he spoke from
Is. i. 3. Showed the great goodness of God in reasoning with men, and our guilt in not knowing and considering. Surely the Lord has placed us here that we may
consider.

2. *Election day.* Numbers came to the window.
The colored men conversed with them through the grates,
which was very unpleasant. I sometimes imagine we
are confined on the brink of the pit and hear the sounds
that come therefrom. O! how lovely do holiness and
heavenly purity appear, when contrasted with the abominable, unholy, and filthy scenes that surround us.

3. Felt strengthened by the promise that " as my
day is so my strength shall be."

5. Had the privilege of seeing my wife and Edwin
Lovejoy.* There were numbers at the door, by whom
we learned the hatred and excitement against us.
Though we are in the lion's mouth we find honey in the
carcase. " Who shall harm us if we be followers of
that which is good ?"

7. Have not been well for the three past days.

8. *Sabbath.* In the afternoon there was a company

* A little son about four years old.

playing cards over our heads, who mocked at and reviled the worship of God. " Father, forgive them."

9.   An unpleasant day : felt gloomy ; but in the evening the love of God filled my heart. The guard take delight in making a noise. They thump and dance over our heads, mocking and deriding our worship. We pity, and pray for them—"they know not what they do." Saw Mr. Craig, from Quincy, at the jailer's door. He went from there to the sheriff's but was not permitted to see us. I feel that this is the very school I need ; and though I sometimes tremble at the danger that surrounds me, yet the promises of God give me strength and peace.

10.   Last night, a Mr. Berry was confined here on the alleged crime of murder, committed in Kentucky, last November.

11.   Mr. Berry obtained bail and left us. He is a slave-holder. I tried to make him acquainted with the principles of abolitionists, the rights of man, and the claims of God. He could not gainsay the truth.

" Let this fact be well considered. A man committed for the crime of *murder*, is allowed the privilege of bail within twenty-four hours of his confinement. And while he was in jail, his friends had free access to him ! besides, *he* was not considered sufficiently guilty to deserve a chain !—while our three brethren, whose offence consisted in offering aid to a few wretched slaves in attempting to escape from their degrading vassalage, were treated with all manner of insult and scorn—made fast to the prison wall with a very heavy chain riveted about the ankle—guarded by an armed force during the whole time of their confinement there—kept on the coarsest fare—denied the privilege of seeing or corresponding with their friends (except Mrs. Work and children),—and not allowed the privilege of seeing ministers of the gospel from Illinois, who called for the purpose—neither allowed to have bail ! !   The offer was, indeed, made to accept of $6,000, advanced in cash, as bail for them; but we were assured that no individual or any number of individuals out of the state, would be

accepted in such a case. And to find any in Missouri,
that would become thus responsible, was out of the
question."—*Quincy Committee.*

12. I feel that the sheriff is cruel in keeping the
letters of my wife and children from me, as some of
them contain nothing but family affairs : but I will not
murmur.

13. My body fails from confinement.

14. Find peace and strength in prayer—feel my
" inward man renewed." Then let this body fail and
die—" this corruption shall put on incorruption, and this
mortal immortality."

15. *Sabbath.* George spoke on the subject of faith,
from the circumstance of Elisha and his servant seeing
the mountain full of chariots and horses of fire. Surely
" they that be with us are more than they that be with
them."

17. Saw Brothers Van Doorne and Record, at the
jailor's. As they were starting for home (Quincy), we
hailed them. They stopped in the middle of the street
—said they were not permitted to speak with us—that
our friends were well and thought much of us. They
brought us fruit and sundry comforts.

The patrols stand in the different streets at night;
each armed with pistols, a club and cow hide. If a
white man passes he is hailed; if a negro, his " pass"
is demanded. If he has none, no excuse will answer;
his shirt must come off and the cow-hide be applied to
his back !

20. Have been unwell. Looked at death. It does
not appear dreadful, though I am so great a sinner. I
love the Savior, his law and service; and though I feel
he would prepare me a mansion on high, I would be
glad to live to train up my children, and to help the
slave ; but " thy will, O Lord, be done," for which prepare me and my family.

23. Last night, heard the guard say—" Since the
d—d rascals have been here, more niggers have run
away than ever before." They mentioned several, for
whom $50 and $100 reward was offered. It makes our

chain light to think that those of others are broken.
We believe that our being here will spread the knowledge that there *is* a road to LIBERTY. Yes, yes, bless
the Lord!

S. S. Glover, at our request, came in to see us, and
spoke respectfully to us. This is the first Missourian,
the blacks excepted, that has done so.

The foregoing is all of Alanson's journal that I have
been able to obtain. It will show of what spirit he was,
and how he bore his imprisonment. He continued his
journal till the day of trial, breathing the same spirit.
Nothing could be found in it but pity towards the oppressor and oppressed.

CHAPTER III.

POETRY, JOURNAL, ETC.

AMONG other letters, I received one from a sister, asking
me the question, why I was in prison?—which I answered
in the following manner:—

I.
"In prison! ah! why is this, my brother dear?
I was amazed and shocked, such news to hear.
What hast thou done?—thy Savior disobeyed?
That thou art thus in chains and prison laid?"

II.
Hark, sister, while to thee the cause I tell,
Why I was bound, and why now in this cell—
Why witnesses who're false are 'gainst me sworn,
And cruel men with rage and malice burn.

III.
A man by thieves was met upon his way—
Robbed, bruised, and weltering in his gore he lay—
And sad indeed the state this man was in ;
No one to help or take him to an inn.

IV.
A Levite passing where the sufferer lay,
Stopped not to pity—hastened on his way.
A priest along the same way chanced to go,
He looked, but left the sufferer to his wo.

V.
At length one came, who on him looked and *fell*,
Poured oil and wine, as by his side he knelt:
On his own beast he placed the man, relieved ;
Conveyed him to an inn, nor pay received.

VI.
" Go, do thou likewise," saith my glorious King,
" Relieve the poor, and out of trouble bring—
Where'er thou find him, lend a helping hand,
And aid him on his way to freedom's land."

VII.
In deep distress a poor man thus I found,
And offered freely to do up his wound ;
The priest and Levite scorned and passed him by—
The neighbors heeded not his mournful cry.

VIII.
Knocked down, and robbed of all, he long had lain,
By cruel men oppressed and almost slain.
With torturing stripes his back was deeply gashed,
Which oft, through spite and malice, had been lashed.

IX.
Thus groaning, weltering, and despised by man,
I heard him loudly call, " Help, if you can ;
To be delivered from this state I long,
And placed where I may sing sweet freedom's song."

X.
I listened while he told his tale of grief,
And longed to find some way for his relief,
My heart with tender sympathy was moved,
And my poor neighbor, as myself I loved.

XI.
I tried to comfort him, and poured in oil—
I told him of Victoria's happy soil—
" I'd like to go," said he, " but here I'm bound,
How can I reach that distant, happy ground ?"

XII.
" I'll gladly help you neighbor on your way—
We'll carry you by night, and hide by day."
" O! this is *good* ! 'tis *good* ! 'tis *good* !" he cried,
" I'll go with you, and with you safely ride."

XIII.
While thus engaged a dreadful voice I heard
Which threatened *death*, if from the place I stirred !
Amazed was I—my hands were quickly tied,
While hardened *robbers* stood on either side ! !

XIV.
Followed by fiendish spirits, black and white,
With hellish rage they vented out their spite—
While hundreds round us rushed, to gaze and rail,
They thrust, and locked me fast within this Jail !

XV.

Such, Sister, is the cause why I am here—
Such, why my voice you can no longer hear.
Did I in this do wrong? or sin commit,
Because I wished this man to benefit?

XVI.

My blessed Savior did I disobey,
When from this man, I crossed not o'er the way?
Because I tried the suff'rer to relieve,
Did I, by doing this, the Spirit grieve?

XVII.

Ah, no—the Dove is still within my breast,
And 'midst the raging tempest gives me rest.
The Savior smiles, and all within is peace.—
The storm and tumult, He will cause to cease.

XVIII.

"Fear not," He says to me—"keep courage good;
I will be with thee through the fire and flood;
You shall not want—I'll be to you a Friend,
And all that's needful, I will surely send!"

XIX.

Blest Savior, in thy word I will confide,
And 'neath the shadow of thy wing abide.
Now let the tempests howl, and hell engage;
Secure and safe am I from all their rage.

XX.

Come life or death—come sorrow, care, or pain—
In him I'll trust, and glory in his name.
" All things shall work together for the best;"
And soon I'll with my glorious Jesus rest.

Palmyra Jail, 1841.

Some extracts from my journal will give further particulars, and show my feelings at that time better than I can now express.

My journal, for the first month and a half is lost—as also all of James's—but the extracts given from Alanson's may be considered as expressing the feelings of each of us. We had but one mind in attempting to aid the slave, and after we were bound among strangers, and in an enemy's land, we felt but one interest. We all rejoiced in our sufferings—each sympathized with the other, our hearts beat in sweet unison, and all were willing to go to the Penitentiary, or *die*, if need be, for the deliverance of the oppressed. At home or abroad, in prison or at liberty, living or dying, we felt but one

desire, and were aiming at but one object—the good of
our fellow-men, and the glory of God.

We had been in jail but a day or two, when one of
the Guard came to the grates one night, and wished us
to sing for them a song they heard us sing once ; it was

> " Awake my soul, in joyful lays,
> And sing the great Redeemer's praise," &c.

It was *new* to them.   And we were reminded of the
Jews in Babylon, whose enemies, said, " Sing us one of
the songs of Zion."   But blessed be God, that we were
not obliged to " hang our harps upon the willows,"—
that we *could*, with joyful hearts, " sing the Lord's
song," " though in a strange land."

July 18. *Sabbath.*   In the morning a crowd came in
to gaze upon, taunt, and try us.   In my chains, with
Testament in hand, I stood before them and preached,
plainly and boldly, deliverance to the oppressed—holding before them the *Savior in bondage*, bought and sold,
whipped and abused, in the person of his " little ones,"
—the slaves—making appeals to their consciences, &c.
One of them, their chief speaker (who will hereafter
speak for himself), tried to form some pleas for slavery,
but they were dams of *quicksand*.

When we spoke of our trust in God, they sneered at
the idea of such rascals trusting in Him.   When we
appealed to his law, for our rule—they said, " You better
just let *that* alone, if you know what is good for you.
God's law is not the standard here in Missouri.   We
have laws of our own.   You better study them !"   When
we told them, " the eyes of the Lord are upon them that
fear Him, and his ears are open to their cry," they
replied, " What had *God* to do in the matter ?   What
does He care for you ?   You better trust in the laws of
Missouri," &c.

I am glad they are so honest as to own, what we have
believed, and are now more firmly convinced of, that the
law of God, in slave states, is *null* and *void*—a *dead
letter*.   Slavery tramples the Bible in the mire, nor heeds
in the least its warning voice !

When Brethren Hunter and Warren came over to see us the first time, they brought us such books as they thought would be suited to our condition—such as the Book of Martyrs, Village Hymns, Greek Testament, Pilgrim's Progress, some Memoirs, Henry and Scott's Commentaries, Christian Lyre, Manhattan Collection, &c., &c. So that we had plenty of reading and music. Considerable of our time was spent in tuning our hearts and voices in praise. At morning, noon, and night, we thus poured out our souls before the Lord.

Our singing, and happy contentment in our prison-house, much annoyed the consciences of the inhabitants of Palmyra. They said, " They are the strangest prisoners we ever had here : " " We never saw such men before : " " Hark, the rebels are singing," &c. But none of these things moved us. Though at times the guard would order us to stop our singing, try to mock or frighten us, as " servants of the most high God," we felt that we were *bound* to praise his name in *every place.*

July 24. A load came from Mission Institute. Brethren Griswold, Kirkland, and Seymour, Mrs. Seymour, and M. C., also Mrs. Work. None but Mrs. W. were allowed to look at us. We could see them walk the street, but could not speak a word to them. This was trying, but the Lord is good and kind in it all. They brought us many little comforts, which we were allowed to have,—straw bed, bedding, &c. After a long time, Mrs. W. was allowed to come in, with the sheriff, jailer, and others. She fell prostrate at her husband's feet, and wept excessively, for some time. At length, becoming more composed, she talked and prayed with us. She begged the sheriff to take off the chain —but no. She asked that they would keep *her*, and let her husband go home,—*no, no* ! The scene was affecting. We tried to comfort her, directing her to " trust in the Lord," and all would be well. Lord, be with and support her.

While they were here, a rabble gathered round, and acted like heathen. Poor, deluded, miserable men ! O, Jesus, sanctify this event to us and to them.—My faith is tried. My heart is sick, at seeing the depravity of man. Had I now no Savior, what could I do? No promises, where could I go? These disappointments are for my good. O, that I may have no will of my own.

Brother G. demanded admittance to us, as our counsel, but was denied.

26. Last night there was a rabble around the jail nearly all night, carousing, and thirsting for our blood. Night gatherings around the jail are frequent.

27. Last night great excitement about twelve runaway slaves. Some went in pursuit of them. May the Lord direct and protect the "outcasts."

28. O, the degradation of man! How sweet is the word of God! Bright and very excellent does religion appear, when I witness the conduct of those who profess it not. May we ever exhibit the true spirit of Jesus.

I should write more if I could get paper. My journal I write on old scraps, and keep it in my watch pocket. "It is all for the best."

31. Time passes very pleasantly.

Aug. 1. This morning a company came, gazed, talked, mocked, sneered. "This," said one, "is a *Gospel ship.*" Honorable appellation! *Ps.* lxxxi. and lxxxiv. have afforded great comfort to us. *Ps.* xci. has been a rich feast. What! *Angels keepers?* Yes. O, precious—delectable—sweet! Of this fountain the ungodly cannot drink.

5. Mr. Warren, and Mrs. Work, and Aunt Terrel called to see us. Mrs. W. was admitted. Aunt T. stood at the door, wept, and begged to see us, but could not. This is strange. Their hearts are made of steel —surely they cannot be flesh. Esq. W. demanded admittance as our counsel, but was denied! They came near mobbing him. Poor deluded creatures, they act more like fiends than men!

6. To M—. "I am glad you can trust me and yourself in God's hands. I am happy in lying there. His promises are as a *rock*, and strong consolation to my soul. I can see no reason for feeling uneasy or being troubled. I know my Father will do just right.

We shall one day see it, and thank him for this providence; then let us rejoice now."

8. The excitement runs high. We are a wonder to them. God will "cause the wrath of man to praise him." Glory to Jesus! I find the Book of Martyrs very interesting and profitable. I am in a palace compared with the condition of the ancient Christians. Compared with them I do not suffer at all.

Sweet Sabbath!

9. Happy to-day. Time passes pleasantly. Said Latimer to Ridley, as they were bound to the stake, " We shall this day light such a candle, by God's grace, in England, as I trust, shall never be put out." God grant a candle may be lighted in *this prison*, that shall not cease to burn, till *slavery* shall come to an end Although we are so small, insignificant, and unworthy, yet I have no doubt God will kindle a fire, that will burn and spread, not only through this region and state, but through the United States, and that will hasten the deliverance of the oppressed and the conversion of the world. O! how unworthy am I to be the brand that shall be burned to cause this light!

Dear Lord, "do with me as seemeth thee good." Let this body be tortured and killed, only spread thy truth and glorify thy blessed name. But leave me not to my own strength. Stand by me: support, and comfort me. We are unworthy to lie here. We do not deserve the honor; but my God can use feeble means, and kindle the flame. Glory to his name!

LETTER TO A FRIEND.

Palmyra Prison, August 9, 1841.

" M.——I feel as if I wanted to express my feelings to you, that you may know what is the state of my mind, and how to pray for me; and I request, that before you read any further, you will retire and pray, that your mind and heart may be in a proper frame to receive and profit by what I am about to say. Lest you may feel that I am disturbed in my mind, you may be assured that it is fixed on God. He is my stay. I feel a sweet peace within, and an assurance that He will do just right.

"To-day I have heard more of the feelings of the people here, than I have since I came. It is amazing what passions can dwell in the human heart.

"Brethren Brown and Turner came here about noon, and we talked with them through the grates. A crowd immediately gathered round, with savage wildness and hellish madness depicted in their countenances. They looked upon Brethren B. and T. with a fiendish, blood-thirsty eye, as they talked to us through the grates. When Brother B. asked, "Are you so filled with grief that you cannot eat your bread?" and I promptly answered, "No, we are happy;" they were cut to the heart, and could scarcely refrain from gnashing on B. and T. with their teeth. Brother B. remarked, "We are all praying for you, and sympathize with you, and believe God will overrule it for great good;" which stirred their rage very much. Brother T. asked James, how he felt about a "*certain subject*," which they had often talked over. James replied, "The same as usual." Fuel was only added to the flame.

"As soon as the brethren left us to get their wagon, they then gave vent to their spite and enmity, still standing under the window, where we could hear. They were running-over full. One man made a flaming speech about our feeling so happy, when we had committed such an AWFUL CRIME!—believed we *lied*—said we must have *hard consciences*, &c. Others, "They are sure to go to Jefferson." Others, "If they are not sentenced for twenty years, they will be hung here. The people will not be satisfied with anything less." Others, twenty-five years. Others thought the people would be contented with a sentence of twenty years. Others, "It will need 100 men to take them to Jefferson," &c.

"When Brethren B. and T. came back, and left the things, they again began to gather, but they drove off before all came. One cried out, "You need not come

2*

with that blacking, for they have gone." They then talked of pursuing them. But I think they did not.

"Such is a sketch of what I have seen and heard to-day. It drove me to my Bible to search for promises, and with them to the mercy seat. For a few moments my mind was a little agitated, but reflection, prayer, and the promises, calmed the tumult of my thoughts, aud brought sweet peace and consolation. I was enabled to roll my burden upon the Lord, and feel that He would sustain me, and grant me all needed grace.

"I feel that we are in the hands of God, and that He will do with us just as shall be for our best good, the good of the slave and the world. I don't know but we may be called to suffer (we have not yet suffered any), and perhaps to *die* for the slave, and for the truth of our Lord. I know that our Father can preserve and deliver us; and *will*, if that will most glorify his name (and I don't wish him to do it unless his cause will be more advanced by my life than by my death). Many holy men and women have been long imprisoned, and killed in many ways, for the name of Jesus, who, to human appearance, were much *needed* in the church, and who promised fair to do much good; but God saw that their sufferings and death would do more for his glory than their lives, and suffered wicked men to vent their fury upon them. He could have preserved them. Lovejoy's death probably did more good than he could have done by his life. I have *expected* that there must be more sacrifices upon the altar of slavery, before it would come to an end, and if God sees fit to select one, so unworthy of the honor as myself, to suffer or die in this cause, I say, *Amen.*

"GEORGE."

James, writing to Brother Turner respecting the same adds, "One said, 'It was a violation of the laws of God and man, as sure as there is a God'—that is our act. Another, 'I have concluded to hang them.' Another, 'I have determined to have them whipped,' and with many similar imprecations did they curse us. When they heard what Brother B. said, they were cut to the heart; and when they saw you were gone, they were ready to gnash on us with their teeth. But as the natural heart is opposed to God, of course it is to all good. Nothing enrages them so much as to hear of our peace and comfort. But our hope is in God. *Ps.* vii., xviii., xxii., and xlvi. *Isaiah* xli. 10—19. God's word, dear brother, appears more and more precious every day.

"When we were first taken into the jail, the jailer said to us, ' This is your house.' " We then *dedicated* it to God, for the time we should occupy it.

"We have good times on the Sabbath. I feel that God is giving us severe lessons to learn, but blessed be his name, it is good to be taught of Him."

Aug. 14. The king of Syria was an enemy to Israel, and to God's people. He sent an army to take Elisha. When Elisha's servant arose in the morning, he saw the city surrounded, and was filled with fear. Forgetting Elisha's God, he cried, "Alas, my master, how shall we do ?" He saw no way of escape. He had no *faith*, and consequently could not see. But what was the reply of one who had faith in God ? " *Fear not*, for they that be with us are more than they that be with them." This was like a Christian. With the enemy were horses, and chariots, and a host ; but with Elisha, the Almighty God, the angels, and the hosts of heaven. Why then should he fear ? What could man do unto him ? O Lord, increase my faith.

Mr. Creathe, a Campbellite preacher in Lewis Co., Mo., is here preaching. Albert says he has a slave, through whose ear he has cut a hole, where he takes hold when he whips him !!—says he has seen the hole himself. How far is slavery behind the Inquisition ?

In conversation with our jailer, he remarked, " It is no place here for a poor man ; he can't get along." No ; slavery crushes him.

16. A few nights since, a woman of vile character spent most of the night with the guard overhead. The next day I wrote a letter to the sheriff, informing him

that it was very unpleasant living so near a brothel, and
requested its removal. He gave the letter to the guard.
We overheard them read it, and say, "Now this thing
is known and she must leave the place," &c. Last
night, Esq. Wilson, captain of the guard, came in with
others, and showed out some of his spite about it. He
had his iron rod in his hand and seemed much agitated
and enraged against me. "Well, is that brothel removed yet?" said he. He evidently came to give us
a severe flogging, but dare not here in the jail. He is
much troubled.

Mr. Bess, the jailer, says they sent her away from
town soon after. So it seems the letter was not in vain.

PATROLLERS.

David foresaw and described them more than two thousand years ago, in *Ps.* lix. 6, 7, and they now answer
the description. In the 8th verse he pronounced their
sentence. They are very despicable characters.

The slaves here on the Sabbath, dress like gentlemen,
They get their clothes by extra work, done on the Sabbath and in the night, and yet "they can't take care of
themselves!" Shame on those who hide under this
leaf.

17. The Lord is my comfort. *Is.* li. 12, 13. Dost
thou, dear Lord, ask "who I am?" I am but dust—a
feeble worm—yet leave me not to fear my fellow worms,
who are also weak and shall die; nor to "forget thee,"
the Lord my Maker, though "the fury of the oppressor"
is great, and he seems "ready to destroy."

The Christian should not live in slavery, but walk at
liberty.

BLASPHEMY.

Last night, one of the guard, talking about our first
letter that was published, said, "It is *blasphemy* and
sacrilege for THIEVES to write such a letter!"

This letter was an affectionate outpouring of our souls

to those whom we dearly loved in the Lord, and with whom we had long "taken sweet counsel;" expressive of our happiness, contentment, submission, faith—asking their prayers, urging them to duty, &c.

Reader; you see how enlightened the inhabitants of slave states are, and what *clear views* of sin and virtue, reverence and blasphemy, they have! O! if you have any pity in your heart, let it move for such pitiable objects.

"Mr. Moore, the rumseller, is nearly as great a nuisance as John was. Charles and Albert seem worse than ever, and to be hardening fast. Dear Savior, preserve our souls safe from their polluting influence. Teach us how to speak and act before them.

Aug. 20. Our circumstances are such as try our souls, and make us feel the preciousness of religious society. There is so much obscene talk—so many foolish songs—and so much trifling nonsense, that, much of the time, we can read with but little satisfaction; and it is often difficult to fix our minds so as to pray with an undivided heart. For two nights past I have had precious seasons, in the silent watches, when all was still, and nothing to disturb. With the poet I can say,

> "'Tis sweet conversing on my bed,
> With my own heart and Thee."

Why should I feel anxious about my friends? Does not my kind Father sit on the throne? Am I not in his his hands? Will He not do right? Does he not know what I need, better than myself? Then for me to murmur, is great folly and aggravated unbelief. He has always done me good; and frequently I have had occasion to thank Him for providences, which at the time looked dark, and I could not understand, and I will trust Him *now*.

THE CHURCH IN SLAVE STATES.

Aug. 21. In slave states, especially, Zion is almost dead—but little signs of life left.

Slavery eats out the very *vitals*. It causes and nour-ishes pride, laziness, haughtiness, cruelty, oppression, de-ceit, fraud, theft, lying, Sabbath-breaking, drunkenness, adultery, fornication, and all uncleanness, murder, and everything that is hateful and abominable in the sight of God! It disregards all his laws—tramples them under foot—sunders, and as it were, annihilates, the principles of the Gospel; and how CAN a church, with such a monster in its bosom, grow in the grace of God? Until slavery dies, there can await the slaveholding church naught but leanness and death. Already is error and delusion sweeping through the land like a mighty flood. O Lord, how long? How wonderful, *wonderful*, that God has borne so long! Surely he hath showed us what is good—" to do justly, to love mercy, and to walk hum-bly with God." But where is this to be found in the slave states? Certainly not in Missouri—not in Palmyra.

22. How delightful the Sabbath morning! How my soul would leap for joy to meet with the saints in the sanctuary? But this is denied me! Is the Savior ashamed of our habitation, or our chains? Glory to God!—*no!* He will come even here and bless us, though man may curse and reproach, and many who profess to love Him, be ashamed to be seen communing with us.

Have taken comfort in reading my father's letter. This morning Alanson talked to us from *Isaiah* lv. 6; very good: I did not know that he could preach so well. In the afternoon, I talked from *Micah* vi. 2, 3, 8. Card playing overhead, and much noise.

23. Morning. The leaven is working—the flame is rising—the fire is spreading! May the Lord fan the flame. Last week we learned, by overhearing the guard, that the people here are much troubled on account of their slaves. Since we have been here, light has gone abroad, and some sparks have found their way into the minds of the slaves, who are beginning to walk in the light thereof *towards the river*. Said Esq. Wilson, " Since these d—d rascals have been put here, the slaves

are going off faster and *faster ;* [good, good—go it my good fellows!] and there are multitudes of *other* rascals, just like them, on the other side, ready to help the runaways along." Yes, yes, Mr. W., and they are multiplying "faster and faster," too. May the Lord protect and carry them through. Shall we murmur that we are cast here? Are we not willing to suffer for the slaves, and thereby for our master? If the leaven begins to work so soon, shall we not rejoice? Yea, Lord, carry on thine own work, in thine own way.

If the Palmyrians think to wreak their spite on all the "rascals" who are like us, on the other side, they will have a long work before them. Let them rage, and foam, and vent out hell's fume—let them imprison, revile, and menace, but let them know also, that the more they stir up fire-brands, the brighter and fiercer will they burn—the more they attempt to extinguish the flame, the hotter will it flash in their faces—the more rapidly spread and consume their two-legged property! Let them go on then. They are but spreading snares for their own feet—preparing shame to cover their own faces—using means to defeat their own purposes, and pull down what they wish to build up. Work away—work hard!

Before breakfast, Mr. Glover came in. He appeared the most friendly and gentlemanly of any one that has been here (our friends excepted), since we came. He spoke like a *friend*—said the sheriff's conduct was altogether unjustifiable—he had no right so to do—that prisoners, may, by law, have paper, &c. The sheriff came in a moment, but could not look us in the face, nor did we have time to speak with him at all. I expect he has what Bunyan calls the *gripes.*

Evening. I know not how to express my feelings, nor in what words to frame my thanks to God, for what I have seen, heard, and felt to-day. My heart is full to overflowing. Bless the Lord for his goodness. My soul exults in Him who orders all things aright, and for his own glory. His kind hand is very plain, his directing providence quite manifest.

The journal description is so lengthy, I cannot copy. A load of our friends came to see us (nine in number), bringing us many comforts, fruit, cakes, pies, bread, clothes, letters, &c. None but Mrs. W. and her children, were allowed to come in, and they were strictly forbidden to say anything to the father, or he to his family, except in a manner that all could hear! This was truly astonishing, and shows the heart-hardening and conscience-searing effects of slavery. They seemed perfectly steeled, and past feeling.

With the other friends we conversed through the grates, with great satisfaction, passing letters to and from each other, while we shook hands through the iron bars. In this way the most of our writings had to be sent out. The brethren and sisters seemed very cheerful and happy. Said one (now my wife), "I come not to weep, but to rejoice with you." And we did rejoice to see them so submissive under the affliction. It seemed to do our friends much good, thus to have an opportunity to see and speak with us, though iron grates intervened.

Among other letters, I received one from my brother in Ohio, written to Brother Hunter. He said, "Tell George I am not 'ashamed of his chain,' nor to call him a *brother*, in any sense of the word." It was reviving. Two of our letters were rolled in a cloth, and baked in the centre of a loaf of cake, so that when we opened the cake, our letters were safe and legible. *Such* cakes we valued very highly. They were rich food—very nourishing. The Lord can find ways enough to give his children all that is good.

Our beloved teacher, Brother Beardsley, informed us that the committee in Quincy, had concluded to employ Esq. Warren, of Quincy, and Wright, of Palmyra. As they did not feel justified in employing another counsel, and as Wright was unwilling to undertake without the assistance of S. T. Glover, we engaged him—Alanson giving his note for two hundred and fifty dollars. The fee of the other two was four hundred dollars, paid principally, by friends.

CHAPTER IV.

THE SLEEPING PREACHER, JOURNAL, ETC.

August 24. Last night Charles dreamed aloud again. (He, in his dreams, talked it all aloud.) We lay and heard him for two or three hours. He preached us a good sermon—adapted to the occasion, and fitted to our circumstances. We were much benefitted thereby, and strengthened in our faith; encouraged to trust in God implicitly, being assured if we have Him on our side, vain are all the efforts of wicked men and devils arrayed against us. He was emphatically a *sleeping preacher*, and a very eloquent one too. Though he is an ignorant, wicked boy, even Demosthenes could not produce finer strains of eloquence—nor Bunyan more sublime and striking metaphors—nor divines more pure theology. It was beyond anything I ever heard; and I trust we shall remember and profit by that sermon as long as we live.

The next morning I wrote down all the principal ideas, as far as I could call them to mind, and give a few of them below for the curiosity of the reader, and I hope profit too.

THE DREAM.

He first seemed to be in a by-way, where he ought not to be, with his mother, his child and another of his companions by the name of George. While there, he espied a huge monster with great horns, and an iron grapple in his hand, coming towards them. They were much terrified; and he felt that the devil had come for him and his child. He seized the child, threw it to his mother, and said to the monster—"Let my child alone, and take me." The mother and child escaped, while he disputed with the devil, who seized him; but he very narrowly made his escape, and, they all got home. After they had talked about what had passed, he consulted with George about going with an army to take all the slaves in the country and free them. He would make peace with slave-holders on one condition only—that they should give up every slave. Said he, "I'll have *every one*, even to a span long." He was very uncompromising with them.

While thus employed in talking, his wife (who was dead), appeared to him, and gave him a letter, in which she exhorted him to repent and meet her in heaven, or he must go to hell—told him that the child must die and be with its mother, &c., which gave him much trouble and distress. He thought of his promises to his wife on her dying bed, and how he had broken them. He talked with his mother, who urged him to repent and prepare to meet his wife. She spoke of his wife's urging him to be a Christian. Now and then he would get out of patience and exclaim, "Mother, do go away and let me alone; you are all the time at me about this subject—do let me alone." At length he confessed his neglect and his sin—said he was sorry—and after much entreaty and persuasion, promised he would do better and serve God the rest of his life, and trust in Him. He then seemed very happy—had great courage and faith in God—was not afraid of the devil and all his hosts—felt he could put them all to flight, and none of them could hurt him so long as he kept his faith in the Almighty God. "I have cast aside the devil's garments and implements," said he, "with which I could do nothing, and have put on God's garments, in which nothing can hurt me."

He then began to talk with George, his companion, who was very fearful and faint hearted :—"You must not be so. You have the devil's garment on, and you must cast it all aside before you can do anything or be happy ; and you must put on God's garments ; then you will not fear." George tried to put the garment on over the devil's. "No; you can't do that. You must take the old garment clean off. It wont go on over. It just fits, and you can't get it on over anything." George tried, but could not get the old garment off. "Try again, pull hard, tear it off and throw it in the devil's face. I had to try hard many times, and kept it on a long time, but bless God, I've got it off and got on a new one which the devil can't look at." George finally got it off and the devil took it away. He put on God's garment, and was happy and courageous. "Now when the devil meets you, look him *right in the eye* and he can't hurt you, but if you look down you are gone for ever. Don't be afraid; *look up ;* look him *plumb* in the eye, and he'll flee.

"With our enemies is only the devil, but with us the Almighty God, who is stronger than all. He has given me a commission to go and fight, and He will be with me, for He has said so (and that is enough), He *can't lie.* I shall conquer. They can't overcome. God will help me, and bring me safely home to heaven.

"George, you must give up all the devil's armor, keep none ; take entirely new ; take God's. There is a trap-door in the heart, and you must turn the heart bottom upwards, and empty out all the filth and bad stuff, and have it filled with good, with God and his Spirit. Do it now.

"You must not attempt to go *round* the commandments ; you must go *straight* and keep them. If you go round them the first you know you will be right plumb in the middle of hell.

"Keep your coat on. So long as you keep it on and your bright weapons in your hand, the devil can't look at you. You can walk right over him."

He was sometimes very oratorical. It exceeded anything I ever heard. It was wonderful ; for when awake he is an exceedingly wicked and profane man. He must have been talking in this way for two or three hours ; so that I have given a mere skeleton of the scene. Could the whole dream be written out, just as he spoke it, it would make an uncommonly interesting, amusing, and instructive little volume.

At other times in his dreams he would be commanding an army, planning and calculating with great shrewdness how to obtain the conquests, pursuing the enemy, cutting bridges, charging with his cavalry on the surprised foe, firing cannon, shouting—"They flee, they flee, hurrah! come on my brave fellows,"—and then, after a victory, calling his officers about him and addressing one and another, praising their bravery, encouraging them and bestowing rewards upon them.

This "sleeping preacher," is a short, thick set, stout mulatto—a Canadian—was engaged in their war skirmishes there a few years ago, where he probably obtained his war spirit. And if he is as shrewd and persevering and undaunted a warrior when awake as when asleep our generals would do well to seek him out and promote him to some *chief rank*, for in his sleep he seemed to understand war tactics perfectly.

His hatred of slavery was inveterate; and from his dreams it was evident that he thought much of leading an army into the South and liberating every slave in the land. At times, in his dreams, he had collected a force and was going from plantation to plantation proclaiming liberty to every one who would join, and thus swelling his army till it was irresistible.

Aug. 25. "In reproaching us do they not reproach the Savior?" (*Mat.* xxv. 40, 45). "They have blasphemed thy name, O! Lord." "How long?" "Arise, plead thine own cause. Remember how the foolish man reproacheth thee daily." (*Ps.* lxxiv. 22).

Surely "the dark places of the earth" (slaveholding dominions), "are full of the habitations of cruelty." It is a system of cruelty as much as the Inquisition.

Said Charles, "It is a common thing for slaves to come upon the boats almost starved and plead and beg for something to eat; will offer their hats or their clothes for something to satisfy the cravings of nature; will work Sundays and nights to get money to buy something to eat!" He says they are often fed on cotton seed!

When I think of separated wives and husbands, parents and children, brothers and sisters; the mangled, bleeding backs; the starvations; the oppressions and labors; the murders, degradations, and ignorance; the innumerable evils and sufferings indescribable; I can but exclaim with the Psalmist—"*Full of cruelty !*" "O, Lord, pluck thy right hand out of thy bosom; let thy arm be exalted and thy name honored in the destruction of this evil."

To-day we talked with Ambrose—Dr. Ely's slave. He has a family of nine children—is buying himself— has to pay nine hundred dollars with interest!—has it nearly paid, besides having worked two years for the Dr. of which no account was made. He was sold to go down south, but ran away, and the Dr. bought him running in the woods. He is forty-one years old, black, and very large. He told us that one of the slaves who betrayed us had run away and there was fifty dollars reward offered for him. "O, they won't run away, they can't be hired to run away." Ah, ha ! Let them be sure of *friends* and see.

The blacks generally seem to sympathize with us; they are getting some ideas into their heads which are new to them.

O, if our enemies knew what they were doing how they would tremble at the consequences. They are fast undermining themselves.

The thought that our being here will advance the cause of liberty is delightful. Let them do what they please with this body, if the chains of the poor slave are broken thereby, I will gladly suffer all that their spite and malice can invent. With the assurance that it will be so, a States prison will be a sweet place.

BLOODY TOWNS.

Aug. 26. *Habk.* ii. 11, 12.—"Wo to him that buildeth a town with blood, and establisheth a city by iniquity." What meaneth this strange, this awful language? How can a town be built with blood? How established by iniquity? Go to ancient Babylon. It was built and enriched by conquering other nations; its glory sustained by the blood of its enemies. It was established by its iniquitous laws. Concerning it the " woe" was fulfilled. It has long since been a desolation.

But come to our own country. Behold our southern cities. They are built and enriched, and sustained, by the gains procured from the blood and sweat and tears of the slave. They are built on *slavery*, and slavery is a system of *wholesale bloodshed*—the blood flows continually.

They are also " established" by such "iniquity" as the sun scarce ever looked upon! Behold their laws, by which they are governed and " established," and well may we blush to think that we belong to the same race.

O! could their cruelty and oppression be fully known! But can they prosper? Is not the cup of New Orleans, of Vicksburg, of Palmyra almost full? The " woe" has gone out against them, and if it is not executed in their overthrow it is fulfilled in their moral desolation, and will be in their eternal destruction unless they repent. Are the inhabitants so generally and entirely sunken in iniquity, and so united together in their wickedness, that there are none to testify against them? Let them not, therefore, think they are secure, for " the stone out of the wall shall cry against them, and the beam out of the timber shall answer it," (or " witness against it," as the margin reads), and proclaim their abominations. God will find witnesses enough to testify against them, and unless they repent there is only *wo !* wo !! WO !!! for them.

Last night Charles preached repentance again in his sleep. He is much disturbed in mind,—Alanson talked with him to-day. He said, " I have so much pressing on my mind that I can't attend to religion." Getting out and getting slaves to Canada occupies all his thoughts.

My journalizing now is all done on old letters, and my letters written on old cards, which I split—writing on the inside with my pencil, and on the outside with ink. " Necessity is the mother of invention."

The effects of slavery are seen very plainly in this State.   Horse-racing is a great game among them.   Private gambling is prohibited, while public and wholesale gambling is licensed by statute!   Fighting, dueling, lawing (or mobbing), murdering, and so on, abound. Children are brought up to be haughty and insolent, and the fine feelings of the soul are totally destroyed.

27.   When I read of the unspeakable pains and tortures so many Christians have endured from the servants of Satan, I can hardly *think* of my condition.   Happy, happy am I.   Thanks to God that I live in this day. Yea, thanks to his name that I am here.

DEVICES OF THE ENEMY.

Doubtless our enemies felt they were waging an unholy warfare.   For, so little confidence had they in the justice of their cause, that they used every means they could devise to call to their aid the united prejudices of the community against us.

At first they branded us with the name of Mormons, than which, *Abolitionists* excepted, there was not a more odious name in Missouri.   This was soon known to be falsely applied.   Then they called us Dr. Nelson's satellites—a name we were proud of—and he had been driven from their midst and hunted like a wolf, fleeing, in dead of night, for his life.   In the papers they published us as dyed-in-the-wool abolitionists.

Some were so zealous in the cause, they went about reporting that the Church to which we belonged had held several meetings, and passed resolutions to come and take us out by force; which caused great excitement and tumult, preparations for resisting, &c.

And when the three men were hung in St. Louis, they published a confession, said to be Brown's, in which he confessed he had assisted eighty slaves to Canada in one year—that he was employed by the abolitionists, and received a large salary, &c.

The Rev. Mr. Bullard came out and published that Brown denied ever saying any such thing, but this was

of no avail.   They were eager to believe that it was so,
and I suppose they succeeded; for it is exceedingly
easy and natural for the carnal heart to " believe a lie."

All these and other causes combining, produced a tremendous excitement all over the country against us.
Even the *little boys* drank in the spirit, and would come
to the jail and try to torment us, knocking on the door
and calling out,—" Ha! there, nigger-stealers, you
think you will steal any more niggers, heh ?"—yea, and
even the *women* would revile us as they passed the jail!

But by this excitement they only burdened themselves,
making it necessary, as they supposed, to keep a guard
of four men at the jail, every night, at an expense of
$1,50 a piece, $6,00 a night, for seventy nights—$420,
beside other expenses amounting in all to nearly $1000
—all to come out of the county.

Again, the more they increased and kept up the excitement, the more light spread abroad, the more the
slaves inquired, heard, and learned; and many times
more than we should have got away, had we succeeded,
bade farewell to Missouri and slavery in consequence of
their foolish zeal to excite public odium against us.

See how God " disappointed the crafty devices" of
the wicked, how He " takes them in their own crafti-
ness," and causes all their " wrath to praise Him,"
while his children sing and rejoice.

CHAPTER V.

EXTRACTS OF LETTERS.

EXTRACT—TO MOTHER BALLARD.

We do not feel to murmur or repine, because we
are here confined, and deprived of former privileges.
No. It is not for us to say what we will do—where we
will go, &c.,—all this we leave with our Father, to di-

rect as will most glorify his name. He best knows
what kind of a training we need—and shall we say to
Him—This is not best? We cannot. We are happy
here—and how can we be unhappy so long as we have
such words, as *Ps.* xviii. 12; xxiii., xxvii. 1—3, 10
—14; xxxii. 7, 8; xxxiv,, xxxvii. 1—8; xlvi. 1—3;
lxxi. 1—8; lxxxiv. 11, 12; xci., cxxi., cxxv. 1, 2, *Is.*
xxvi. 3, 4; xliii. 1—3; xlix. 25; *Matt.* v. 10—12.
Rom. vii. 28, 35—39; and many others? These are
a *few* of our cordials—our tonics—our balsams—our life
preservers. Just read them carefully, and see if they
are not sufficient for *every state.* Although our chain is
a *very large* one, yet it feels very light. I sometimes
forget I have any chain on my leg. I hardly think of it.
Mother, come and pray with us in our palace. Come
and see how we keep house. We are highly favored.
We not only have a cook, but our victuals and drink are
even brought to us, so that we are not obliged to step a
foot out of the door.   Yours truly,

GEORGE.

The following was written to Rev. Moses Hunter on
a margin, cut from a newspaper:

Palmyra Jail, Aug. 28, 1841.

DEAR BROTHER H.

You see we have to rob the edges of newspapers
in order to get paper on which to write to you. I have
kept my journal on scraps of old letters, bits of newspapers, &c., ever since I came here. The paper which
you left with the Sheriff, we cannot get. It has been
more than three weeks since we had an opportunity to
speak with him. But if his conscience can endure his
conduct, we can easily bear what he sees fit to lay upon
us. I think he will view his conduct in a very different
light, at the great day of solemn trial. It seems he is
determined to prevent us from obtaining justice. May
the Lord have mercy on him.

The jailer appears quite friendly. He is willing to do
all he *dares* for us. We are watched very closely. The
guard annoy us very much. Poor men! I pity them.

2

Many of the colored men appear like real friends, and take a deep interest in our case. Some of them will get a few ideas, which I hope they will improve to advantage. They frequently converse with us through the grates, and some of them appear like sensible men.

God will take the cause into his own hands. Let this comfort our friends, though we go to the penitentiary, or be assassinated. Our bodies, our earthly ease and comfort, are nothing compared with God's cause. Let God's will be done, and let ours yield joyfully to his.

I think it will be well to have a number of the sisters here on the day of decision. If we are acquitted, their presence will have a tendency to restrain violence. The Lord will reward you for all your trouble, and many poor slaves will rise up and ' call you blessed.'

Yours,
GEORGE.

The following letter was written by P. C. L., of Palmyra, who is said to belong to the Episcopal Church; (at any rate, he professed to be very pious when he talked to us). It was written for the St. Louis Republican.

THE MISSOURIAN'S LETTER.

Mr. A. B. CHAMBERS:

DEAR SIR,—From an editorial which I observed in a late number of yours, in regard to the Abolitionists which have been lately apprehended in this county, I perceive you have been led into an error in saying they were Mormons. They are Presbyterians, and are the satellites of the notorious DR. DAVID NELSON, formerly of this county. Two of them are students of his; the other is a man of family. You will remember that this same reverend gentleman was driven away from this county, some five or six years since, for disseminating *Abolition* doctrines.

When these men were first arrested, I was under the impression that they were kidnappers, and that their object was to get the negroes off and sell them; but I am perfectly convinced that they are DYED-IN-THE-WOOL ABOLITIONISTS!! They talk freely and openly on the subject,* and say that the laws of God are superior to the laws of man.

On Sunday I called on and conversed freely with them. They are quite conversant, and one of them is studying for the pulpit as I am informed.

They have prayer night and morning, and one generally gives a short discourse on the Bible. I never have, in the whole course of my life, seen such deluded creatures! They say that they are fully resigned to their fate—that God will protect and defend them—that in doing what they were about to do, they were endeavoring to set free a portion of God's creatures, who were in bondage contrary to his will.

Speaking of Dr. Nelson, he says,

But would you think he had the impudence to make an appointment at Philadelphia, a small place near Marion College, to preach, on last Sunday. News of this fact was brought to town (Palmyra), in the early part of the week, when two or three large companies were formed in different parts of the county, to go and take him out of the pulpit; but I am happy to say he left the county on Saturday, for had he remained and attempted to preach, HE WOULD HAVE BEEN HUNG AS HIGH AS HAMAN!

A large company, however, went to the College to make an examination, but as I said, he left the day before. In justice to Marion College, allow me to say, that it is in no way connected with these *vile fiends*.

We are opposed to mob law in Marion, but there *is* a point beyond which lenity ceases to be a virtue. We are *determined* not to be harassed by this monster in human shape. We do not want to see one of our old and valued citizens stabbed, and nearly murdered as Dr. Bosley was, a few years since, and that on Sunday, by the same gang, and that too under the guise of religion.

Respectfully yours, P. C. L.

* See Chapter III., July 18.

Can it be possible that the slaveholder's religion is the same as ours? "I tell you nay"—as far from it as light is from darkness. Who is the man that is most abominated in a slave state? Why, he who dares to live by the *Bible*, and act' out its holy principles. "Well, do not slaveholders go by the Bible?" No; by the Bible!—*no*, no! Themselves being judges, the laws of their States are far superior to all the laws of God. Who is called a "monster," "fiend," &c.? Why he who "let the oppressed go free," and then called on his neighbors to do the same! He who would rebuke their abominations—pointing out to them a better way. Believe me, dear reader, for I speak that I do know, there can not be a greater abomination to slaveholding Christians than a *Bible Christian*. I have not merely heard so—or conjectured it—or believe so—I have *seen* it—I have FELT it. O, pray that the Spirit of God will open their eyes.

THE DR. BOSLEY AFFRAY.

Dr. Bosley is said to have been "nearly murdered by the *same* gang"—the Abolitionists. The circumstances, if my memory serves me, are about as follows. Dr. Nelson was preaching in Palmyra in 1835 or 1836. While thus engaged, Dr. Bosley advanced to take him from the pulpit. William Muldrow, a *slaveholder*, but friendly to Dr. Nelson, attempted to hinder him, a which Bosley drew his pistol on Muldrow, and Muldrow drew his dirk and stabbed Bosley.

EXTRACT FROM JAMES'S LETTER.

One of our counsel told us it would be a violation of the laws of Missouri, to read either the Declaration of Independence or the Bible, to a slave! How plainly their laws are at war with God! I have thought that slaveholders will soon have to commence a law-suit against Jehovah, to see whether his or their laws shall stand. But the contest would be unequal—the Almighty will overturn their system of iniquity.

It may be a satisfaction to you to know our individual feelings, in regard to the step that brought us here. I do not repent it, nor have I any doubt respecting the morality of the act.

JAMES.

EXTRACT FROM ALANSON'S LETTER.

I think I can see the hand of God in it. I now know how to feel for those who are separated from their families, and bought and sold like cattle—how to sympathize with the slave in all his afflictions, better than I ever did before.

I have often thought I would give my life and strength to the cause of the slave. If He who is infinite in wisdom, sees that I can do more for the cause by being for years separated from my family and those I love, shall I murmur? *No;* in humility I will rejoice, that I am accounted worthy to suffer for well-doing.

Palmyra jail is not a gloomy place. I have had many happy moments here, which I shall not soon forget.

When I look at myself and the dangers that surround me, I tremble—but when I look at the promises, I find confidence and peace. Thus far I have found my strength sufficient for my day, and in this promise I will continue to trust. Though men have bound us with this chain, and guards are prepared to take our lives, if we attempt to escape, yet I feel that it is a *kind hand* that holds us here; and that when our great Redeemer shall have accomplished His purposes of mercy. He will deliver us. Be not anxious for us, but pray. Through the prayers of Christians I trust our imprisonment will be for the glory of God, and the speedy release of many in bonds.

We have the sympathies of the slaves, and who knows but the "blessing of those ready perish" may come upon us? May I ever esteem *it of more* value than the favor of the oppressor.

A. WORK.

TRIAL IN PROSPECT.

Palmyra Jail, September 4, 1841.

Not knowing what will be the issue of my trial, I desire to record a summary of my feelings, that it may be
known what they are, should I suddenly be killed or
thrust into States prison.

And 1st: I do not regret the step I took more than
seven weeks ago ; nor have I at any time been sorry for
it, although thousands condemn and call me a thief,
rascal, liar, and all that is vile and abominable—though
many who love the Lord, and feel for the slave, and are
my friends, disapprove of my course, yet I cannot see
wherein I acted contrary to my master's direction or the
spirit of the Gospel. My conscience approbates my
course.

That helping the poor is *right*, I have no doubt ; and
although the slaveholders may plead it is taking their
property, I feel, and am bold to affirm, that there is no
such thing as their having property in man. It is all a
sham. The slaves, by the law of God, own themselves,
and if we can relieve them in any proper way, we are
bound, by the laws of our king—by the bonds of humanity—by the feelings of mercy—by the spirit of the
blessed gospel—to do it. The reproaches, insults, and
menaces that have been heaped upon me—the close
confinement, dragging the heavy chain, and being denied
the many privileges which even their own law allows,
have not in the least altered my principles concerning
the rights of the slave, but on the other hand, have much
strengthened them.

I have not felt sorry that I have had to lie here so
long. I have blessed the Lord, and will continue to
bless Him for placing me here. As long as I live, I expect to praise Him for it, and trust all my friends will
have occasion to do the same.

At the time I was taken I felt a little troubled for a
moment—so sudden was the transaction—but my mind
soon became composed ; I lifted up my heart to God,
committed myself to his care, and said " Father, glorify

thy name." Then, as ever since, I felt assured that He would overrule it for his own glory, that He had kind and wise designs in permitting it, and that " all things shall work together for good," to those that love Him. I have all along desired that his name may be glorified and the greatest good accomplished, and felt the assurance that this would be the case. I felt, and still feel, a peace within, a comfort, and a satisfaction, in leaving all in his hands. 'Tis

> " Sweet to lie passive in His hands,
> And know no will but His."

There have been times, since I have been here, that have tried my faith, and I have been almost ready to despond ; but betaking myself to the promises, and the weapon, " all prayer," I have been strengthened and encouraged, and would look up and say, " My Lord and my God." The days I have spent within these walls, have been happy, memorable, and profitable days. Time has passed sweetly and pleasantly away. The glorious Redeemer smiles upon and communes with us. He has spread before us the rich tables of his grace, and on their loaded bounties we have feasted. I now feel a confidence and joy in committing my whole cause into his hands, that He may plead it, and order all things according to his will, that knowing that it will be best for me, for my friends, and for the world. Can I not rejoice ?

It would be very pleasant to be restored to dear friends, and with them again enjoy the privileges of the sanctuary, of prayer and praise ; but if this is not my Savior's will, I hope I may not be left to desire it, nor feel dejected, though long deprived of it.

It has long been my prayer that God would do with me just as He saw best. I have expressed a willingness to labor in any part of the vineyard where He shall direct. If He has work for me in a States prison why should I not be willing to perform it, and rejoice to run at his command ? I do, yes, and I will " rejoice in the Lord and joy in the rock of my salvation." This I know,

that wherever my Master sends me, He will be with me
to counsel, support, and grant all needed grace; and no
good thing shall I want.   He will be more to me than
father or mother, brother or sister—more than any or all
earthly friends.   He will also be more to them than I
could possibly be myself.   I joyfully commit them to
his will.   The fury of my enemies will not be in vain.
Truth will be elicited—light will go forth—interest will
be excited for the slave—and the great cause of liberty
advanced.   If this be the case, then what are years of
toil and exclusion from the world and from Christian
society?   I go CHEERFULLY—I go GLADLY.   Pray for
me daily—that I may " be strong in the Lord"—exhibit
his spirit in all circumstances, and be useful to others.

Yours in the gospel,
GEORGE THOMPSON.

CHAPTER VI.

JOURNAL.

THE COMMAND.

AUGUST 28.   " Remember them in bonds as bound with
them."—*Heb.* xiii. 3.

Those who have never been bound can better sympathize with those who are, by imagining themselves in
the same condition.   They will then *feel* for them.   We
here can, in a small degree, " remember them in bonds
as bound with them," *from experience.*

1st.   We know how the chain *feels.*

2nd.   We know what it is to be at the will of another;
to do as others say; receive what they see fit to give;
eat and drink what their will supplies, and await their
pleasure.

3rd.   We understand what it is to be forcibly separated

from wife, children, parents, and friends, and denied the sweetness of their society.

4th. To live in uncertainty—not knowing to-day what they will do with us to-morrow.

5th. To be looked down upon with scorn, reproach, and contempt, by men, women, and little children.

6th. What we now suffer is for trying to benefit the poor, down-trodden slave.

O, that we may feel for them more than we should have done had we not been placed here. I do. I believe I shall.

This evening a man was brought here from Waterloo for fighting. Said he, "If it had not been for whisky I should not have come here." His head was bound up, having been cut in the affray. O! cruel avarice! that makes such deathful drink! What multitudes are slain by this monster! O! the misery!—beggared families—broken-hearted wives, and desolate children!

29. Just after breakfast a gang of seven came in, some with clubs, one with a great book under his arm, and among them the magistrate and constable. Amazement filled our minds. What was coming, we could not conjecture—but soon, said one, "Where shall we begin?" And another, "We've come to see whether you have anything with which you can get out!" Then they searched every nook and corner—turning things upside down—rummaging the beds, trunks, drawer, &c. They have not had the least occasion to suspect any such thing as our desiring to get away.

I expected they would search our papers—but as the Lord would have it, they did not read one—though they saw them in the drawer.

They seem to know no Sabbath, except for wickedness. In the morning we were much disturbed. Many came to the window, with whom the others talked and laughed till nearly noon. It was very distressing to hear such nonsense and folly on this blessed day—but here we are confined, and all we can say seems of no avail. We could neither read, nor think to profit. Dear Lord, it is said of thee, "He preserveth the souls of his saints."

3*

O! look upon us surrounded by wickedness, and save us from its contaminating influence. At noon talked from *Is.* lv. 2. A very quiet afternoon—was much benefited by the word. James preached from, "What shall I then do with Jesus?"

Whatever may come, I feel to say with the prophet *Habakkuk*, iii. 18—"Yet will I rejoice in the Lord, and joy in the God of my salvation." *Ps.* lxix. 19 is a comfort to me. The Lord knows all my wrongs, and my adversaries are all before Him. He knows their hearts, and just how to deal with them.

SLAVE WOMEN IN PALMYRA.

It is a common thing here for women to chop wood, and frequently, have I seen them thus engaged on the Sabbath. (I suppose their masters were in *Church.*) A great part of the water that is used in Palmyra, is carried a considerable distance by slave women, on their heads—and many of them carry their large washings to and from the public spring in the same manner. (The town is chiefly supplied by a fountain.) Thus slavery not only robs, and oppresses, but turns even *females* into beasts of drudgery and burden.

OUR REASONS FOR SUSPECTING THEM.

To-day, the slaves we would have helped, were here, among many others, who came to see us. They looked very much ashamed, and seemed to regret what they did, since they have ascertained that we were friends, and wished to do them good. But we have not the least hard feeling towards them—would just as soon help them to freedom as any others, though they may have voluntarily betrayed us, as some say. We have rather felt inclined to think that it was whipped out of them, by their masters—yet there are some things which strongly favor the former. It is said that the one who was foremost in the affair, belonged to a genuine *kidnapper*—if so, he may have feared we were like his master, and consequently betrayed us. And it is a well known fact, that slaves in general are taught that abolitionists are their worst *enemies.* It is not therefore to be wondered at, that they should be suspicious of them, till this idea is corrected—and this has been, and will be one good result of our imprisonment. The slaves will learn the true character of abolitionists, and fly to them for help from every quarter.

Another thing, that favors the idea that they betrayed us. The slaves informed us, that they got together one night—tied the one who was leader in the matter, to a tree, and gave him *fifty* lashes! so incensed were they at him, for treating in such a manner, those who loved them.

Again, one of the very slaves who assisted in taking us, (and for it, received large pay from the people), as soon as he learned our intentions, and that in Illinois were friends to help him, left his kind and generous master, to *try* and "take care of himself!" I trust he will succeed.

But whether they did or did not, voluntarily betray us, it matters not to us. We are, by this event, settled for a time *in their midst,* for which we bless the Lord. We will continue to seek their best good.

Aug. 31. "Commit thy way unto the Lord; trust also, in Him, and He shall bring it to pass." We are at times much puzzled to know how to get our letters to our friends, and often pray that the Lord will open ways for us to communicate with those we love. To-day Brethren William Vandoorne, and John Brown came over, and contrary to all that has been before they were allowed to come in with our two lawyers. Brother Vandoorne seemed to understand our straits, and while we were talking with the lawyers, &c., he with his hat in his hand behind him, backed up before us, and before Charles (to whom we had given most of our papers), and we cast in our offerings, unobserved by our enemies

FRIENDS—ENEMIES RAGE.

Sept. 1. Another load of friends came over—brethren and sisters. Mrs. Work came in while the rest were in the wagon under the grates of our window. We had but just passed our letters, shaken hands through the double grates, and spoken a few words, when they were ordered away from the window. Many gathered round as if to devour them. Their wild stare, and unmannerly conduct was such as might be looked for among a company of savages. Our brethren and sisters in the street, and we fast to our huge chain, united in singing some of the precious " Songs of Zion." When we began to sing, the people in greater numbers gathered round, and many went away in a rage, cursing, and almost gnashing their teeth! O! what a spirit is that, which is so *envious* at the happiness of others! What a heart does it show when a man is filled with rage, and fury, by seeing those who are the objects of his spite, happy in the Lord, and rejoicing under reproaches! When I see the fury of those who would devour me —the great numbers of great men, of all classes who are uniting against me—their resolutions and determinations, almost like that of the forty, who " bound themselves with an oath, that they would neither eat nor drink till they had killed Paul"—when I see all these things, and hear their threats, and then remember that they are magnifying themselves against God, it is very comforting to know that He can put his " hook in their noses, and his bridle in their lips," (*Is.* xxxvii. 29), and lead them where—and as He will—and cause all their rage to magnify his name.

SLAVE WHIPPED.

Sept. 4. Last night a slave passing the Jail, was ordered by Esq. Wilson to stop. " Where are you going ?" " My master sent me after the Doctor." " It is a d—d lie !" said Wilson—" Pull off your shirt." " I can't do that," said the slave, and took hold of Wilson. The guards came to his help, and held the slave while Wilson gave him twenty lashes ! " Now go home," said he. " I shan't, I shall go after the Doctor," replied the slave, and ran, Wilson pursuing him.

Shortly after Ambrose (Dr. Ely's slave), came along, " Where are you going?" bawled out Wilson. " It's none of your business," replied A——, and as he was very large they dared not attack him. Two others came along with clubs in their hands, and Esq. Wilson thought his safest way was to let them alone. O! the abominations of slavery! How innumerable are its cruelties!

Sept. 5. My faith fastens on the promises more and more strongly; and yet the blessing of being restored to liberty and friends, seems almost too good, and too great, to expect. I am unworthy of it, but will cast myself into my Savior's arms, to do with me as seemeth good to Him. His word is very dear and sweet to-day. Talked from *Ps.* xxvii. 1—5. It gave me comfort and peace. With the assurance that the " Lord of Hosts is with us," " I will not fear." " For in the time of trouble He will hide me in a pavilion, and set me on a Rock."

The " Book of Martyrs," has afforded me much comfort and strength in prospect of suffering. As we were singing, a Palmyra *lady* passed by. " Hark," said she, " the *rebels* are singing." The Lord open her eyes, and have mercy. The Sun is about to leave us. Farewell, " King of Day." Shall I greet you again, on a Sabbath, in Missouri? I shall see you where it is best. Amen.

EXTRACT, FROM A LETTER TO THE CHURCH JUST
BEFORE THE TRIAL.

Dear brethren and sisters, I still ask you to remember us at the " throne of grace." Don't put any trust in man. There is no hope in an arm of flesh. There are many who have risen up against us, and who are laying deep their plans, in certain expectation of our condemnation. They will spare no money, nor efforts to accomplish their end.

But " with us is the Lord our God." Don't think our lawyers can help us, unless God be on our side. Think of Hezekiah and Sennacherib—of Paul and Silas, and of Peter. Read the accounts, and look only to the Lord. Let there be much fervent prayer while the trial is advancing. Pray that Jesus our great "counsellor" will direct the whole.

Of some of those who shall come as witnesses, it may be required to testify to our former character. Esq. Glover thinks if that is established, it will be sufficient, and no more will be required. We wish W. J. C., to recollect very particularly the conversation between him and James and the two slaves, to show that the slaves *wished* to go—that there was no intention of taking them against their will. Wright and Glover think this very important. We shall want those to whom James related the facts, and conversation, and his intentions—who knew our feelings and motives, as they have heard us express them, to testify to our *motive*—that it was to set them across the river, according to their own desire, and not against their wills, nor to make gain of them. Perhaps testimony may be required as to the time we had been in Missouri. May the Savior direct you all. Come filled with the Spirit, and relying on God.

GEORGE.

I will here remark, that many came over prepared to testify on all these points, but for reasons which will hereafter appear, not one was examined—our lawyers all considering it perfectly unnecessary. The particulars will be given in their order.

TO A FRIEND.

M——, how would you feel to see your father, mother, brothers, or sisters put up, and knocked off to the highest bidder ! O, have we felt for the poor slave, " *as bound with him ?*" Did Christians realize their condition ; O, how differently would they act ! Wherever we go, " let us cry aloud."

SALE OF HUMAN BEINGS !—JOURNAL.

Sept. 6. I know not in what words to express my feelings—my mind is filled with mingled emotions of amazement, indignation, pity, and horror. At noon, eight or ten horses were sold, at sheriff's sale, and then a woman and her child, for four hundred and sixty-five dollars—lastly, a man for five hundred and seventy-one dollars! Of such things I have often *heard*, but never before *saw* them. O! the scene!

A crowd gathered round, and these immortal beings —bound to eternity, bought with the sweat, groans, blood, and death of Jesus Christ—destined to heaven or hell—bearing the impress of their Maker's hand—possessing feelings, emotions, and affections like ourselves, and the consciousness that they were *born* with the "inalienable rights of life, liberty, and the pursuit of happiness"—*these* were set up, cried, and knocked off under the hammer, to the highest bidder, for gold and silver!

Am I among human beings? Am I in a civilized country? Can it be that I am among those who profess to be the servants of the blessed Redeemer, that meek and lowly Lamb! Am I in a community where the Bible is read, and its principles professed? O, what is man! Where are his feelings of propriety, of mercy, of reason, of justice, of humanity? What do they think their fellow-men are? Have they any thought of an eternity—of a judgment—of a righteous, holy, and just God? Do they expect to meet these proceedings at his bar? There, do they expect to see the poor slaves they thus buy and sell, and be charged by the Judge with buying, selling, and abusing Him, in the person of his children? What *can* they think? What have their hearts become? And what will become of them? Is there a *heaven* for them?

Poor slaves! what must be their cogitations, while being thus bid off? And what must be the state of a community—how distorted, how sunken in vice, and corruption and wickedness—how far gone, and almost past recovery—how ripe for the judgments of heaven and how deserving to be cast into the darkness of deep oblivion and eternal night, that can allow, practise, and *justify* such awful abominations by *law* and by the *Bible !* and who imprison and kill those who oppose their iniquity !!

And yet what are northern, compared with southern

slave states? O, my country, my country! Is there
any mercy for it? How is God insulted, and cast away
(so to speak), when MEN are looked upon, and treated
as the *brutes!* And yet multitudes who profess to be
Christians, yea, the *ministers of the gospel!* are engaged in this hellish system of barbarity—and worse
than heathenish cruelty, and heaven-daring, insulting
abomination! O! heaven spare.

Are they followers of *Christ?* Are they on the road
to the Celestial City? And are the upper regions to
ring with songs from such beings? But I forbear. "O
that they were wise, that they would consider their latter
end," and these things also in view of it. May God
have mercy on them, open their eyes, melt their hearts,
and cause them to repent. May I have right feelings
towards them. I can pray for them.

THE MISSOURIAN'S LETTER, AGAIN—PRISON REFLEC- TIONS.

Sept. 6. Read the letter, written by P. C. Lambert
—and a strange one it is to be written by a professor of
religion. Dr. Nelson, that meekest of men—very harmless, and who would not injure a fellow mortal for a
world—whose whole soul is filled with love to God and
man—who thinks of naught but heaven, and doing good
to a lost world—he is called a *"monster in human
shape!"*

Does P. C. L., expect to sing in heaven? Let him
know that this "*monster*" will be there (he is already
there before him). Abolitionists, whose hearts burn with
love to their fellow-men—who are trying to benefit, help,
and comfort the poor, and who rebuke the iniquities of
slavery,—they are called "*vile fiends.*" If such be
"fiends" God increase the number, and fill the earth
with them. This man, no doubt, anticipates a seat in
the mansions on high. Yet how will he feel, and all
others like him, when they see "a multitude that no man
can number of these "vile fiends," coming up before the
throne, and striking their harps to the praise of the Lamb?
They will *surely* be there, and can such men as P. C. L.,

be happy in their presence? Will their notes of praise at all harmonize? But there is no discord there. Can they sing the same song? There is only one there. Then what will they do? Will a portion of the upper region be set apart for them? Will they be *colonized?* Ah! *no.* There is no place in heaven for those who cannot love ALL MEN. I fear many will find their heaven to be *hell.* O! the Church! Lord purge it.

Of us he says, " I never saw such poor deluded creatures." Deluded? Bless God for *such* a delusion! O! that it may rapidly spread, till all the Church shall be under its influence. Happy delusion!

O! how Slavery blinds men's eyes and minds! They can see nothing good or lovely in a person or plan, that does not.uphold their " Domestic Institutions." The more faithful a man is to them, the more he is despised and persecuted! And should the glorious Redeemer again appear, and pass through the slave dominions, doubtless he would be looked upon as the greatest " fanatic"— " insurrectionist," and " monster in human shape," that ever trod God's footstool—would be despised, hated, and " hung as high as Haman," without " Judge or Jury," by those who " worship the great goddess," and fear lest " the hope of their gains" should be taken away! Shall I then repine, and think it hard that I must lie here so long? No, *no!* I bless the Lord for this chain. It looks sweet to me. I shall never forget it.

COURT.

On the 6th of Sept., court commenced, but our case did not come on till the 10th. There were three reasons for its delay. First: It took some time for the Sheriff to hunt up men for Jurors. Second: Confident of the weakness and injustice of their cause, they had sent to St. Louis, for one Crockett, who was paid a large sum, by the voluntary contribution of individuals—and our trial must be delayed till he arrived. But the third, and perhaps most prominent reason was, they could not, for a long time, find any indictment against us, for it had become universally acknowledged, by friends and foes, that we had broken NO LAW of *Missouri!* And what to do they knew not. To send us to the penitentiary they were determined, but the *how* puzzled them for a time. Said the States Attorney to a brother lawyer, " I wish you would help me a little. I have a difficult case on hand. I can find NO LAW on which to predicate an indictment against these men, and yet an indictment *must* be made out in some way!" Yes, but none but the distorted mind of the slaveholder could have devised the plan. For how is it possible to indict a man who is obedient to the law? And, " Where NO LAW is, there is NO TRANSGRESSION"—divine authority for it.

Said a lawyer to Esq. Glover, after he had made his plea for us, and was retiring from the court-house— " Well G., you have made it perfectly *clear*, that these men have transgressed NO LAW of the State."

Said Wright in his speech—" If we have *no law* to inflict punishment upon these men—if we have over-looked this point in our legislations, let justice take its course—release them and send men to Jefferson who will *enact a law*, and thus guard against all future de-predations of the kind. At Jefferson only, can this defect be supplied."

To our trial many of our friends from Quincy and vi-cinity came, with whom we had frequent interviews through the grates, while waiting from day to day for our case to come on. Those who could not come, wrote, assuring us of their sympathy and prayers.

THE ABOLITION STAND.

While waiting in daily expectation of our trial, I wrote the following on the bottom of the drawer to our stand, with my pencil, that after we had gone it might act as an Anti-Slavery lecturer where the living voice would not be heard.

ADDRESS.

" Wo to them who decree unrighteous decrees (such as slave laws), and establish iniquity by law," (such as buying and selling men—parting wives and husbands, parents and children—causing men to work without wages, the hire of whom crieth unto the Lord for vengeance). Let every one engaged in this system of hellish iniquity be afraid and tremble, for the judgments of heaven hang over their guilty heads, and will quickly fall upon them unless they repent.

O! man, "flee from the wrath to come." "Escape for your life." Ruin is nigh. "What thou doest, do quickly;"—for unless you humble yourself before the eternal God, there is no heaven for you, but an awful, eternal hell.

The slaves are God's poor. All their sufferings are noticed by Him—every stroke of the whip is recorded —every groan counted—and every tear bottled up by their Maker, to be brought up against you at the solemn judgment. How will you answer? What will you say for yourself? You will be speechless.

I pity the fate of a slaveholder. If there is a low place in hell, an enlightened slaveholder will occupy that place. He will be cursed by men and devils.

I pity the children of slaveholders. They are trained up for oppressors, upon whom God will pour the " blackness of darkness" for ever and ever.

I pity a patrol. This office is cruel, low, mean, and heart-hardening.

Dear stand,—You have been very kind to us in our confinement. For your valuable services we are very thankful. As we are now about to leave you, we bid you farewell, and send you into the world a single-handed abolitionist, to preach deliverance to the captive, to rebuke men for their sins, and warn them of their danger. Cry aloud to high and low, rich and poor—spare not. May you do much good and be protected. We commend you to the mercy of the people. May many of the oppressed be delivered by your means.

I pray some eye may fall upon it, and that good may result by the blessing of the Lord. "How great a matter a little fire kindleth."

68   A DEVICE—THE RABBLE.

TREATMENT OF OUR FRIENDS.

Though many of our friends were present in **Palmyra**
for nearly a week, yet, by the " good hand of God upon
them," no one was injured.   And wonderful, as it may
seem, the large body of " dyed-in-the-wool," abolition-.
ists were generously entertained by the citizens.   Mr.
Muldrow, keeper of the Temperance house, invited Mrs.
Work and other ladies to make his house their home
during the trial.   Mr. Wilcox, a tavern keeper, gave the
use of a house, and fuel, to all who desired to occupy it.
I rejoice that I am able to speak some good of those who
desire our destruction.   One of our witnesses, whose
testimony was deemed very important, was pursued by
a company, and very narrowly escaped with his liberty,
at the risk of his life.   By some means (perhaps by
some Illinois traitor), it was ascertained that he was with
James at the time the agreement was made to meet and
help the slaves.   They had determined to take him, and
send him to Jefferson with us (merely for *speaking* to a
slave) !   Their plan being known, by one who felt
friendly, he was advised to stand on Illinois soil as
soon as possible.   He fled, and barely saved himself.

On the night of the 9th, the rabble made considerable
disturbance—collected a company of " certain lewd
fellows of the baser sort," and marched round through
the town singing, huzzaing, and deriding our friends, till
the Lord came upon them and smote one of their number, making him groan and cry aloud, and thus they
were dispersed.   How easy for God to smite them all !
They made their boasts that if we were cleared, we
would get a great flogging, before we could get out of
town.   How vain their threats !   " The Lord is on my
side.   I will not fear what can man do unto me ?"
Dear Savior, stand by me.

THE CLOSET MOTHER.

Said mother B., as she stood and talked with us
through the grates, " If my John (who was dead), was
there, I should feel that I could do more for him, by

staying at home in my *closet*, than by going into court to
testify for him !" This is an excellent spirit, it shows
that she knows from whence help must come, and a confidence that she should not be turned empty away. Ah!
give me *such* to plead my cause—those who go to the
fountain of help.

Some seem to think we cannot be so happy here, as
at liberty. I know of no two months in all my life, to
which I expect to look with so much real pleasure, as to
these. Sweet walls! sweet chain!

THE SLEEPING PREACHER AGAIN.

To-day he had a long dream about delivering the
slaves. As he fell asleep and dreamed in the day-time,
we had a fair opportunity to observe all his motions, as
well as hear his words—and a more amusing sight I
never saw. Sometimes he would be in one position,
levelling a cannon at the enemy; then he would be
riding on horseback, spurring and hastening with all
speed, calling upon his troops to follow.

Said he, with great energy, " Slavery *shall* be done
away, or *I* will die." His whole soul seems to be bent
on this one thing. This is his fixed determination—
asleep and awake. O! that every abolitionist had his
courage and perseverance. But how few are ready to
die, or even suffer a little for the poor slave! They are
willing to avow themselves the friends of the despised,
so long as they are surrounded by others who plead their
cause ; but as soon as they find themselves among the
enemies of the slave, they are still and afraid.

Said Charles (in his dream), " If no one will go with
me, I'll go alone, in the strength of God, and shall prevail. The slave *shall be free !*" May all have this
spirit as respects spiritual weapons, and go forward—
single-handed if necessary—determined never to cease
crying aloud, and using all their endeavors, till every
chain is broken, or life is extinct. O Lord ! gird up thy
people for the work. Prepare me to go forth, and labor
successfully for the downtrodden.

EXCITEMENT.

During the two months we lay in jail previous to trial, our fame had spread far abroad—and the farther it extended, the more exaggerated and false the statement became; so that great excitement prevailed over the country. The prejudices of the people were aroused against us, and great indignation was manifest on almost all countenances. When court time came, multitudes assembled from far and near. The old and young, black and white, rich and poor, all seemed enlisted—here a company and there a group—some staggering *like a* drunken man, others cursing and mocking. Some seemed very anxious to get into the jail, where they could lay hands on us; but God restrained them. They evidently waited from day to day, with much impatience, to see us brought forth, eager to get a view of such notorious disturbers of their peace.

It would be a great wonder, if, in the midst of such a furious gang of wolves, a few feeble lambs (our friends), were not destroyed, if we did not call to mind the promises. From these, we should have expected just such a wonderful deliverance.

CHAPTER VII.

TRIAL AND CONVICTION.

On the day previous to our being brought forth, our attorneys, Warren and Glover, came into the jail, and read to us our indictments. And I almost regret I have not a copy of them, for the reader—but it is best I should not have. They were strange things indeed, and would show very clearly, to what extremities slavery was driven, when obliged to resort to such measures for its support. The principle, by which they were governed,

seemed to be, " If we have not *right*, we have *might* on
our side, and go to the penitentiary they *shall.*" In my
journal, respecting it, I recorded,—" What the result
will be I cannot tell, but it does appear as if, in making
out their indictments, they lacked common sense. I can
say with Paul, ' Neither can they prove the things
whereof they now accuse us ;' unless they suborn witnesses (which a number did), and then I am sure they
will have the worst of it."

There were three indictments. The first took the
broad ground, and charged us with STEALING four or
five negroes—being utterly false in many of its circumstantial statements. The second charged us with an
attempt to steal them. The third, with having formed a
combination, *intending* to make an attempt to steal
them—both the latter, as false and ridiculous in their
statements, as the former.

At first, our counsel thought of trying me alone on
the latter indictment, as this was the lightest, and I was
only an accessory in them all—but finally concluded
there would be no manner of danger in taking us all
together, on the first, feeling confident that justice could
do nothing with us. We consented to be thus tried.

" May our faith be greatly increased, and continue to
increase, as we advance through the fiery ordeal. May
we have His spirit, " who, when He was reviled, reviled
not again—when he suffered, He threatened not, but
committed Himself to Him who judgeth righteously."

SHACKLES OFF.

Sept. 10. *Noon.* Truly they are many who are gathered together against us, to destroy us. What are *we*,
that we should attract so much notice ! A little before
twelve o'clock, they came, and knocked off our fetters,
with hammer and chisel. We were then led out to the
gaze of hundreds, who, no doubt, expected to see something very wonderful. They were a sight indeed !
Such running, and crowding, and stretching, and climb-
ing—such eyes, and mouths, and expressions of wonder
and amazement. we had not before seen ! O ! what mad-

ness! What folly! What meanness! They seemed
almost ready to devour us.

Thus surrounded, we walked to the court house, each
accompanied by a guard. In a few minutes, court ad-
journed, and we returned to our palace, safe and sound.
This is the first time, for more than fifty-eight days, that
I have taken a natural step. I feel like a bird out of its
cage, now that we can walk about our room with freedom.

Evening. Have been before the court—house crowded—windows, doors, stairs, &c., all full, while many
could not find a place. After a long time the Jury was
chosen,—all of whom, with one exception, had made up
their minds from previous report, and under oath, confessed themselves *prejudiced* against us, but thought they
could decide according to justice, which was, in their
view, the Penitentiary. Such, reader, was the *impartial jury,* before whom we were tried!

WITNESSES.

Against us, were three or four witnesses sworn
—and for us, about six. As Esq. B., an old man,
whose head blossomed in white, came forward to be
sworn in our behalf, one of the rabble behind us, exclaimed, " there goes the daddy of all Abolitionists."
But though so many of our witnesses were sworn, when
the testimony and confessions of those *against* us were
heard, it was deemed wholly unnecessary to occupy more
time in the examination of our witnesses; as the testimony of our *enemies* was considered abundantly sufficient to clear us from the indictment.

In their first testimony, many things were stated, positively false, and which the witnesses must have *known*
to be so. . For example, Wm. P. Brown testified that
he heard Work and Burr tell the slaves that they had
sent off four negroes about four weeks ago—that they
had sent off a good many negroes, who were all doing
well, &c. The Devil could not have told a more abso-
lute falsehood. Nothing of the kind was ever uttered
by them. Two weeks previous to our arrest, we *had*

helped one on his way, and that was *all*. Again Brown said, when he presented his gun, Burr sprang, and said "Lord God!" and appeared to be near *fifteen* feet high ' Burr made no such expression. The "*fifteen feet*" is a sufficient comment on this testimony.

Again, he swore, that when he came to the bank, I was paddling. I had my fishing pole in my hand, and was standing in the skiff, just ready to draw my captive from the watery element, when he approached and threatened to shoot me. Again, he swore it was dark, there being a *fog*, so that he could not see a man at any distance. The *fact* is, it was a very bright night, and the moon was shedding her silvery rays most beautifully upon the earth. And many other statements, which I will not mention, were just as false—statements respecting what *we* said—what *slaves* said, &c. When cross examined by our counsel, he said, "I told Paris, Allen, and Prince (slaves), that there were some men from Illinois, who wished to assist them in getting their freedom, and that if they wished to go, *they had* MY PERMISSION *to go with them!* They said they did not wish their freedom. I told them to go with Anthony, (a slave)—and where he was going—and that if they saw any man who wished to aid them in getting their freedom, that they had *my permission* to go with them! That I would meet them before they got to the River. I did dot *direct* Anthony to go, but I *knew* he was going. I did not know that John went, but John was present, when he told all his boys, that they might go, if they desired. We gave the negroes five dollars apiece, for their conduct, and some more money was made up for them in Palmyra afterwards. I gave these directions to my negroes, at my home, in the yard, before they went. I told them to go where Anthony had appointed to meet them—the prisoners—at the river, I told Allen to go, and get hold of the skiff, and hold it. I also stated to Wiseman, the directions I had given to my negroes. I don't know that the prisoners had ever seen the negroes before, nor do I know that any agreement had been made to meet the negroes. I never had any communi-

4

cation directly or indirectly, with the prisoners, prior to
the time I took them. I had no control over Woolfolk's
negro. Woolfolk was not at home. I do not know
that John heard me, when I said that as many as wished
to go had my permission, but he was present in the yard
and heard me."

Reader, what think you of sending men to Penitentiary for twelve years on such testimony? It needs no
comment.

Mr. Quinn was examined. Among other things he
stated that he saw Burr two weeks before our arrest, in
Boulman's field, where he was at work. When he left
he did not go in the *precise* direction given to him, he
did not go in any *road*." Cross examined. He said,
" Burr did not speak to the negroes, and there *was no
road*, to go in the direction my uncle gave him. He was
in the *field*, and there *was no road !*"

Reader, you may consider this as a specimen of the
circumstantial evidence brought against us. Look at it.
Because, perchance, Burr did not go in the *precise* course
he was directed; because, in a field where there was no
road he varied a little to the south, what is the conclusion? Why, that he wanted to *steal the slaves !*

Another thing. When the witnesses were cross examined, our counsel were particular to enquire from
whence they derived their information (on many points).
They were obliged to confess, "*from the slaves !*" By
the laws of Missouri, a black man's testimony against a
white man, is of no avail, and yet here, they were lug-
ging in testimony after testimony, as *if* they saw or
heard the things themselves, when, lo ! " My negroes told
me," so and so.

Crockett, the St. Louis lawyer, saw that the most of
the testimony of the witnesses was likely to be shown
to be but the mere say-so of the negroes, and he remonstrated strongly against our counsel asking such questions.

Mr. Boulman, an old man, tottering on the brink
of the grave, was examined, but what he said, merely made sport, and a roar of laughter in the assem

bly—and I deem it not necessary to fill my pages with trifling nonsense. For want of room, I am obliged to omit much I otherwise should desire to lay before the public.

Sept. 11. Last night as we were talking together, one above cried out, "Shut your mouths there below, and go to sleep." They had been playing cards and carousing, so that we could scarcely sleep at all, and then because we could not sleep on account of their noise, and were passing the time in conversation, their hearts were so filled with spite and envy, that they grudged us even that happiness. O, what a spirit. But such worketh slavery.

THE PLEADING.

The States Attorney [Abernethy], made a short speech, venting out his hatred to abolitionists—classed them with Mormons, yea, with the notorious land pirates, John A. Murrell's gang, holding us up as terrible creatures, and making appeals, to excite the prejudice and hatred of the multitude, who were already so charged therewith, that they could scarcely contain themselves.

In his speech he compared the slaves to sheep, and liberty to salt;—said that enticing away the slave by spreading the offer of liberty before him, was just as really larceny, as tolling away a man's flock of sheep by salt.

Glover followed him with a clear, forcible, and argumentative speech, showing by various illustrations that what we did could not, in any sense of the word, be called larceny. His illustrations and references I cannot call to mind. He made some thrilling appeals to the jury with regard to the importance of justice—beautifully introduced the case of Aristides—referred to the house in which we were assembled as being called a house of justice, &c.—acknowledged that the rights of the people had been invaded—but there was *no law* forbidding it, and consequently they must patiently and nobly bear the wrong, till legal steps could be taken to prevent such things.

He made the case very plain; but their hearts were so filled with deep-rooted prejudices, and their minds so blinded to everything that does not uphold slavery, the jury appeared to see no force in his reasoning.

Anderson followed Glover. He volunteered his services, and talked very wickedly. His whole speech was merely a wild, boisterous harangue against Abolitionism and Mormonism (classing us with the Mormons), appealing with great spirit to the malice and prejudice of the jury and crowded assembly present, that he might make our punishment more sure. He fought hard against God, against his truth, his poor and his 'little ones'—against righteousness and all reason, mercy, justice and humanity. It distressed my soul exceedingly to hear a professor of religion (I was informed he was such), talk thus; and I could, at the time, but raise my heart to God in his behalf. O! that his eyes may be opened. Once (as I am informed) he professed to be a warm friend of Dr. Nelson and of the poor slave—but he has laid aside such feelings, and, as his own slave testifies, is now worse than ever—more oppressive to the slaves, and more bitter against those who plead their cause. He plead strongly for slavery—made exciting appeals, and seemed to desire ardently our long imprisonment.

Shall we meet him in heaven? How will he look upon us and sing with us there? Unless his feelings change from those expressed, he could not be happy with us. The Lord will make it all right.

Alanson and myself wrote him a very plain letter, which he published, to increase the prejudice against us, and augment our suffering.

Warren next made a lucid speech—showing clearly, by a variety of familiar illustrations, that what we did, could not be called larceny. He was an Illinoisian, and much prejudice prevailed against him in Palmyra, many supposing him to be an abolitionist. Yet he plead boldly. That his arguments might have more force, or to secure his own safety, he told them—" I have never yet passed for abolitionist on either side of the river."

Whether he was an abolitionist, I cannot say—but this much I can say for him—he and Moses Hunter were the first of our friends whom we saw after our confinement. They both prayed with us in the jail ; and there, in the presence of the jailer, guard, &c., he prayed for the " oppressed" as not one half of the abolitionists would dare to.

Wright followed, making the closing speech in our behalf. He was quite lengthy but not tedious. He took up the statute, and, from standard authors (so received on all other points even in slave states), demonstrated to every unprejudiced mind, that upon no possible principle of legal interpretation, could our conduct be called larceny—that there was no law whatever in Missouri touching our case.

He took up the facts, and showed that we had no intention to convert said property to our own use—had no self-interest in the matter, but desired only the benefit of the slave. In every point of view, from legal rules, legal principles and examples, he in numerous ways brought out the same truth.

Said he—" I appear before you as a friend to our institutions—as a citizen of the State, and as a *slaveholder,* but also a defender of justice. I believe those men were honest in their intentions, and really desired to benefit the slave. I have no doubt that they think themselves persecuted, and, should they go to the penitentiary, will feel that they are martyrs, and that their crown will shine brighter, and their song rise higher on account of what they now suffer. I despise an abolitionist, and their conduct too, but I plead that there is *no law* to hit the case, and therefore they should not be punished. Our only way is to send men to Jefferson who shall make provision for the future.* Let justice take

* The following law was passed and approved by the Governor more than three years after we were confined in the Penitentiary.

" If any person shall forge for any slave a free pass, or place in the possession of any slave any paper or thing whatever, by which such slave may the more readily escape from his master,—and any person who may abduct or entice, or *attempt* to abduct or entice any slave away from his master, such person shall, for every such offence, be subject to its course," &c. He plead nobly, though he was a slaveholder. None but those who were determined not to see could help seeing the truth, as thus spread before them in meridian brightness. He showed that the slaves were so far from being in *our* possession, and under our control, that we were in *their* possession, and that they were in the possession of their masters, acting according to their commands, and under their control—and instead of our stealing them, that they stole us.

It was now evening. After an intermission of half an hour, we again assembled, and Crockett made a display of his ingenuity in evading argument, blinding men's eyes, and causing justice to fall in the streets. His speech pleased the rabble very much, but was not in accordance with the *law*.

For the information of the reader, I will mention the great lever by which he overturned, in the minds of the jury, all that had been brought forward from standard authorities, by our counsel. From a great many references, they had shown what *was*, and what was *not* larceny—and that the present case could not from any definition, or principle, or example, be construed into larceny. But a very easy way to get round all this, had Crockett, by simply saying that "*England* had no *slave* property, consequently all these examples that have been brought forward, have no application to this species of property, and are wholly irrelevant!!!" Amazing! what a discovery! Where is the school-boy that does not know that England DID have such kind of property, when the laws were *made*? And yet, this palpable absurdity was swallowed by the mass, as an unanswerable argument.

His speech continued till near midnight, on Saturday; we then returned to our habitation, to spend the Sabbath.

an indictment in any court in the State having criminal jurisdiction, and, on conviction thereof, shall be confined in the Penitentiary of the State for a term of years not less than five nor more than ten."—Sec. vii.

Reader, the above is a true copy from the State Records, signed by the Speaker of the House, President of the Senate, Secretary and Governor of the State of Missouri, March 27, 1845. And we were locked in the Penitentiary, Oct. 3, 1841. Judge whether we were transgressors of their laws.

JOURNAL.

Sept. 12. After the scenes of the past week, the care, anxiety, and suspense in which we have been held —surrounded by gazing crowds, who poured their anathemas upon us, and thirsted for our blood, how delightful to be again enclosed in our room from the multitudes! Yea, how sweet to meet another Sabbath, when we can draw near, and pour out our hearts into the bosom of our Savior. Though we are yet in suspense, it is good to have this day, to study our bibles and pray. The result is yet uncertain. It is now in the hands of the judge and jury, and they are in the hands of God—and I am sure He will lead to that decision which will most advance the cause of liberty and truth. Feeling this, and desiring only the advancement of that cause, why should one anxious thought possess my bosom? They say they must punish *us*, to deter *others* from the like, and put a stop to such proceedings—but how vain! Why cannot they see that the more they punish, the worse it will be for them? For they will only increase the number of "these vile fiends," an hundred fold! Well, if Jesus be with me, I can bear the reproaches and insults of man. Confinement will be liberty; the prison, a palace; stripes, sweet-oil; hard labor, rest; separation from friends, tolerable; and death, in forms frightful, will be glorious.

In ourselves, in our friends, in our lawyers, in man, there is no help; "our help is in the name of the Lord." "Man's extremity is God's opportunity."

SENTENCE.

Sept. 13. Monday morning, we again went before the court. After the different instructions were given to the judge, and he had charged the jury, that we were *guilty*, &c., they retired a short time, and returned with a verdict of "*Guilty, and twelve years in the penitentiary.*" Clapping of hands, and shouts of "good, good," filled the house. Though they had so strongly declared they would hang us, if we were sentenced for less than twenty years, they appeared to be satisfied, when this sentence was pronounced. " There," said one, " we've got clear of mobbing them!"

OUR GALLOWS.

So general was the expectation, that they could do nothing with us, by law, that a mob had been organized, who had erected our *gallows,* provided ropes, blacked their faces, and were ready to take us at a moment's notice, in case we were acquitted, and hang us on the spot! Reader, do you believe this? It cannot be doubted. I have abundant testimony, printed, oral, and optical. On this point I shall let the Missourians speak for themselves.

Yes, there were *twenty* men, at Palmyra and Hannibal, who, in the sight of God, were (and if living are), guilty of our *murder!* They are *murderers* in the light of *God's* law, and *as* such, they will be tried and condemned at the great tribunal, unless, before that time, they make their peace with the Judge. We pity them, we pray for them—" Father, forgive them, for they know not what they do."

BILL OF EXCEPTIONS—FROM THE COURT RECORDS.

" And this being all the evidence in the cause, the counsel for the prisoners ask the court to instruct the jury as follows :

" That before they can find the defendants guilty, they must, from the evidence in the cause (and from no other source), find the following facts :

" 1. That the defendants had possession of the slaves. And, to constitute a possession in them, of said slaves, the jury must from the evidence in the cause, find that the defendants exercised authority to restrain the movements of the slaves, or (the slaves being present), claimed the right of control, dominion, or authority over the will of said slaves.

" That if they find that the defendants were so possessed of said slaves, the jury must also find, from the evidence in the cause, that at the time of becoming so possessed of said slaves, it was the intention of said defendants, to convert the property in said slaves *to their own use.* If on the contrary the jury shall find from the evidence in the cause, that the defendants were in the control of said slaves or in the power of said slaves, or that when the defendants and slaves met and while they remained together, the defendants claimed no authority over said slaves, nor exercised any, but met the slaves on equal footing, as free men, they ought to find the defendants NOT GUILTY

" They ask the court further to instruct the jury, that whether Anthony met the defendants, with or without the consent of his master, still, to constitute a *taking* of said slave, by the defendants, the said slave must have been in the possession of said defendants, as before explained—and that even such possession cannot authorize the jury to find defendants guilty of larceny unless the jury can also find from the evidence in the cause, that at the time defendants had the intention to convert the property in said slaves, to *their own use*. That a conversion to the use of said defendants cannot be made out, by merely showing that the defendants were willing and desirous to give *aid* and *assistance* to said slave or slaves in crossing the Mississippi river, and in pursuing their journey to Canada, but that there must be an intention to *sell*, or *hire*, or retain said slaves *for their service*, or otherwise to exercise acts of *ownership* over said slaves."

The record proceeds—" Which instructions the court refused, and instructed the jury that the *agreement* to meet the slaves for the purpose of aiding them in obtaining their freedom, and their meeting under that agreement constituted a taking! To which opinion of the court, in refusing to grant the instruction asked by the counsel, for the prisoners, and deciding that the agreement to meet the slaves, constituted a taking, the defendants except."

The attorney for the State moved the court for the following instructions :

State of Missouri, against George Thompson, James Burr, and Alanson Work, for larceny. The said State, by her attorney moves the court to instruct the jury :

1. That if they believe from the evidence in this cause, that James Burr and Alanson Work *did* steal, take, and carry away the slaves, as charged in the indictment, or any one of them, and George Thompson was in any way aiding or abetting as charged in the indictment, then they must find them all guilty, as charged in the second count of said indictment.

2. That if they, the defendants, Burr and Work had the slaves, or any one of them under their control or government, and while so, caused the said slaves to take one step, then the taking and carrying away was completed.

3. That if the defendants fraudulently intended to deprive the owners of said slaves, of the property and labor of said slaves, and to confer the same on them (the slaves), the defendants

or any third person or persons, other than the said owners, that is sufficient to make the stealing, taking and carrying away, larceny. That if the jury believed there was a taking, it is no difference whether the taking was effected by physical, or moral force, if the force was sufficient to effect the object intended.

5. (Erased).

6. That if the jury find from the evidence in this cause, that the defendants, James Burr and Alanson Work attempted to steal, take, and carry away the slaves, or any one of them *as charged in the indictment*,* and that George Thompson aided or abetted in such attempt, but failed in executing said attempt, then they must find them, Burr and Work, guilty of said attempt, and George Thompson guilty as accessory before the fact of said attempt,"—which (instruction) was given by the court. To which opinion of the court in giving the said instructions for the State, the defendants by their counsel also excepted. After verdict, the defendants moved in writing for a new trial as follows.

STATE,	*Indictment* for larceny.
vs.	of slaves
BURR, WORK, AND THOMPSON,	

The defendants by their counsel, move the court for a new trial.

1. Because the court refused proper instructions asked by the defendants.

2. Because the court gave improper instructions on behalf of the plaintiff.

3. Because the verdict is *against evidence.*

4. Because it is *against* LAW.

5. Because the punishment is *excessive.*

GLOVER AND WRIGHT, *for def'ts.*

Which motion the court also overruled, and the defendants excepted to the opinion of the court in overruling said motion. The defendants then moved in writing to arrest the judgment in the case, as follows:

STATE,	
vs.	*Indictment.*
BURR, WORK, AND THOMPSON,	

The defendants move the court to arrest the judgment in the above cause.

1. Because the declaration is bad.

2. Because the judgment is for the wrong party.

GLOVER AND WRIGHT, *for def'ts.*

But the court also overruled said motion, and defendants excepted,

* This is wholly gratuitous and false, for there was no such charge in the indictment by which we were tried—the charge was broad STEALING —the *attempt to steal* was a separate indictment altogether.

and prayed that their several exceptions to the opinions and decisions of the court as aforesaid, might be signed and sealed, and
made part of the record in the cause. This is done accordingly.

Teste.   { P. H. McBRIDE, *Judge*.
         { P. RUCKER, *Clerk*.

(A copy.)

From the foregoing, the reader will get a pretty
good idea of the circumstances in the case, as also of the
flagrant injustice we suffered.   The exceptions and instructions of our counsel were contemned, and utterly
rejected—our appeal for a new hearing refused, and every
motion in our favor vetoed by the judge.

We remained in jail until the 17th, when we went out
to receive our sentence from the Judge.   After hearing
it, we appealed to the Supreme Court of Missouri—and
obtained a respite of two weeks, while our counsel could
go to St. Louis, where the court was sitting—but the
Supreme Judge utterly refused to have anything to do
with it, and would not allow the appeal.   Thus our
twelve years stared us fairly in the face ; but by the grace
of God, we were enabled to meet them undaunted and
unmoved.

Let me here remark (what the reader must have observed), that it was evident through the whole of our
trial and imprisonment, we were not looked upon nor
considered as common *State felons*, but as *abolitionists*.
It was contended by *no one* that we intended to *steal* the
slaves in the common acceptation of that term.   Every
body acknowledged us as " *true blue*" abolitionists, who
desired only the good of the slave.

NOVEL DECISION.

During the course of the trial, it was contended and
decided, that a man on the East bank of the Mississippi
river, might steal another on the West bank !   It was
not necessary that he should even see, or speak with the
slave ; if, by any means, by moral suasion, letter, or
signs, he helps a slave to freedom, who had of his own
accord run away from his master, he is guilty of
grand larceny !   If a man in Quincy lets it be known

that he will help slaves on their way, after they have crossed the river—and this information spreads among the slaves, so that hundreds take shelter under his roof; what is the decision of a court of justice in Missouri? Why, that he STOLE them all, though he may never have seen one of them till they called at his door for help. Nay more. If he only sends word into Missouri to one slave, and that slave spreads the news to others, that in Quincy are friends who will help them—as many as will come—they come—others help them on their way —he sees or speaks to none of them—what is the decision in Missouri, by lawyers, judges, and juries? Why *he* STOLE them all! How? pray. "Why he placed the SALT before them!"—"Salt! salt!—Sheep! Sheep!" is the great hue and cry, for an illustration on this subject.

Hereafter, reader, you shall have more as novel decisions as this, by Missouri courts of justice.

OUR MURDERERS AGAIN.

As this subject is in close connexion with our trial, I will close this chapter with testimony on the point. A man writing from Palmyra says, "There is a determination on the part of the citizens, should they be cleared, in consequence of any flaw or technicality in the law, *not to let them go unpunished.*

"This, I think you may put down as a settled point— and I am of the opinion that it would be far better for the prisoners to be sent to the penitentiary, than to be turned loose here—for there is no telling what scenes might be enacted. On one day I heard the above sentiment expressed on several occasions by as respectable gentlemen as there are in the county. Suppose, sir, that those men had been cleared, could not every man in this community have done the same with impunity? Most assuredly, and I repeat it—I should deeply deplore to see these men loose, in Palmyra, for there is no telling what scenes might be enacted."

I am thankful I can inform the public " what scenes" would have been " enacted" had we been cleared.

Rev. Wm. Beardsley, writing for the Oberlin Evangelist, says, " We have been assured by respectable people in Missouri, that there were many at the court, prepared and fully determined, in case they were not convicted, to assassinate them on the spot."

A minister, at the time he wrote, living at St. Louis, and acquainted in Palmyra, handed us, in the Penitentiary, a letter (hereafter to be introduced) in which he says, " I believe the Lord overruled the affair for the preserving of your lives—for had you been acquitted, you all would have certainly been murdered! The infuriated mob, with their faces all blacked, had prepared the gallows, and even the ropes for your execution! O! tell it not in Gath—publish it not in the streets of Askelon!

After we had been in the Penitentiary, nearly four years, a man who at the time of our trial (I believe he was present) lived in the adjoining county, said to us, " To your trial, twenty men came from Hannibal prepared to *hang* you in case of an acquittal. When the sentence was announced, a *magistrate* said to his fellow, " There we've got clear of mobbing them !''

Reader, turn back and read their repeated threats, their oaths and curses, and then judge if I speak falsely. " Lord, lay not this sin to their charge."

CHAPTER VIII.

JOURNAL AND LETTERS.

TWELVE YEARS IN THE PENITENTIARY.

Sept. 13. " Father, not as I will, but as thou wilt." " Glorify thy name."

If that is the field of labor for me—if most for my good—if best for my friends—if the cause of Christ

needs it—if abolitionists need it to stir them up—if the
poor slave needs it—if it will be for the best good of the
world—" if my crown will shine brighter in heaven, my
song rise higher," and be sweeter—then *Amen!* I
shall be acquitted at the great and supreme tribunal of
the universe.   Then my dear Savior will act as judge,
and the world will see and acknowledge the justness of
my cause.   Then those who are now my enemies, and
rejoice and clap their hands at my condemnation, will be
covered with shame and everlasting confusion, unless
they repent.   Then all things will be set perfectly right,
and *to that court I appeal!*

I had laid my plans, and was looking forward with
joyful anticipations to the time when I should stand on
heathen ground, to proclaim the gospel of Jesus.   But
if these plans were not in accordance with my Savior's,
let them be frustrated, and his fully carried out.

I have dear attachments at Mission Institute, but I
leave them to accomplish my Redeemer's will.   I
have aged parents, dear brothers, sisters, and friends,
but gladly leave them to follow in the steps of my Captain, and of the innumerable company of those who
have suffered for Jesus' sake.   I feel unworthy to be
thus honored, but am willing my Master should make
me just such an instrument to roll on his cause, as he
sees fit.

Should I be confined twelve years to toil, shut out
from Christian society and privileges, I will say with
David, "Though I walk through the valley of the
shadow of death, I will fear no evil, for thou art with
me."   Yes, Jesus will be with me there.   "He will
never leave me, nor forsake" me.   When I walk through
the "midst of trouble, He will revive me"—"through
rivers of sorrow, they shall not overflow me"—through
the "flame, I shall not be burned," for He is with me.
"There shall no evil befall" me, for He shall "preserve
me from all evil."   He shall "preserve my soul."

If I go to Jefferson, I go as innocent a man (as to this
crime) as ever suffered from the spite and malice of wicked men.   Their own law condemns them, and God's

law pronounces sentence upon them, unless they repent.

Well, let them do their worst, they can't hurt us. They cannot give a guilty conscience, nor keep us from communion with God, nor shut from our hearts the consolations of the Holy Ghost. They cannot bar heaven against us nor take from us the golden harp, nor pluck our crowns from our heads. No; still "Blessed is the man who trusteth in the Lord, and whose hope the Lord is." I pity those who would injure me—I pray for them—I forgive them, and hope they may find forgiveness with God. O for a spirit of greater love to, and more hearty forgiveness of enemies.

The grace of God has sustained me during the trial; my heart has been calm, and my mind composed. At the time of the sentence, our minds were unmoved and our countenances unchanged. The multitude gazed to see us blush and drop our heads, but were disappointed. Jesus did not forsake us at that trying time. I felt then, and still feel the preciousness of trusting in Christ, of leaning upon his arm, and committing all to his care.

To-day, through the intercession of our counsel we received a quire of paper, that we might write letters to some of our friends before going to the Penitentiary.

During much of the time, of those two weeks, we were engaged in writing letters—some of which shall be soon forthcoming.

A FREE MAN MOBBED.

14. This afternoon, Charles (the sleeping preacher), went out and was cleared—no prosecutor appearing against him, nor indictment found. He started to go over with Stephen (a student), but a mob pursued.

They have long threatened abusing him, when he should get out, and no sooner is he clear, than the human bloodhounds are in close pursuit! This is but a specimen of the spirit that exists here—that slavery germinates and fosters. The cause of their hatred to Charles, was doubtless his enmity to slavery. Mark! though he was honorably discharged, and had injured no

one, he could not, with safety, stay there one nour—
and yet "we are opposed to mobs in Marion!"

MOB IN CINCINNATI.

Heard, by Stephen, that there has been a mob in Cincinnati—some killed—property destroyed—and great
commotion. Our nation appears to be drawing very
near a crisis. It seems almost ripe for ruin. The sufferings of the slave, and the blood of the martyrs, cry
loudly to heaven for vengeance.

That slavery is soon to fall I have no doubt, but in
what way, I cannot tell. I fear men will not listen to
truth, sufficiently to lead them to see and put away the
evil peaceably; if they will not, then, by the judgments
of God they will be compelled to give it up. He can
easily find means to put away the system; and may the
time be hastened. Let God use those means which will
most glorify Him. These commotions, mobs, concus-
sions of States, casting honest men into prison, and
other events of like character, evince that something
uncommon, unlooked-for, and that will cause "the ears
of men to tingle," is *near*. Lord, turn and overturn,
till the nation and church are thoroughly purified.

THE BROKEN WILL.

15. Harry, the shoemaker, is a slave. His old master, at his death, left in his will that Harry should be.
free. But as soon as he was dead, before he was buried, his children contrived and destroyed the will, and
still hold Harry as a slave.

Such is the case with many. I have heard of numbers; and there is not an honest, enlightened slaveholder, that can deny that such cruel injustice is common in the slave states. Nothing is too bad for the spirit
of slavery to do.

Albert's first master willed him free at the age of
twenty-five. Since then he has been sold again and
again. They have tried their utmost to sell him south,
so that he could never get the will; but he is a little too
smart   he knows too much, and doubtless will

get his freedom, by will, or "leg bail." His mind is well-filled. This Albert was sold south—ran away— was taken up and put in Palmyra jail—was there during all our time—learned to write—took lessons on liberty —and, shortly after our departure, slipped by the jailer, as he came one evening to bring his supper—called, with his companion, on our friends—and went safely to Victoria's domain.

UNBELIEF AND FAITH.

16. At present the way may seem dark to some of our friends, and because they cannot *see* the reason of this dispensation, may feel discouraged. Let not this be the case with any. There is no cause for being cast down. Only believe that God knows and will do what is for our best good, and we shall rejoice in all his ways.

Joseph might have thought his treatment a strange providence ; he could have brought up many plausible reasons why it would have been better for him to be with his father and friends, but he trusted in God. Though he could not see, yet he believed and was happy, and useful in his prison—in a land of strangers. Had he not believed, he would have made himself miserable, and perhaps pined away, and sunk into the grave. Unbelief banishes peace.

Behold his father. How very different. He has no faith. As soon as a dark cloud arises, he is in trouble —puts the worst construction on the providence of God —looks at the dark side, murmurs, frets, repines, and makes up his mind to "go to the grave mourning." He was unhappy—had no peace ; for his unbelief had completely shut out peace from his soul. Friends, believe, where you cannot see. Rest in God, and you shall be kept in "perfect peace," though the earth should pass away.

Though Jacob chafed and vexed himself, yet God went forward with his wise and kind purposes. Joseph was separated from home and friends for perhaps twenty years. Jacob, all this time, made himself wretched by unbelief, when he might have been contented and happy, by only exercising confidence in God. But after a long time he showed the old father his folly in being so concerned and irreconciled.

Great good was the result of this strange providence —not only Jacob and his family but *nations* saved and God glorified! How much sweeter this blessing would have been to Jacob, had he all the time felt a firm confidence that all would come out for the best.

Then let not my parents feel and say as did Jacob— "An evil beast hath devoured him. George is, without doubt, rent in pieces." "I will go down to the grave mourning," &c., but let them trust in God and be quiet. Let them feel that He is wiser and more kind than they.

Let not M. feel as did Martha and Mary of old when their brother died—"Lord, if thou hadst been here. my brother had not died,"—as if their happiness all rested on their brother. Here was unbelief. They did not acknowledge the hand of God. Because their brother died, their hopes were all blasted, and they were filled with anxiety and trouble. Let her remember the words of the Savior—"Said I not unto thee that if thou wouldst believe, thou shouldst see the glory of God?" Let none fret and murmur. The glory of God *shall* be seen—therefore let all be satisfied, composed, and trust in Jesus.

Though I go not down to Egypt to feed with temporal bread or save the temporal lives of millions, yet, if I go to Jefferson, there is no doubt that thousands will be delivered from worse than Egyptian bondage, and fed with spiritual bread, and made to inherit eternal life in consequence. More broken hearts than were in Jacob's family will be bound up and comforted,—many an old mourning father will be made to rejoice upon his son's neck, and to say—"Now let me die, since I have seen thy face and thou art yet alive." In many a family will there be "heard music and dancing," because he that was as dead has come again, and the lost has been found—of many places shall it be said, "there was great joy in that city," because the oppressor's arm has been broken, and liberty to all proclaimed through the land.

Shall I then fear to go down to Egypt? (Jefferson?)
No! No! "Lord, here am I, send me."

TAKING THE SLAVE'S PLACE.

"Thou shalt love thy neighbor as thyself." How
shall this be applied to the slave? If many can be released from their sufferings for years, by my taking, as
it were, their place, then does not this principle require
me to do it cheerfully? At any rate I am willing to
wear the chain—endure the frowns and threats—perform the toil, and suffer the smartings of the lash, if
this will ease them of their burden.

Although going to the penitentiary is not exactly taking the slave's place, yet it is suffering with him, and
for him, and will shorten the time of his bondage. If
in this way, more than in any other, I can labor effectually to break his chain, then let Jesus take me, use me
in his own way, help me to "gird up the loins of my
mind," that I may bear up manfully under all.*

THE LAST VIEW.

After our sentence, many of our beloved associates
hastened, day after day, to take their last view of us in
this world. Load after load came and gave us the parting hand, the farewell look, and the affectionate benediction. The clank of our chain, and the united voices,
of those kindred and dear, made music sweet, while
they in the street, and we in our dungeon, together
praised the Lord, and sought his blessing and protection.
O, precious seasons!

As I write, my mind recalls the names of many who
then beheld us for the last time. One, and another, and
another, were soon called to their rest. Our beloved
Moses has gone; good old David walks in white; Isaac
and Samuel are no more; Brother Francis is with Jesus;
Reoecca has long sung with the angels; little Ellen
(Alanson's youngest child), quickly pined away and sank

* Though my journal was written as expressive of my own particular
feelings and views, it is believed it as heartily expresses the feelings of
the other brethren as my own.

into the grave, sorrowing for her father;—while many
have been wafted to distant nations, to proclaim the glad
tidings of salvation.

Though bars of iron prevented our near approach, our
spirits rejoiced in secret fellowship, while we anticipated
the happy meeting above, where foes can never more
approach.

On the 18th of Sept., Mrs. Work with all her family
made a visit to the Jail—came in—and while the little
ones embraced their father, and each bade him farewell,
O! where is the heart that would not melt? Yet Palmyrians could look upon the scene unmoved. Slavery is
very familiar with seeing parents torn from their children, and families sundered. Such things are common,
every-day occurrences, and not regarded.

I believe Mrs. Work came once more, before we left
—some came still later, but for the last week of our time
there, no one came—having heard that we were gone.
Expecting every day that some one would be over, we
wrote many things both in the way of journal and letters,
expecting an opportunity to send them by our friends;
but no friends came, and they all fell into the hands of
the enemy, and most probably were committed to the
flames. Our books, watch, &c., after a long time, were
given up.

Before our trial, a minister, Brother B., from Illinois,
came to see and converse with us, but was not allowed
to come in. We spoke a few words through the grates.

On the 17th, Horatio Foote came to see us, but was
denied the privilege. He went to the sheriff: "No."
He went to the circuit judge: "No admittance." And
he went home, without seeing or speaking to us.

In a *religious* town, and yet a prisoner not allowed to
converse with a gospel minister, nor receive from him a
word of counsel and consolation. Now mark. On the
very next day, *two men* [Missourians], were allowed to
come and talk with us, in defence of slavery; while he
who wished to enquire after our souls' welfare was excluded. One of the two was formerly a methodist
minister, but is now an *editor*, and probably came in to

talk with us, that he might have something to attract notice in the columns of his paper.

The following is the substance of our conversation : "What are your feelings under your trials ?" " We are perfectly resigned, contented, and happy." " Do you think your conduct was right ?" " Perfectly so." " By what rule was it justifiable ?" " By the commands of the Bible, and the whole spirit of the gospel." " Will you please state more definitely ?" " Love thy neighbor as thyself,"—" As ye would that men should do to you, do ye even so to them,"—" Do good unto all men," &c. " What do you think of Philemon's case ?" " There is no difficulty in that, for Onesimus was Philemon's *own brother*, and not a *slave*." On this he argued some time, " I have been accustomed to believe that Onesimus was a *runaway slave*, and that Paul sent him back to his master." " All very natural, sir, but read the chapter, and see what it says (v. 16), ' Not now as a servant, but above a servant, a *brother beloved*, specially to me—but how much more to thee, both *in the flesh*, and in the Lord ?' Sir, the phrase ' in the flesh,' can mean nothing more nor less than an *own brother*. Read again (v. 18), 'If he hath wronged thee, or oweth thee aught,' &c. Can a *slave* owe his master ? The probability is, sir, that he was a younger brother, bound out to his older brother, Philemon." It was a new idea to him altogether, and he was taken in a way he was not expecting—was confused, and could not say much ; for there it was, right before his eyes ; deny it he could not. Perhaps he had read the chapter hundreds of times, and preached from it frequently to slaves, and others ; yet slavery had so blinded his eyes, he never had seen the plainest undeniable meaning. He had been looking for something with which to bolster up *slavery* and not for the simple truth—and is not this the case with the majority of slaveholding ministers?

OUR CHAIN AGAIN.

Sept. 18. Before dark they came and put us in chains again, not the old one, but one not quite so large. It was a large ox chain. One of us at each end, and James in the middle, about five feet apart.—This is the one they expect us to wear to Jefferson. What their object can be I know not, unless it is to spite and harass us all they can, while they have the power; for surely they cannot feel that there is any danger of our getting away, and they must know that we have no disposition so to do. This is by the sheriff's orders, a professed brother in Christ!

Remonstrance was in vain, nor had he courage to come and speak with us, but sent word, "It must be done." Is it uncharitable to say, "And Felix willing to show the Jews a pleasure, left Paul bound?" But I will bear it patiently, for heaven will be the sweeter for the trials of earth. We have been free from our chain eight and a half days.

SLAVEHOLDERS' RELIGION AND CATHOLICISM.

I very much fear that much of the religion of the slaveholders is like the religion of Bishop Bonner and the Catholic clergy in the times of the persecutions, about the year 1500. Then, if a man called the Pope *Anti-Christ*, &c., he was at once, without judge or jury, condemned as a heretic, and not fit to live. So now, if a man go into a slave state, and open his mouth against the awful abominations practised—if he " cry aloud and spare not," or if he even drop a word or remark in favor of *abolition*—if he does not uphold their " domestic institutions"—if it is seen that he is against slavery—why then, no matter what his character may be, though ever so meek, humble, inoffensive, and devoted to doing good, he is denounced as unworthy to live,—mobbed and killed, imprisoned or driven from the state. The more holy the man, the fiercer their rage.

There certainly is a great similarity in the *fruits* of the two religions—whether they are the *same* religion, the Lord be Judge.

TRUSTING IN GOD.

Sept. 19. " Whoso putteth his trust in the Lord shall be safe ;" and again, " shall be made fat."

Situated as we are—in chains—among enemies who devise our hurt ; separated from dear friends, and denied the privileges of God's house—watched with an eagle-eye—reproached and reviled—not knowing what a day may bring forth—expecting, in chains, to be hastened to the confinement of a penitentiary, under the care and treatment of whom we know not—there, for years, to be shut out from all religious society ; perhaps to be denied even speaking or writing to our friends ; excluded from religious privileges ; in speechless toil to spend the day under a driver, and by night alone with Jesus—thus situated it is beyond utterance blessed, sweet, and glorious, to commit ourselves and cause into the hands of our faithful Redeemer. It gives a peace " the world cannot take away"—a " joy unspeakable and full of glory."

20. " If thou faint in the day of adversity thy strength is small."—*Prov.* xxiv. 10. That my strength is small I am conscious ; yet I trust the grace of Christ will so strengthen me, that I shall not " faint." For he has said, if I " wait on him with good courage," He " will strengthen my heart." I have waited on Him and have not fainted. I will wait upon Him, and trust I shall not faint. His promise is *sure.*

O ! that none of my friends may faint, but trust in the Lord in adversity as well as in prosperity—yea, we hardly know whether we do really trust in Him till adversity tries our faith. We should then be thankful for circumstances which put our faith and principle to a test. They show us what we are—teach us ourselves—bring out our real hearts. Adversity is calculated to promote in us unfeigned humility ; to increase our dependence on God—our patience, love, faith; and to separate us from the world and all creature objects. It shows us who are our true friends ; for

" The friends who in our *sunshine* live,
    When *winter* comes, are flown ;
And he who has but *tears* to give,
    Must weep those tears *alone.*"

It teaches us to be thankful for prosperity; we learn the *worth* of it; and when restored again to health, friends, and comforts, we shall prize and improve them. Thus sickness teaches us the worth of health—losses and destitution, the value of possession—bereavements, the greatness of the blessing of friends, parents, husband, wife, and children—persecution, the blessedness of peace and quietness—and by imprisonment, we learn the importance of *liberty*.

Such being the beneficial results of adversity, shall we shrink back from its approach? Oh! no; for "blessed is the man that endureth temptation, for when he is tried he shall receive a crown of life."

> I welcome, then, the piercing blast,
> For Oh! though sharp, 'twill soon be past,
> And swiftly waft me homeward too:
> Let tempests blow and billows roll,
> My Captain will their rage control,
> And He will bear me safely through.
>
> I welcome dungeons, pain, and shame,
> Yea, welcome death, for Jesus's name.
> If I may reach his blest abode,
> In tribulation I'll rejoice,
> In persecution tune my voice,
> And glory in the path He trod.

Moreover, adversity not only teaches us, as nothing else can, the preciousness and worth of the promises, but gives us a claim to them, bringing us into circumstances for which they were especially provided, and to which particularly adapted. Says Meikle—"He that suffers under the greatest load of afflictions, has a right to the greatest number of promises: and whenever he loses another enjoyment, he has a right to another promise, which makes up that loss with a redundancy of goodness." But I need not enlarge. The whole tenor of the Bible teaches us that adversity is profitable if rightly improved—sent in love, and only designed to "do us good in the latter end," and "make us partakers of his holiness."

The universal testimony of the saints is that their most afflictive days have been their best days. They all sing, it is good to be afflicted,—sweet affliction, that brings Jesus to my soul.

LETTER FROM ALANSON, BEFORE STARTING FOR JEF-FERSON.

BROTHER TURNER:—

You expressed the opinion that we did not realize what it is to go to the penitentiary, or that we looked upon it in too light a manner. Thinking it may help me to endure with patience whatever awaits me, and be a satisfaction to you and the dear friends, who have manifested their kind feelings to us while here, I have concluded to give you a brief history of my feelings, that you may be the better able to judge of my preparation to go to the penitentiary.

When I started on the expedition that has brought me here, I felt confident that it was right, yea, and duty, to help those who want help. This confidence has given me a quiet conscience at all times. When we first fell into the hands of our enemies, and they, with their guns at our breasts, threatened to shoot us if we stirred; when they had us in their power, and Brown stepped back and said he would shoot *me* anyhow, I felt startled. And when I came to realize my condition and the prospect before me; not knowing what to expect—hearing the threats of those who had us in their power, some of whom were for hanging, some for shooting; some for one thing and some for another; when these prospects flashed across my mind, my condition appeared dreadful. And then my *family* !—my wife forty miles from home —my little children *alone*, waiting in anxious suspense the return of their father—all came pressing on my mind with such force, that for the first week I was unhappy.

The thought that I might, if acquitted, fall into the hands of the mob, my body be whipped to a gore of blood, or my life be taken away by this or some other means, at times made me tremble. But feeling conscious that my motive was " to do to others as I would they should do to me," I continued to commit myself and

5

fami.y to God, in fervent prayer, feeling that *He* was my only hope.

Our friends furnished us with books. In these I found food and strength. In studying the Bible, I found it " a lamp to my feet, and a light to my path." In it I learned that the " Captain of our salvation was made perfect through suffering;" and that if we " would reign with Him, we must also suffer with Him." These and kindred passages, together with the account of the sufferings of Christians, as given in the Book of Martyrs, reconciled me to my "light afflictions." When I heard my Savior saying, " Let not your heart be troubled, neither let it be afraid;" when I heard the word of God in almost every chapter—" Fear not," " Be not dismayed," " I will be with you," " I will help you," " Not a hair of your head shall perish, and nothing shall by any means hurt you," " When thou passest through the waters I will be with thee, and through the rivers, they shall not overflow thee," " When thou walkest through the fire thou shalt not be burned, neither shall the flame kindle upon thee," &c., my fears were allayed. And when I read Mahan's Christian Perfection, and saw the *full redemption* there is in Christ—how He has made the fullest provision for all our necessities of body and soul, for time and for eternity, that infinite love and wisdom could devise—when I saw that infinite faithfulness was pledged to fulfil the " exceeding great and precious promises" to every one believing in them, and when I could plead these promises with confidence, I felt my strength renewed, and my mind girded to meet the conflict.

I committed myself to the Lord, and prayed that He would deliver me out of the hands of my enemies, or that He would allow them to triumph by sending me to the penitentiary, or to wreak their vengeance by taking my life, or in any other way that would glorify his name, and most benefit the slave. With these feelings I went before the court, and was "not greatly moved" during the trial, as the prospect appeared for or against us.

When the jury gave their verdict, and all eyes were

turned upon us, to see the effect, by the grace of God, I looked them in the face with composure.

And now, if it is my Heavenly Father's will that I should go to the penitentiary and labor for twelve years, separated from my family, from his ordinances, and people, I know that He has wise reasons—some purposes of mercy to accomplish; and as He has hitherto given me strength according to my day, I feel that I can trust Him for the future, and that He will prepare me to endure to the end, or open the prison door, in his own time and way. Now, dear brother, is my confidence misplaced? Have I any reason to murmur, be cast down, or to fear what man will do to me? I trust that you, and all who sigh and pray, and labor for the slave, will answer, no.

I learn that my condition, on account of my family, excites sympathy even in the hard heart of the oppressor. But why should it? They can see the slave separated from *his* family, and all the ties of nature sundered in respect to him, without one feeling of compassion. Let them first learn to show pity at home, and I shall need none. I now feel my interest, my life, my liberty, my all, identified with those of the slave. I design to search for some pillar on which slavery rests, and through the prayers of God's people, hope to be endued with power from on high to lay hold of it, and if I perish, perish Sampson like.   A. · Work.

Doubtless the foregoing letter will be read with interest by every reader.

I regret that henceforth, our history, feelings, &c., must be drawn chiefly from my own writings. The journal for all, was kept by myself. Each of us wrote letters frequently, yet these are for the most part lost, and many of my own I have not been able to get, so that the history will necessarily be incomplete. However I trust it will not be unprofitable.

Palmyra Jail, Sept. 14, '41.

DEAR PARENTS, BROTHERS, AND SISTERS :

"I suppose you have had many anxious thoughts about me, since you heard of my confinement in this jail. Let me say, dismiss your anxiety, your carefulness, and your fears. ALL IS WELL, Yesterday, our trial closed, with a verdict of guilty, and twelve years in the penitentiary. Be not troubled. 'The Lord reigns.' Shall not the Judge of all the earth do right?" Yes, I am satisfied with his dealings with me. Be assured that the things whereof I am accused, are not true.

They have tried but failed to prove them, and passed sentence *contrary* to their own laws, though in perfect accordance with their prejudices and their malice. I go to Jefferson, remembering that I am but treading in the steps of my Captain, and of an innumerable company of saints who have been persecuted and killed for doing good. I go with cheerfulness, to be a partaker of the *slaves'* sufferings, and to "fill up that which remaineth of the sufferings of Christ." I go, feeling that I have done right. In view of these things the Penitentiary seems a sweet place—the toil, rest—the confinement, liberty —the years, a few days—the disgrace, a great honor. My spirit they cannot confine, my thoughts they cannot chain. They shall soar on high, and dwell in the celestial region : I shall lack no good thing. If my plans are all to be frustrated, *Amen.* I will not love my parents, brothers, sisters, plans, attachments, more than my Savior ; but gladly leave them all, to fulfil his most blessed will. My sentence is twelve years, but we do not expect to remain that length of time—if nothing else can be done, slavery will probably cease before that time, and *then* we shall come out.

I enjoin upon every one to plead the cause of the poor slave—to "cry aloud, and spare not," to exert yourselves to the utmost, to deliver the poor, and speed on the day of universal liberty.

Not one Christian in Palmyra has been to converse with us, *as* a Christian. Our friends at Quincy and

M ssion Institute, have been very kind; they have spared no pains nor effort, to make us comfortable and happy. Since we have been here, unceasing prayer has been offered by multitudes, that God would glorify his name. The time spent here has been very precious. We have had a prayer meeting, night and morning— and on the Sabbath, usually two sermons. I shall ever look back to these days with pleasure,

GEORGE.

Of the previous and following letter, I give merely extracts, as much of the sentiment is similar to that ex- pressed in Alanson's letter, and in my journal.

LETTER TO THE OBERLIN EVANGELIST.

Palmyra Jail, Sept. 15, 1841.

DEAR BROTHER :

It no doubt seems strange to you, to see me date my letter as above, and strange it *would* be had not our Sa- vior, more than eighteen hundred years ago said, " Be- hold the Devil shall cast some of you into *prison*, and ye shall be *tried*," and did we not remember that the apostles, and thousands of the ancient Christians, were cast into prison " for the name of Jesus," and " for con- science toward God." Remembering these things, it is not strange, that the devil should even *now* cast God's " little ones" into prison. We are told " It is through much tribulation we must enter into the kingdom of God," and " all who will live godly in Christ Jesus, *shall suffer persecution*," yea, the time cometh, that whosoever *killeth* you, will think that he doeth God service."

I am not at all astonished to see days of persecution commence. I have expected them. I have felt that they would come, before the poor slave could be deli- vered : and that some must make up their minds to be sacrificed upon the altar of slavery, and if *I* am thus to be sacrificed, I submit cheerfully, rejoicing that I am counted worthy to suffer shame for the name of Jesus.

I am happy. I never expect to look back to any portion of my past life with greater joy and satisfaction, than upon the time spent in the *chain*. The Savior has been our constant companion, to whom we have had great delight in approaching. He has poured into our souls the consolations of his grace. His love has cast out fear, and our souls have been kept in peace.

If I am to labor for years in prison to satisfy the spite of blood-thirsty men, be it known that I go gladly and triumphantly, knowing that truth will prevail, and great shall be the good resulting. May thousands arise in my stead—the cause roll on with power, and the Lord arise, and cut short the work in righteousness.

For the truth and the slave,
Yours truly,
GEO. THOMPSON.

THE SLAVEHOLDER'S PLAN.

Sept. 20. This afternoon a slaveholder came to the window, and wished to know how we felt. He expected to find us cast down and sorrowful, but was much disappointed and amazed, when he found us cheerful and contented, in view of twelve years in the Penitentiary.

Said Alanson to him, " I expect that every stroke I strike there, will be knocking down your goddess. The man replied, " I think not, but perhaps you may do the State some good by your labor; I confess that slavery is wrong—that it is an evil, and should be done away, by enlightening the mind, and getting legislators to enact *laws* against it." Granted. But *how* are your minds to be " enlightened?" Already, you have laws against a word being spoken, or a book circulated, on the subject ! If a man dares to open his mouth he is mobbed and abused. You have closed your eyes, stopped your ears, fortified your hearts, and seared your consciences against every approach of light on the subject, and *how* are your minds to be enlightened.

The man thought he could show us a better way, to do away the evil, than helping slaves away from their masters, but he soon saw that there was no hope in his way of operating, confessed his ignorance of the Bible, and that he did not govern himself by that book. Undoubtedly this is the case *generally*, with slaveholders, and the supporters of the system—they are ignorant of the Bible.

THE ACCUSATION—LOOK AT IT.

Sept. 21. Slaveholders accuse abolitionists of enticing their slaves to run away—of exciting them to rebellion, &c.,—mob them for their principles, imprison, kill them, and pass laws to prevent their speaking or circulating their pamphlets on the subject; and yet come out and declare *publicly* in their paper (Missouri Courier), and even in this time of great excitement, that the " notions of these fanatics only tend to rivet still closer the chains of servitude upon our slaves—they are doing more than any other class to fasten the chain on the African slaves," &c. What logic! How alarmed lest they cannot get the slaves off their hands! How they groan to be delivered from the burden! Oh, what hollow-heartedness!

The whole community thrown into an uproar and consternation, because *three abolitionists* are among them, and yet they are only *tightening* the chains of the slave! Are they indeed so anxious to get rid of slavery? Do they so ardently desire to have every chain broken, that they so *dread* the presence of an abolitionist, lest he should *retard* the day of liberty? Ah, no. If they desire the continuance of slavery, and these fanatics are doing so much to *rivet* the chain, surely they should rather *court* their presence, and *thank* them for their assistance in holding the slave. Such is the true specimen of the logic of slaveholders and supporters. What nonsense.

ABROGATION OF GOD'S LAW.

Sept. 22. How true are the words of David. *Ps.* 119, 126, " It is time for Thee, Lord, to work, for they have made *void* thy law." Surely slaveholders have so done. They have not only been careless and indifferent towards it, as is the case with many wicked men

—do not care whether it is obeyed or not; but they have made it "*void*,·' as to the government of their actions—it is of no force or account in managing slaves. They have, as it were, *done it away*, and enacted in its stead, those coinciding with their lusts, and base passions—laws which encourage and reward wickedness —discountenance and forbid mercy, truth, and righteousness. All the multiplied and awful warnings, and alarming denunciations against oppression, are entirely disregarded, and laws directly opposite enacted in their stead!

God says, "Go preach the gospel to every creature." They *forbid* its being preached at all, to more than half their population; and forbid the preaching of the *whole gospel* to any! God says "Teach your children." They forbid and make it a penal offence to do it. God says, "Let every man have his own wife." They forbid it. "What God hath joined together let not man put asunder." The law is universally disregarded. "Do good unto *all* men." They won't allow it. "As ye would that men should do to you, do ye even so to them." For doing thus we are here in prison. "Love your neighbor as yourself." Because we *did*, we are sentenced for twelve years to the Penitentiary. "Be merciful." Because we were, the country is in array against us, and would destroy us. "Deal justly—love mercy." Justice is a mere *name* among them, and their mercy is cruel as the grave." "Judge the fatherless, plead for the widow." They condemn and tread them down, and persecute those who do plead for them. God made man in *his* own image. They, by law, make them brutes, property, chattels. "We ought to obey God rather than men." They tell us, "God's law is of no account here—you better just let that alone, and think of the laws of Missouri." We tell them, "the Bible forbids such and such things." "Well, well," say they, "the laws of *our land* and the Constitution of the United States grant us such privileges. God's law is not our rule."

And so in almost every thing have they made *void*

God's holy law. They have *legislated it away*—it comes not into their code. It is quite *obsolete.*

Surely, Lord, it *is* time for Thee to work." They profess to *love* Thee, and to regard Thy word—it is a professedly Christian community, and yet behold how they insult, reproach, and mock at Thy law. "What will become of Thy great name," if they are thus suffered to triumph? O, arise, and come forth, for the vindication of Thy honor, the establishing of Thy law, and making it *honorable.* Let thy right hand be exalted, and the glory of Thy name be greatly magnified. Defend Thy little ones, and save those who put their trust in Thee.

Reader, you are well aware that the above sketch is very incomplete—that "the half has not been told" you. The list may be extended almost indefinitely!. Truly God's law is "*made void.*"

"The slaves are contented and happy, and could not be hired to run away!" So say slaveholders to abolitionists. But what is their testimony in a crowded court house, when trying to condemn three abolitionists? The State's attorney compared slaves to sheep, and liberty to salt. Said he, "they would as readily follow a man who held out liberty before them, as sheep would follow a man who gave them salt." And who does not know the readiness of sheep to follow salt, and the strength of their appetite for it?

Thomas Anderson, a lawyer and slaveholder, testified, "It is only necessary to give them *any* hope of liberty, and they are ready to escape. They love liberty more than sheep love salt," &c. Glover testified to their love of liberty, and how they often show this love by trying the fleetness of their feet. Wright, a lawyer and slaveholder, contended that they were men—were rational and immortal beings—that the love of liberty was, by the Deity, implanted in their hearts, and could not be got out ; and many other such things which I do not now call to mind.

If the slaves do not love liberty, then why so much effort to keep them down ?—why such severe laws, and pun-

ishments against them, to keep them from running away?
Why so much terror, alarm, excitement, and rage, because an abolitionist is found on this side of the river?
Ah! they are afraid the slaves will hear a word about
liberty and Canada, and that then it will be impossible
to keep them. Their only way to hold them, is to keep
them in the darkest ignorance, and this is done by legislation.

Why are we sentenced for twelve years to the penitentiary? Because the slave loves liberty. Why so many
advertisements and rewards in the papers—so much
effort and pains to find the slaves? If they do not love
liberty, surely they will come back. Why are slaveholding cities filled with patrols by night? And why
cannot slaveholders sleep at night? Ah, the slave
loves liberty, and they know it! Don't love liberty!
What a libel on human reason and common sense.
Their own mouths, conduct, spirit, laws, condemn them,
and proclaim to the world that the slave DOES love liberty?

The remainder of my jail journal probably fell a victim to Palmyra flames. The above is the last record
that I have been able to find. A few extracts of letters
will close the first division of this work. I insert them
because I think they will do good.

TO A FRIEND.

I am satisfied with God's dealings thus far, and ever
expect to be with all his providences. I have "rolled
my burden upon the Lord, and He has sustained" me.
While the trial was advancing, and when the jury were
out, I waited to hear the will of my Savior, and when
known, how should I feel but resigned, composed, and
satisfied?—and what do but rejoice in that will? I do,
yea, and I will rejoice. Let me lose sight of myself,
and look to the general good.

What are twelve years' labor, compared with the imprisonment and torture of ancient Christians? What,
compared with the life of toil, and suffering of the poor
slave? Shall I hesitate to suffer with them? Ah no.

The way not to be dejected and discouraged, is to look at the promises, the end of life, the good to be accomplished; and not to ourselves and selfish interests. Forget these.

TO THE SAME.

True, we are under sentence of twelve years in the penitentiary, but what of this? Surely, it will not hurt us; it will only purify and better prepare us for our heavenly abode.

We feel that our separation is an affliction, but must we not call it a "light affliction?" Comparing it with what Jesus suffered for us—the apostles, and primitive saints, for the name of Christ—with what the poor slave suffers—with what we deserve—can we call it more than a very "light affliction?" Surely we cannot. But how shall we conduct ourselves under these afflictions. Paul tells; 2 *Cor.* iv. 18: Look not at ourselves, our sufferings, and our prospects; but at "Jesus, who endured such contradiction of sinners against Himself, lest we be wearied, and faint in our minds." Look at his sufferings, and his conduct under them. Look at his promises—their faithfulness, richness, fulness, all-sufficiency; look at heavenly and divine things—the mansion, the crown, the harp, the white robe, the innumerable company, the *Lamb.* Looking at these things we shall forget our sufferings, and be filled with peace and joy, substantial, soul-reviving, satisfying, and eternal. *Rom.* viii. 18. But looking at, and dwelling on the things "seen," our troubles, &c., we shall forget the promises, Jesus, and the glory prepared for us; and be earthly, fretful, unhappy—because the things "seen are temporal," and cannot furnish that enduring food for the soul, which the "things unseen and eternal" afford. Well, what are the consequences of thus conducting ourselves under these "light afflictions?" Why, they will seem, as they really are, "but for a moment," and shall "work for us a far more exceeding and eternal weight of glory." See how Paul labors to get words to express the fulness of his soul.

There is also a sweet promise in *Ecc.* viii. 12, " It shall
be well with them who fear God." Believing this will
give us peace and joy in all possible adverse circumstances. Can we not fully trust our Savior's word?

We need not fear being crushed, or killed by the rod,
so long as we lean on Jesus. Knowing that the rod is
applied in love, by our Father, let us not faint, but embrace and kiss the rod, which shall make us " partakers
of his holiness."

May some afflicted soul profit by these hints.

The following is considered important for every
Christian to understand and feel. Because this idea is
not understood and felt, is the cause of nearly or quite
all the baneful influences arising from broken plans,
disappointed hopes, &c.

TO THE SAME.

How often have we prayed that God would make us
useful in the world, to the greatest extent of our powers. We have said that this is all for which we desire to
live. We profess to desire the glory of God more than
anything else. This is all right. And have we not
given ourselves up to Jesus, to direct and do with us just
as He sees best? Is not He wise? And does He not
know perfectly all our abilities, and qualifications, and
circumstances? Does He not understand fully, just
where we are calculated to labor with the greatest success; and where it will be most for our good, the good
of our friends, and most for his glory? Then, if we
have given ourselves up to Him, to dispose of, and use
for his glory and the greatest good of mankind, let us
fully believe in our souls, that He will place us just
where we are most needed, where we shall be
most useful, and where we shall most honor and
glorify his name. If we have no will of our own,
we shall be perfectly satisfied with all the will and dispensations of our Savior, in whom we repose implicit
confidence. We shall rejoice to go just where He sends,
do what He assigns, and suffer what He lays on us;
not doubting, for one moment, that we are in just the

circumstances where we shall accomplish the most for our Redeemer.

Though He may place us in circumstances that seem adverse, and dark clouds gather around as—though we cannot see how good will result, yet, let our confidence in his wisdom and faithfulness be unshaken, feeling assured that He will bring it out just right—and just as we would have it, did we know all the circumstances and results as He knows them.

Forget ourselves, our interests, our plans, and rejoice to let Christ take and make us instruments to carry on his plans and interests, in his own way. Be perfectly swallowed up in God's will—ready for anything. This will give a quietness, peace, and joy, that nothing else will. And let me assure you, this quietness, peace, and joy, I feel in my soul in view of all that is before me. It banishes anxiety and all uneasiness, while I patiently wait for, and desire only God's will to be done. I have an unshaken confidence that He will do "all things *well*." With these feelings, it is out of the power of earth and hell, combined, to make me unhappy. If the greatest good will result (and can we doubt it) ? by our suffering, our long imprisonment, why then, our desire is accomplished—our request granted, and why not rejoice ? Is it for *us* to say, in what way we will be useful? We are in the Savior's employ—let Him direct, and we will sing,

> "Only thou our leader be,
> And we still will follow thee."

I have not a doubt, that if the Lord sends me to the penitentiary, more WILL be accomplished, than could possibly, by me, in any other way.

My Savior calls, and I rejoice to obey. Keep close to Him, and He will keep close to you.   GEORGE.

LETTER OF INTRODUCTION.

To the Warden of Missouri Penitentiary, Jefferson City.

Palmyra, Sept. 20, 1841.

DEAR SIR :—This will be handed to you by Messrs.

Work, Burr, and Thompson, who have been confined in the jail of this place, for some months, on a *charge* of taking some slaves, with intent to set them at liberty— on which charge they have been convicted, and sentenced to twelve years' imprisonment under your care.

They have solicited me to say to you, what is their true character and standing. I can say that I have known them only since they came to Palmyra jail, and in the relation of counsel, who defended them on their trial.

That they have sustained a good reputation heretofore, I have no doubt, from all I can learn. I am of the opinion that they are *conscientious* men, and mean to do right, according to their views of right. I think, sir, they would be *incapable* of stealing, in the common acceptation of that term—and what they have done, has been induced by mistaken opinions of duty in regard to the subject of slavery—they being *practically* and *emphatically* ABOLITIONISTS. They having requested, I could not withhold from persons situated as they are, a statement of what I have been satisfactorily induced to believe, was and is their true character.

With great respect, I am sir,

Your most obedient servant,

S. T. GLOVER.

The jailer also wrote a letter to the Warden, commending our good conduct while with him, approving of our character, &c.

The Judge also wrote to the Warden, stating that he believed us honest, conscientious men, who meant to do right in what we did—and he believed if we were at liberty, would do the same again. He thought we should not be treated as common felons, as other prisoners, but more leniently, &c. And yet this same Judge was a wicked man, and so prejudiced, and hard-hearted, that he did all he could to convict us. No thanks to him for thus recommending us to the Warden, for the Lord pressed it out of him.

After our trial, a committee was appointed at a public

meeting in Quincy, to collect and publish all the circumstances in the case. They did so. A pamphlet of thirty-seven pages, one thousand copies, was published. A few remarks from that work, and I close this chapter.

They say—"That they are honest men, all who have been acquainted with them will testify. We believe them incapable of a departure from what they deem a course of integrity and honor. We know the men— have witnessed their correct course of life, and the closeness of their walk with God.

" They have hitherto been distinguished for uprightness of character, for benevolence, and purity of life, and for their zeal in every work of reform, and especially in the cause of human rights. The standard by which they aimed to regulate their lives, was not public opinion, not expediency, but Heaven's own statute book, for which they maintained the most sacred regard, and made it their constant study. And in marking out their course of conduct, their great inquiry seemed, not what would please others, or be to themselves a source of present advantage, but what was right, what was duty, what was in fact the will of God. They emphatically ' Remembered those in bonds as bound with them,' and they have been heard, while engaged in prayer for their emancipation, to entreat the Lord that if thus they could more effectually aid in delivering the enslaved from bondage, they might themselves wear the chain,"—and blessed be God, we HAVE worn the *chain.*

PART SECOND.

CHAPTER I.

JOURNEY TO THE PENITENTIARY.

THE morning of the first of October, 1841, was cold and very stormy. We arose as usual—but about nine o'clock we were called to start for Jefferson. A crowd again assembled to take their farewell gaze at us. The rain was pouring down almost in torrents, but the stage came, and we, after bidding the jailer adieu, were seated, on the middle seat—the driver before, and the sheriff behind us.

A guard of six or seven men, armed with pistols, dirks, &c., on horseback, accompanied us. The cause of this great force, was an expectation on the part of the sheriff, and others, that we would be waylaid by a large company of our friends, for the purpose of rescuing us from their hands. We told the sheriff he need fear nothing of the kind—for our friends were not of that disposition. We had repeatedly requested our friends, that let the case be as it might, there should be no physical defence in our behalf.

Let me here state, that since my release, I have been informed that there were men in Licking county, Ohio who at the time of our arrest, were ready, and very eager, to head a company, for the purpose of going to Palmyra, demolishing the jail, and effecting our rescue. They probably would have advanced with the project, but for the disapprobation and opposition of my friends in that county—who did what they could to discourage any such measures—and told them that *we* would not come away in such a manner, if they should go—and the plan was abandoned.

I heartily rejoice in having parents, brothers, and sisters, who would sooner see me lie in prison, than give countenance to any such illegal, mobocratic suggestions of such ferocious, hot-headed *friends*.

Our sheriff, JOHN JORDON MONTGOMMERY, was a member of the Presbyterian church in Palmyra. Though during our confinement in jail, he shunned us, now he was obliged to look us in the face with shame and blushing. He thought the subject of slavery was a very delicate subject, and was quite reluctant to talk—but we discussed the question to some extent, at various times. He looked upon Dr. Nelson as a very bad man—not fit to live!

I asked, "Do you think that what we did, *unchristianized us?*" "I do," was the bold and unhesitating reply. So much for the opinion of a slaveholder as to what religion is. This, connected with his views of Dr. Nelson, will give the reader a little idea of the vast difference, there must be between the religion of slaveholders, and that of the Bible. His opinion did not at all change our views of the character of our conduct.

In the stage we read "Clarke's Promises," "Mahan's Christian Perfection," and the Testament, which tended to keep our minds tranquil, and gave us much comfort. Where we stopped at night, we found a large Bible, and as we sat before the fire, in chains, the gazing stock of the neighbors who ran together to see the sight, we read the thirty-first Psalm. The reader will there find some very precious promises, upon which our souls laid hold, and were strengthened.

As we stopped for dinner, the sheriff, &c., ate before us. While thus waiting in a separate room, the landlord came and talked quite freely. He began,—"Well, we slaveholders will have a great account to render, will we not?" Yes, sir, you will indeed. He acknowledged the evil of slavery—that they would be better off without it—it was a curse, &c., "but *how* are we to get clear

of it ?   The evil has been entailed on us, and now what can we do ?"   " Let the oppressed go free"—" break every yoke," and " pay the hireling his wages."   Just stop oppressing them—let them go.

At our next stopping place for the night, Alanson left an Emancipator, hoping and praying, that the *spark* might kindle into a *flame*.   We could walk, by all stepping together—and we frequently refreshed ourselves by our musical marching step.   It was very pleasant to be able to walk in this way, after being so closely confined to the side of the old jail, so long.   We felt that God was with us, to comfort and support.   Into his hands we committed ourselves and our cause, with the unwavering assurance that " *all was well.*"   With this confidence we were cheerful and happy.   The promises were unspeakably sweet and precious, on which we feasted.

The sheriff would not believe we were satisfied with our condition—thought we would run away, if we had an opportunity.   I told him I was so far from going unwillingly, that if I were left alone, I would go directly to the penitentiary, and tell them I had come as a *convict*, to take up my abode with them, for twelve years. But this was what slaveholders could not believe.   It was a spirit of which they knew nothing.

THE SABBATH.

The morning of the third day, was the Sabbath.   We remonstrated with the sheriff against travelling, but he was unfeeling, and only tried to insult us.   " You might have attended to your business, then, and staid on your own side of the river."   Alanson thought we ought to refuse to stir a step—but James and myself, said it would be of no avail, they would put us in, and take us any how—accordingly we made use of our own strength to get in and out of the stage.   We afterwards regretted so doing—felt we did wrong, and sought pardon from God.

It was a very trying day to our souls, but God in great mercy, stood by us.

SLAVEHOLDERS, AND BIBLE RELIGION, AGAIN.

As we came in sight of the huge and dismal walls. one of the guard, a professor of religion, came, and said to us, " Your happiness for this world is now at an *end.* You may be happy in a world to come, but you will see no more happiness below."

Reader, see how little slaveholders know of the power and excellency of the Gospel. The very first princi- ples, are so far from being understood, that he who *practises* them, and *acts out* the spirit of religion (which is benevolence and love to all mankind)—is branded as a criminal, and looked upon as having forfeited all right to liberty, and the privileges of the gospel—and as utterly incapable of experiencing further peace and happiness on earth ! Amazing !

Of the power of the gospel to support, and cheer, in times of trial and darkness, he seemed to have no con- ception ! Poor men! how they are to be pitied ! North- erners, do not censure them too severely. Their gross *ignorance* calls for the exercise of charity—" they know not what they do." 'Tis true they have the Bible, but they can't read it intelligently—they read it, but they don't understand its meaning—and they understand not, because they will not,,for their eyes are blinded, and their hearts hardened.

I informed the poor man that my happiness arose from a source beyond the reach or power of mortals to affect —that it was of such a nature as not to be destroyed by outward circumstances—and that it was not in the power of any man, or body of men, to make me unhappy. Thrust me into prison, afflict, torture or kill, they could, but still I should be happy, so long as my trust was re- posed in God. But such doctrine was beyond his com- prehension—" it was high—he could not attain unto it." I hope he may be so fortunate as to be " happy in the world to come"—for here, he certainly cannot be happy with such lean, low, heathenish views of what religion and happiness are. And I suppose that Missou- rians are an *enlightened* people, when compared with the great mass of the *South !*

THE MISSOURI RIVER.

In the afternoon of the third day, we came to the Missouri River, opposite the city of Jefferson, and the penitentiary. A messenger who went over for the ferry boat, reported that the abolitionists had come, and a multitude crowded the bank to behold the sight.

While waiting on the boat, we read the fourteenth chapter of John. Our hearts were comforted, and our minds composed by the sweet words, " I will not leave you comfortless" (there in your dungeon), " I will come unto you," &c. We believed the gracious words, and rejoiced.

A large concourse awaited our arrival, on the opposite bank, that they might meet and welcome to·their city, those of whom they had heard so much. The mass of the male population, old and young, rich and poor, bond and free, were there—each one striving eagerly to get one view of an *abolitionist !* And from their running, and gazing, it was evident they expected to see something wonderful.

So elated were the people at our arrival among them, that many followed in our train, while others ran before, and on either side, like so many obedient servants, rejoicing to show their master honor, or homage to their king. I think the arrival of the President would not have caused greater " joy in that city."

CHAPTER II.

THE CHANGE—EXAMINATION—FIRST APPEARANCES.

A MULTITUDE attended us to the prison ; and the office was crowded, while we were loosed from our chain, stripped, examined, recorded, one side of our hair cut close—arrayed in shining colors, and another chain put upon each of us! It was a trying time, but Jesus said, "Fear not." The Warden was insulting, calling us kidnappers (he had not yet read our letters), &c. The overseer stood before us with his great knife and pistols, while the guard, with muskets, kept the door! One might infer from their conduct, that they looked upon us as altogether another species of beings. But one who was present, afterwards said, "I was there, and looked upon you as three lambs led to the slaughter." He was anti-slavery, but dare not speak out.

It was now evening—the prisoners had all retired—everything was still, and dark, and dismal, as we were conducted to our *cell!*

Soon, we were separately brought before the wardens, and overseer, in the "guard-room." One of the wardens was so drunk, he could scarcely sit up—and he did the most of the talking. We were "questioned in many things"—and things with which they had no business. They wished to know all about the "under ground railroad" (but could not get the information)—how many slaves we had helped away—what were the principles of Mission Institute—if abolition was not the principal doctrine—if they did not conceal slaves there —if that was not the object of the Institution—what were the doctrines of abolitionists—what we had studied, and meant to do, &c., heaping upon us opprobrious epithets, and curses—threatening, insulting, and trying to frighten us into a confession of *guilt*, with, "If you don't acknowledge you are guilty, I'll take you down, and give you forty lashes!" at the same time swinging his hickory cane, and shaking it in our faces—his eyes flashing fury.

We were treated very ungentlemanly—charged with lying when we told the simple truth, in the honesty of our souls; and then threatened with punishment—denounced as worse than highway robbers, cut-throats, or wholesale murderers, and as meaner than chicken thieves —threatened with having our tongues wired—*and other things too vile and wicked to repeat.*

THE RULES.

1. " You must not speak to any prisoner, out of your cell, nor to each other in your cell."

2. " You must not look up at any visitor—if it is your own brother; if you do, I'll flog you."

3. " You must always take off your cap, when speaking to an officer, or when an officer speaks to you."

4. "You must call no convict, ' Mr.' "

When I was before them, I used the expression, " Mr. Burr." " No, no; there are no *Misters* here." " Well, brother Burr, then." " No, there are no *brothers* here." " Well, what shall I call him ?" " Why, *Burr*, in just the roughest way you can speak it." Frequently afterwards, we were checked for applying Mr. to a convict.

With the repetition of these rules, we were threatened with severe punishment upon the violation of them ; and charged, " carry yourselves straight."

We were then locked in our cell for the night; but soon the overseer came and spoke very kindly—told us what we must do in the morning—what would be expected of us, &c. He said, " There are many bad men here, but if they behave, they will be treated well; for every man here is treated not according to his character, but according to his conduct." I asked if we could write to our friends. He said, " Yes, but you better not be in a hurry. Wait a little, till you see how you like the place." He said we could write once in two or three months. I asked if we could keep a journal. " I guess not," was the reply. And my journal for the first year and a half, was kept on the bedstead, old boards, and blank leaves, by recording, sometimes a word, sometimes two or three words, and sometimes a sentence or two—just enough to bring the occurrence or scene to my mind—with the date.   In this way I noted nearly every important occurrence or change ; and after about two years, commenced writing out in full, all that had transpired from the time we came to the penitentiary; and from that work, written in my prison cell, I now copy—so that the reader may, for the most part, in the remainder of this narrative, consider the writer locked in his cell; and there, while others were wrapped in slumbers, describing and commenting on the scenes he had witnessed.

THE FIRST NIGHT.

That evening (the first), was a trying time to our souls —our faith—our constancy; but our God, on whom we had leaned, in whom we had trusted, and to whom we committed our cause, did not leave us wholly to ourselves—otherwise " our feet had slipped, and we hat sunk beneath the deep waters,"—but even then, we could lift the heart to heaven for support, for faith, for Christian boldness. And when " we cried unto the Lord, He heard and delivered us from our fears." I believe Alanson and James stood the shock with more composure of mind than I did, and were enabled to speak with more boldness; but even my weak heart was enabled to look upward, trust in God, and roll my cares upon Him. It was indeed a *squally* time—the clouds were very dark, and our prospects gloomy enough. Doubtless we " should have perished in our affliction, unless God's word had been our delight." But glory to his name, faith pierced the dense darkness, and showed us a Father's hand behind. It opened our ears to hear a Savior's voice, saying, " I will surely do you good"—" Be strong and of good courage"—" No man shall set upon you to do you hurt."

We laid us down to sleep, but were suffered to indulge ourselves but little in such enjoyment, being awakened and disturbed by the shrieks, and groans, and pleadings of our fellow-prisoners, in the guard room, adjoining our cell. Capt. William Burch, the drunken warden, had come in from his revels, towards midnight; he dragged the sufferers from their beds—it being of little consequence with him whether they were guilty of any misdemeanor or not, and was giving vent to his cruelty by putting them to the torture. To hear them scream, and see them writhe and smart under the strap, or the paddle, was to him a rich and sumptuous feast.

And such things were repeated night after night, for hours together. Sometimes the whole evening, and then the hours of midnight, and then again before the morning dawn, would be thus occupied, driving slumber far from us, and almost making our hair stand erect on our heads, while we lay in suspense, expecting every moment that our turn would come next. But the good hand of our God saved us from their hellish madness.

In the midst of these fears and alarms, it was sweet to go to the mercy-seat, and pour out our hearts before the Lord, cast ourselves upon the promises, and invoke his merciful protection.

THE FIRST MORNING.

As the prisoners were all in their cells, when we were brought in, we knew nothing of the appearance and sound of things, till we were aroused by the rattling of bolts and locks, the slamming of iron doors, with a dismal, hollow sound, as it echoed through the hall, and the music of chains, as of a multitude of oxen walking over a bridge with large chains hanging from their yokes! Strange sounds were these to us, and the conviction that they were produced by human beings almost startled us. But still more were we shocked when with our eyes we beheld the scene. O, it was heart-rending! Out of upwards of ninety, the majority were in chains—some with one, fastened to the ancle, and suspended from the loins—some with two, one on each leg, and suspended in the same manner; and others with large fetters on the feet, besides two heavy chains, one on either side, obliging them to take very short steps. We also, with ours, contributed to the harmony.

Soon it was generally known that the " Three Preachers," (this was the name by which we were designated for a long time, by prisoners and citizens), had come; and it was truly amusing to see how eagerly every eye was turned upon us, with a gaze that refused to be satisfied. They had learned all about us, by the horse thief mentioned in part first, who came a month or so before us; and also by the newspapers, which contained our letters, and other things respecting us.

That day we remained in our cell the most of the time, but were allowed to walk about the yard in the afternoon by ourselves. As we looked at each other with our striped clothes, and cap, and sheared heads, we could not refrain from laughing heartily, and remarking, " Well, you make a pretty good-looking convict."

OUR CELL.

We were all allowed to be in one cell. This was a great mercy. Had we been separated and scattered among the wicked, I know not what would have become of us. But God knew our weakness, and need of each other's help, and in his great compassion, constrained these wicked men, to treat us in this respect, kindly, beyond our most sanguine hopes.

What was their motive, I cannot say. We attribute it all to the hand of God. They may have thus kept us together, to keep us from contaminating the other prisoners with our principles—for according to their charges, the principles of a *highwayman,* or wholesale pirate, were harmless, compared with ours. Be that as it may, we felt very thankful to God for this peculiar expression of His favor towards us. There being such a very bitter spirit against us and our principles, we should have supposed they would be eager to do all they could to keep us apart, if perchance they might overcome us single-handed, and get us to reform, and renounce our errors. But God suffered it not; and blessed be his name.

Our cell is twelve feet by eight—arched—brick, and plastered—a window, on hinges, in the corner at the top, defended by two large iron bars—an iron door, about four feet by twenty-two inches, with a thick wooden door on the outside. When we went into it, there were two beds—one double, and one single one. The covering of the double bed, consisted of two small, very poor, and thin Indian blankets, under which Alanson and myself *tried* to sleep; but the cold would frequent-

6

ly so molest us, that we could sleep but little the whole
night.   They were both too thin, short, and narrow—
but these, or nothing.   The covering of James' bed,
was one Indian blanket, *too short at both ends*—in which
he would wrap himself, and shiver away the lingering
hours, till called again to his task.   At work we could
keep warm.

After a time, James obtained permission, and fixed
the double bedstead wide enough for us all.   In this
way we fared a ·little better—for we could take turns
getting into the middle.   If an outside one was becoming frost-bitten, he only had to request the middle one
to exchange places awhile ; and we were ever ready to
oblige and accommodate—for each knew how to sympathize with the other.   So far from murmuring, we had
great cause for thankfulness—for many were in a worse
condition than we.

THE ILLUMINATED CELL.

I.

I've often heard of prison cells,
And dreary things, supposed they were :
Where gloom, where darkness only dwells,
To fill the pris'ner with despair.

II.

And such they are to *carnal* hearts,
Who have no Savior and no God—
The day rolls slow—the night departs,
And leaves them still a *drear abode.*

III.

But glory to the eternal King,
Who brought me to this little cell :
Sweet pleasure *here* I find can spring,
For here my *God* delights to dwell.

IV.

A hallowed, consecrated place—
A bethel is my little cell :
The heavenly Dove descends with grace,
And blessings, more than tongue can tell.

V.

The Father, and the Son, come down,
And with me make their blest abode :
Not all the honors of a crown,
Equal the presence of my God.

VI.

He sups with me, and I with Him—
He feasts my soul with heavenly love—
And while I eat my food so plain,
He pours the manna from above.

VII.

Not king, nor prince, finds such delight,
With all his daily, sumptuous fare,
As I within my cell, at night,
When breathing out my humble prayer.

VIII.

These iron doors, and bricken walls,
Do fail to keep my Savior out—
He comes, and listens to my calls—
Says, " Peace to thee, my child,—fear not."

IX.

In peace, I lay me down to rest,
While angels hover o'er my head:
And while with welcome slumbers o.est,
They keep their stations round my bed.

X.

When morning gilds the Eastern sky,
I early rise to sing and pray :
My Savior still I find is nigh,
Who never leaves me, night or day.

XI.

Let monarchs have their wide domain—
And men of state in mansions dwell—
Let worldlings shining dust obtain,
But give me *Jesus and my cell.*

OUR FOOD.

All went to their cells to eat—their food being brought to them by the cook. We had " bread and flesh in the morning," and at noon ; at night, bread and water. Now and then beans or some vegetables for dinner. Our bread was cold, hard, heavy corn bread —our meat, generally bacon—which we had to eat with our fingers—no knives or forks were allowed.

From April to November, we worked from one to three hours before eating breakfast, which gave us a hearty appetite for our corn bread and bacon. During the rest of the year, we generally ate before it was light, so as to be ready to work as soon as we could see. And I am sure it would have put to the test the delicate tastes and stomachs of many who have been accustomed to their dainties—yea, and of many of the hardy farmers too. Imagine a man locked up in a dark room, and his victuals brought to him—he knows not what, nor how prepared—whether clean or dirty. Imagine hog's ears and feet half-cleaned—eyes, hearts, livers galls, and lights—many times quite offensive to the smell—and all these to be separated and divided by the fingers and teeth, in the dark—and a pretty good idea may be had of the poor prisoners' manner of living for weeks and months together. This is no fiction. We *know* it to have been a *reality*. And yet this, with contentment, and the blessing of the Lord, was " better than a stalled ox, and hatred therewith"—For " a little that a righteous man hath is better than the riches of many wicked." And feeling, as we did, that it was the good and wise providence of God that placed us here, and that the same kind hand ordered all our circumstances—meted out to us what we should eat, and what we should wear, we received it as from heaven, with thankfulness, contentment, and love. But let it not be inferred that such has been constantly our kind of living. By no means. Though there have been times when we have gone for days without being able to get even a piece of corn bread—living on little, bitter, cold, potatoes, and fat, or stale bacon; yet, in *general*, our food has been sweet, wholesome, and not unpalatable to us—though many complained and were continually finding fault with the living. The fact was, they did not like *prison* life.

For this coarse fare we were prepared, by previous discipline while at liberty; so that the change affected us but little, in comparison with the other prisoners. Many who have been accustomed to the dainties and luxuries of life were immediately taken with diarrhea, loss of appetite, and were sick much of their time. Thanks to heaven for our Mission Institute training in this respect.

WORKING.

In the course of two or three days we had commenced
our twelve years' task for the suffering and downtrodden.
Alanson was put at the chair business, which was his
steady employ for fifteen months—except that he stocked
now and then a pistol or gun, or did some other occasional job.   James went at his trade, carpentering,
worked mostly inside the walls—but also in the city
considerably, building and finishing houses.

I was first put in the brick yard—assisted in setting
and burning a kiln.

Thus we were now "under way," had fairly commenced our onset upon the *Arch-Monster*, feeling that
every blow we struck fell directly at the roots of the
great American Upas tree—at the foundation of the
Pedestal—the vitals of the Goddess—the *life* of *slavery*.
With this confidence, we worked with light hearts and
willing hands.

In the course of two or three weeks, I was sent to the
city, to work with the masons; was thus engaged for
about a month, building ice-houses, brick dwellings,
&c., sometimes carrying brick or mortar, then laying
brick or stone.   It was pleasant to be *allowed* to work
after so long confinement.   It seemed to brace up our
systems very much.

When it became too cold to work at brick and mortar,
I went to chopping.   A company of us, perhaps twelve
or sixteen, went about three miles—took our dinner with
us, and returned at night.   Chopping wood and splitting
rails was hard, but pleasant work.   It was an exercise to
which I was well accustomed, and in which I took delight.

I also worked in December, in the city again, lathing
a large building.   At one time, I was cutting up corn;
then at the stone quarry; then following the wheel-
barrow—was at this and the other—hither and thither,
till February, at which time I was put at the turning
business, and followed it mostly, for upwards of one
year.   At intervals, I was working with the masons,
then with the carpenters—bottoming chairs, &c., &c.

My principle was to learn all I could, in whatever kind of work I was engaged, feeling that it could not injure, but might be of much use to me.

When we thus worked outside of the walls we were accompanied by a guard of from one to four men (according to our number), with pistols and muskets, who were sworn to shoot the first man that attempted to run away ; but of their powder and balls *we* had no fear, for we gave them plainly to understand, that as we had been openly thrust into prison, we should not leave them until we were permitted to depart in the same manner.

THE FIRST SABBATH.

In the morning we were let out, as usual, and after washing, &c., we were locked up again in our cell, where we spent most of the day, having one Bible among us. During the morning the overseer came round to each cell, examined our clothes, enquired if we had enough to eat, generally, &c. Then, soon the washman came around, and brought the clean shirts and other clothes, if any were needed.

In the afternoon, the cells were all opened, above and below, and every man took his seat (on his stool), in front of his cell, for preaching. It was a singularly looking congregation, indeed. Some had their caps on, and blankets wrapped round them ; some, with only pantaloons and shirt on, others warmly clad, and many loaded down with chains, while a man, with his musket, stood to guard us !

In time of prayer, *all kneeled.* The minister (an Episcopalian), stood at the far end of the hall, above, where he could see the most of his hearers, and preached a short but good discourse. To us it was a rich feast, having been so long from the sanctuary ; for as bodily hunger makes palatable the coarsest food, so spiritual hunger gives a relish and sweetness to the most common instruction, which to the satiated, would be very insipid.

Our chaplain was not hired, his services were volunteered ; he usually came once in two or three weeks—

sometimes only once in six weeks, and once we were about four months without any preaching.

The prisoners generally sung, and gave good attention. They were pleased to hear preaching for a number of reasons.

1st. It was a *change* to them, and helped to wear away the Sabbath's lingering hours, for the most of them had no book, and the Sabbath to them was a tedious day.

2d. They looked upon the minister as a *friend*, and one who sought their good, while the officers and visitors were viewed with abhorrence, as those who only delighted themselves in their misery and disgrace.

3d. They frequently would gain some intelligence of what was going on outside.

4th. The sermon would afford them matter to talk about, and to many, the ideas were altogether new, while others would listen to find something at which to cavil and mock. A *few* gave attention, to gain instruction in the way of duty and the precepts of the Bible.

OUR SECOND SABBATH.

It was a trying one. In the morning, while we were eating breakfast, the overseer came and called James and myself out of our cell—for what we knew not—but followed our keeper, and were taken outside with a company, and marched towards the brick-kiln, which was then burning. I then saw what was wanted, but knowing the desperate character of our drunken warden, we did not feel it duty, at that time, to stop, and refuse to go further. We knew also, that it was a generally received opinion, that a brick-kiln could not be burned, without encroaching on the Sabbath—we knew no better, and supposing that *some* must be thus occupied, we made up our minds to go forward, and spend the day as profitably as we could. I had with me, my little " heavenly manna," upon which my soul feasted, nor was the " *mercy seat*" barred against us in these unpleasant circumstances. Jesus, to our complaints gave audience, and said, "Fear not, thou shalt not be burned,"—" I am with thee."

In the afternoon, the chaplain passed by, on his way to the prison, to preach, but none of our company could go. This is the only time that either of us has been called on to work on the Sabbath, though many are *obliged* to labor on that day.

With regard to burning brick-kilns on the Sabbath, we saw it *proved* again and again, that there is no need of taking one moment of the Sabbath for this purpose. Scarcely a kiln has here been burned more than five or six days. They generally put fire in, about Friday or Saturday, and stop about Wednesday or Thursday of the next week, occupying universally less than a week; so that a kiln may easily be sufficiently burned between one o'clock, A. M., Monday, and eleven P. M. Saturday, if time is improved.

We observed that it took a little over five days, to burn the one at which we assisted. Learning that fact, we should not have consented to burn another on the Sabbath, upon any condition, or for any consequences.

Before I advance further, let me give the reader a concise view of the characters under whom we were placed, and by whom surrounded—that thus our circumstances may be better understood.

CHARACTER OF OFFICERS (PREVIOUS TO FEB. 1843).

Already, I have given a *broad hint*, as to this, but will specify further.

The wardens were both ungodly men—awfully profane—very blasphemous, and regardless of the temporal and eternal welfare of the prisoner. Oaths and curses seemed to be almost as natural to them as their breath, and yet they pretended to disallow swearing in a convict, and said they would *punish* for so doing. What consistency!

They had no regard for the Sabbath. During the Summer season, scarcely a Sabbath passed, but the brick yard hands and others were ordered out to work, a portion of the day. Also within the walls, there was noise, pounding, and confusion.

Though our minister came so seldom, yet even then it was often the case that twenty or thirty hands were outside at work, till meeting was through. If he wished to preach to those not at work, well and good, but if he was not satisfied with this he must stay away.

One evening, a man sat in the chair shop reading "Clarke's Promises," which James had lent him. Capt. Burch came in. "What book is that?" "A prayer-book." "It's no place *here* to say your prayers, you should have said them before you came here." At another time, an old man—unwell—was sitting by the stove, unoccupied, and I gave him "Mahan's Christian Perfection" to read. Soon Capt. Burch came into the shop. "Ah! you've got a reading school here, have you?" and took the book from him. "Whose book is this?" "Thompson's. Is there any harm in it?" "It is not for every one to read," said he, and looked at *me*, with a fiery savageness that seemed to say, "You better take care how you lend your books to other prisoners," but he uttered nothing. Turning to James, he said, "Here, Burr, take that book, and *keep* it."

One evening I had finished my work, and was sitting by the light reading my Testament. Capt. Gorden came along. "Have you nothing to do but read?" "I have finished my work, sir." "Well, when you have nothing else to do but read, go to your cell!" At other times, James and I have been ordered to put up our books, when we have been reading our Testament or Promises, going to and from work—walking correctly in our place. Suffice it to say, "They feared not God, nor regarded man;" but took great satisfaction in doing what they could to degrade and unman those in their power. The guards for the most part, were wicked, profane, dissolute men, and *these* were the men placed over others to *reform* them.

CHARACTER OF PRISONERS.

Undoubtedly a few have been sent here unjustly, by

perjured witnesses, but the majority are bad men.
Here are collected the licentious, debauched, profane,
thieves, perjured, counterfeiters, gamblers, highwaymen,
burglars, liars, vagabonds, infidels, scoffers,
ned,   man-slaughterers,   rakes,   sabbath-
breakers, murderers, anti, and pro-slavery men, &c.—
from the youth of sixteen up to the hoary head of sixty-
two years—under sentences of from two to ninety-nine
years.

Some acknowledge the truth, and pay respect to it,
while the multitude treat it with carelessness and contempt. Of the most it may in truth be said, " Whose
God is their belly, who glory in their shame, and who
mind earthly things," " having the understanding dark-
ened, being alienated from the life of God, through the
ignorance that is in them, because of the blindness of
their heart. Who being *past feeling*, have given themselves over unto lasciviousness, to work *all uncleanness*
with *greediness*." " Having eyes full of adultery, and
that cannot cease from sin, beguiling unstable souls ; a
heart have they exercised with covetous practices, cursed
children, which have forsaken the right way, and gone
astray ;" " counting it pleasure to riot in the day time.
Spots and blemishes, sporting themselves with their own
deceivings"—" as natural brute beasts made to be taken
and destroyed—who speak evil of the things they understand not ; and shall utterly perish in their own corruption." " These are murmurers, complainers, who
walk after their own lusts,"—" raging waves of the sea,
foaming out their own shame—wandering stars, for
whom is reserved the blackness of darkness for ever,"—
" having no hope, and without God in the world."

With such characters we have been obliged to associ-
ate, to work, to eat ; and by such influences have we
been surrounded. What, but the grace of God could
have preserved us from being contaminated, corrupted,
consumed ? Truly, had it not been for " the form of
the *Fourth* with us," long before this we should have
been devoured by the raging flames of corruption, into
which we have been thrust. The hand of the " Angel"

has been manifest at every step of our way, from the first to the last ; the path has grown brighter and brighter; and many have been the wonderful deliverances from evil—some of which I shall mention in their places. Enough has been said to give a tolerable idea of our situation, for more than a year. In the midst of such darkness we felt ourselves called upon to shine as lights—to walk circumspectly and humbly with God.

FLOGGING.

When Brother Edward Turner was talking with us at our jail window, about coming to the penitentiary, he remarked that we would probably find Missourians *semibarbarians.* We have found the saying fully verified. As our cell was next to the guard-room, we could hear the charges, the threats, the curses, the rage of the officers, and the blows they inflicted. We could hear the cries and groans of the poor sufferers.

Flogging was very frequent during the time of Gorden and Burch—though the worst of it was before we came—yet afterwards it was awful enough.

For trifles, and often for nothing, men were called up, and received ten, twenty, thirty, forty, fifty, one hundred, or more strokes, with the strap or paddle. The sufferer had his hands tied together, and placed over his knees, where they were held by a broomstick or cane, passing through behind the knees. Thus, lying on his side, stripped to his skin, he received the strokes. To get up, or straighten himself, was impossible, until the inquisitor drew the stick from its place.

The strap was of thick leather, about one inch wide, and two feet long, sometimes tied to a short handle. It did not break the skin, but bruised and mashed it till it turned black and blue. The paddle was a board about two feet long, six inches wide, one end shaved to a handle, the other bored full of holes, every one of which would raise a blood-blister, where it struck the flesh. It was very severe. The reader probably is aware that this is a common instrument of torture among the slaves holders. One man was so dreadfully mangled that his flesh matterated and putrified, and became so bad, that he was under the doctor's hands for some time, and was unable to sit down. I believe his charge was an intention or agreement to run away, though he did not make the attempt.

Often, two, three, or more, would be flogged every night, week after week, month after month. Sometimes the whole day would thus be occupied. The greatest rascals, and those who could lie the most smoothly, generally came off with the lightest infliction. Many a time have we heard the scream of " Murder, murder! O, have mercy—have mercy —do, do have mercy !"— and the reply, "Stop your noise, or I'll kill you." Many times, when they could not make them cry out or beg, they would then whip them for that. " You stubborn rascal, I'll see if I can't make you *holler ;*" and the instrument would be applied again. Whip them because they do scream, and whip them because they won't— that's the way !

Thus we were obliged to hear the storming and profanity of a drunken fiend, connected with the yells, shrieks, and cries for mercy, of our fellow-prisoners; and thus we were frequently disturbed, when on our knees in prayer to God ! Often we would be compelled to stop praying till the noise was over. It was almost enough to make our blood run cold, to listen; but hear it we must. Frequently, Burch would come in at ten or twelve o'clock at night, drunk, and satiate his hellish appetite, by ordering up some one or more, for nothing, and putting them to the torture.

No doubt men often deserved correction, but there was no mercy for many who suffered very unjustly. " There was no flesh in his hard heart. It did not feel for man." But these days are past. And O, what a scene will the judgment bring to light !

For a week or more, at the first, we felt such a restraint, from the exceeding strictness of the rules, that we only prayed in secret, and talked but little. Gaining a little more strength and boldness, we ventured to pray together, in a whisper, which continued for some time—though a whisper would not suffice, frequently, to give vent to our full souls. We ventured to converse more freely, though at the risk of being punished—for we could easily be heard in the guard-room, where they slept—or in the hall, where they were frequently walking, even if but a slight noise was made. But becoming more bold still, our evening prayers were uttered *aloud*, so that we " prayed, and sang praises, and the prisoners heard us." It was a very frequent thing for the guard, and others, to collect under our window to hear us sing and pray—whether from a desire to overhear something, of which they might make complaint, or from other motives, we know not. But from that time, and onward, we poured forth our souls, without much restraint—for ourselves, our fellow-prisoners, our officers, the slave, the church, the world. And I have often wondered, why we were *not* called up, for our conversation or our prayers—but the mystery is all solved, by one expression, " *It is the Lord.*" His restraining hand alone held them back, and by his hook He led them.

We spent much of our long winter evenings (when not at work), but especially Sabbath evenings, in " singing the Lord's song in a strange land." In this delightful exercise we were not forbidden to indulge. While Alanson and James were at work evenings, (before I commenced night work), I feasted my soul, " in psalms, and hymns, and spiritual songs, singing and making melody in my heart, unto the Lord." When the *moon* shone brightly, I improved my time in reading by my heavenly Father's candle—so holding my book as to catch the reflection from the wall. This was a rich feast. To do it I would often have to stand on my bed, stretching and leaning, in order to get to the place where it shone on the wall—but it was *sweet*. Why was it so sweet to read a few words? Why? Why is bread sweet to a hard working man, at night, when he has toiled all day without any food? Reader, if you " know not the heart" of a prisoner—of a convict, perhaps you cannot understand this—but go into Missouri, a slave, be taken, and locked up in a prison—forced to toil from light till dark—and you will comprehend *why* it was so sweet to us to read a *few* words in the Bible. We carried our little books in our pockets, and read them, by the way, while at our dinner, and when we had a few moments leisure from our work—much of the time my Testament lay pressed to my heart.

THE FIRST PENITENTIARY LETTER.

On the 18th of October, Alanson wrote to his wife, giving an account of our circumstances, feelings, &c. (This letter—as also *all* of Alanson's—has been lost, so that the reader cannot be entertained therewith.) There is a very singular circumstance connected with it. He gave the letter to the officers on the day it was written. But it was not mailed, till the twenty-seventh of November, more than five weeks after. And probably they would not have sent it then, had not God quickened their memories a little, by burning down the large centre building. The letter was mailed the very next day. They were withholding from "the widow and fatherless," that comfort they much needed, and which they were anxiously waiting for—"The Lord saw it, and it displeased Him." And he has promised to *hear* the "widow and fatherless" when they cry unto Him, and to plead their cause, with their enemies. Take care, how you lay oppressive hands on God's poor!

I had many times asked for paper, to write a letter home. About the last of October, I obtained it, and wrote. Extracts will show my feelings at that time, better than they can now be described.

THE LETTER.

Jefferson, Oct. 30, 1841.

Much Beloved Parents:

Through the great goodness of God, I still enjoy the privilege of addressing you. And although I write under circumstances peculiar—under such as I never before addressed you—trying to the soul, and to our confidence in our Redeemer—and which no doubt have caused you many moments of anxious solicitude, and painful reflections—yet *I am happy* in my Savior. 'And though my outward man perish, my inward man is renewed day by day.' I rejoice that I can yet endeavor to administer comfort to your aching hearts : and to prevent your " gray hairs from coming down with sorrow to the grave." I am contented and happy. I came here cheerfully, and shall remain contentedly. I have no desire to leave till the *set time.* The hours and days pass rapidly away. They seem very short.

Dear father, for a number of years past, you have denied yourself and worked hard to help me a little. Should I remain here twelve years, and have my health I can *support myself*, and save you that expense, or you can give it to others who need it.

Should I here be sick, I shall be taken care of. I am in the hands of the Great Physician, " who knoweth my frame"—" who healeth all our diseases." He " will strengthen me upon the bed of languishing, and make all my bed in my sickness." "He doth not afflict willingly, nor grieve the children of men"—but " for our *profit*," &c. Then do not be anxious about me. He is more tender than earthly parents can be, and better knows our wants than earthly physicians.

Dear mother, do not let my circumstances make you unhappy. Go to Jesus, "casting your care on Him— He will sustain you." Do not feel that George is wretched, being deprived of the comforts which you enjoy—for I have all the comforts of life that I need Whenever you think about your son, for whom you have toiled, and exercised so much care and anxiety— of whom you have had high hopes, that he would be *useful* and cause you much pleasure in your declining years, I want you to feel that he is *happy.* If in this world, happy in every situation, for " I have learned, in *whatsoever* state I am, therewith to be content." If in the world to come, still happy, and rejoicing in God with joy unspeakable, and full of glory."

Dear parents, let the words of God to Abraham,

come to *your* hearts as from a wise and faithful **Father,**
" Let it not be grievous in thy sight concerning the lad."
Though you cannot *see* the why, believe.   Let faith
show the hand of God; and may you be able to say
with Laban and Bethuel, " The thing proceedeth from
the Lord"—and if from Him, then surely we should not
repine, but rejoice.   Do not feel that " all these things
are against you"—but " trust in the Lord, and wait patiently for Him," and soon you shall see wise reasons
for so doing.   Rest down upon the promises.

We truly live in a changeable world, and God's
" ways are not our ways."   When my mother brought
me forth, and nursed me in her arms, spent anxious days
and sleepless nights watching over me, instructed and
corrected me, led me to the house of God and the Sabbath school, and did what she could to make me happy
and useful—when she saw me growing up, and her hopes
centered more and more upon me—when she saw me
renounce my sins, and choose the Lord for my portion—
when she heard me in the prayer-meeting, and listened
to my voice at the family altar—when she read my letters from a far distant land, little did she think that she
had brought forth and was training a son for the *Penitentiary !*

When my father held me in his arms, to be baptized
into " the name of the Father, of the Son, and of the
Holy Ghost,"—when he dandled me on his knees, as I
ran to his embrace, after his return from labor—when he
taught me to work, sent me to school—worked hard to
feed and clothe me—when he corrected me for my faults,
and I began to be a help to him—yea, when he rejoiced
to see me turn my mind to the subject of preaching the
gospel, and leave the paternal roof, to prepare for that
work, little did the thought possess his mind that he
should soon hear of George being in the *Penitentiary !*
Yet such is the case.   *I am here.*

And, dear parents, had you thought in what a sinful
world we live, when you baptized, instructed, and prayed
for me—when you saw me bow to Jesus, and leave my
lovely home, to prepare to preach Christ, among the

heathen, and had you recollected the words which the Savior spoke while on earth, you might have thought that such a thing was possible.

Yea, considering such passages as the following, it would have seemed very *probable*. *Matt.* v. 11, 12 ; x. 17--25 ; *Jno.* xv. 19, 20 ; 1 *Cor.* iv. 11–13 ; *Mk.* viii. 35 ; x. 29, 30 ; *Jno.* xvi. 2, 33 ; *Rev.* ii. 10 ; *Acts* xiv. 22 ; 2 *Cor.* vi. 4, 5 ; xi. 23–27 ; 2 *Tim.* ii. 12 ; iii. 12 ; 1 *Pet.* ii. 19–21 ; iii. 14–17 ; iv. 12–19.

Please read these and let your minds be quiet. We " know not what a day may bring forth," nor should we be anxious. The apostle has said, " be careful for nothing," &c. I pray that you may receive all the comforts and consolations of the gospel ; " cast your burden on the Lord and be sustained." I know, dear parents, it must be trying to your faith, but read *James* i. 2—4 ; *Pet.* i. 5–9 ; *Rom.* v. 3–5 ; *Heb.* xii. 6–13.

How often have you punished me when it was painful to the flesh ; and I perhaps fretted and cried about it, thinking it was very hard thus to be whipped ; yet you saw that I needed it, and you did it in kindness and love to me, and for my good—and now I thank you for the same. " Shall we not much rather be in subjection to the Father of spirits and live ?" He desires our good infinitely more than we do, and knows just how to bring it about. He will do nothing to injure, but all He can to benefit us. " Now the just shall live by faith." What then if we cannot see the reason of all God's dealings, yet let us have faith in his wisdom. Did you always give a reason to your little, ignorant, inexperienced children for all you did ? So our heavenly Father does not always now give us the reason—the why—but He has said, " What thou knowest not now thou shalt know hereafter," and this should satisfy us.

I hope my brothers and sisters will profit by this providence. Tell them, from me, that if they were once deprived of the privileges of the sanctuary, as I am, they would feel the importance of improving them.

For your comfort read *Ps.* xxxiv. 7–10 ; xxxvii. 3–7 ; xli. 1–3 ; xlvi. 1–3 ; lxxxiv. 11, 12 ; xci. 1–16 ;

cxviii. 5–9; *Prov.* xii. 21; xvi. 3; xviii. 10; xxviii. 25; xxix. 25; *Is.* xliii. 2, 3; *Job* v. 17–27; *Jer.* xvii. 7, 8; *Rom.* viii. 28; *Phil.* iv. 4–7, 13, 19. Just believe that God means what He says in these and all the promises, and you shall be kept in peace.

Your son,   GEORGE.

CHAINS OFF.

After we had been here just one month, Alanson and James were called into the guard-room, on the evening of the third of November, and their chains cut off. Capt. Gorden was present, and spoke kindly. He asked Alanson about his family; whether they had any property; how he thought they would get along, &c. A. replied—"I think the people of Missouri will not keep me here twelve years, as I have injured no one." "But you intended to, or would have done it, had you succeeded. I have no fault to find with your conduct. There are many bad men here, and you will need to be careful," &c.

To James he said, "I know that slavery is wrong, but it was entailed on us by our forefathers, and we can't help it. We would be as glad as anybody to get rid of it, but we know not how. I have no doubt that you were honest in what you did; and there are thousands, the same way, who are good men, they mean no harm, but they are *abolitionists.* But would you think it harm for a man to steal your bench planes? Would it not be wrong?" James replied, "I do not look upon a slave as a set of tools—as a chattel—he is a MAN." "Would you run away?" "No. I will not go without an honorable discharge." "I have been watching you since you came, and I am satisfied with you. I have no fault to find with your conduct. You have conducted yourself like a man," &c.

Capt. G. is a slaveholder. His is only another evidence of the dishonesty and heartlessness of slaveholders, when they say "they wish to get rid of slavery as much as any one,"—"know not how," and yet perseveringly refuse to hear or read on the subject.

THE RUNAWAYS.

About the first of November, as I was walking home
from the chopping, about three miles distant, with twelve
or twenty others, in double file, with a guard before, and
two behind, with their muskets, two of the hands, as we
were passing a thicket, dropped their axes, and suddenly
broke into the woods, bounding through the thicket with
almost incredible swiftness.   Each had on a chain, but
the thoughts of liberty made them light and nimble.
Both were in danger of being shot, but the love of
liberty nerved them to risk even their lives.   The sensations produced in my mind cannot be described by
words.   One was wounded and taken ; the other escaped.
That evening the wounded man was punished very
severely, and another heavy chain put on him.

As we started to come home the next night, an old
guard, a professor of religion, said to us, "Now boys,
the first man that breaks the ranks, I swear by my Maker,
I'll drop him dead."   But he had no opportunity to glut
his blood-thirsty appetite.   While going to and from
work, I read my Testament, or "Manna."   One day I
worked at the quarry, loading waggons.   There were
about five of us, and a guard.   We had our fire, and
nothing to do, more than half the time.   I had my Testament in which I was reading, by the side of a rock,
when one said to me, "Come here to the fire, and read
to us."   So I went and preached to them awhile.   But
it being not a very orderly audience, I chose rather to
retire in the cold, from their noise, and hold uninterrupt-
ed communion with God, in his word.   That day I read
the Gospel of Mark through in that way.

OUR LIBRARY,

At this time, consisted of three Bibles, furnished by the
overseer (many had none), Mahan's Christian Perfection,
Village Hymns, Clarke's Promises, and Mason's Heavenly Manna, which we brought with us, and were
allowed to have, after asking for them repeatedly.

On the Sabbath, we sung, read, and prayed, with much

comfort and profit. From Christian Perfection, we took turns in reading a lecture aloud. Let me here say, that that book has been a source of unspeakable peace and consolation to us, amid our trials. Its sweet instruction —its lucid explanations of the promises—its presentations of the provisions of divine grace, have cheered, strengthened, and encouraged us to trust implicitly in God. And for hours and hours have we stood and read it by moonlight. I have followed the reflection on the wall half round my cell, holding my book so as to catch the rays, as the brightness gradually moved round the room.

THE FIRE.

On the night of the twenty-sixth of November, we went to bed as usual, but were awakened by the cry, "Fire! fire!" We arose, dressed ourselves, committed our bodies and our all to a Father's care, and waited patiently his will, being assured that He would do all things well.

The centre building, adjoining the cells, containing various work-shops, had taken fire, which placed the nearer cells in imminent danger; but God suffered not a hair of our heads to perish. Our preservation was very providential—we being next to, and almost under the flames. We could look out of our little window and see the raging element just above us; the sparks and cinders falling directly upon the window; and we not knowing what moment the wall that towered above us would fall with a crash upon our cell. But God can secure his little ones, and bring them safely through fiery trials and threatening dangers. "Blessed are all they that put their trust in Him."

The prisoners were quickly alarmed, and that saying was verified, "In trouble they will call upon me;" "In their affliction they will seek me early." Such screaming—such crying for mercy—such praying, I never before heard. Locked in their cells, and not knowing but the next minute would wrap them in flames, and send them quick to the presence of their Judge, they were importunate, with loud voices—some calling upon God, and others begging for some one to let them out—others still, with their broken bedsteads, endeavoring to knock open the door—while others were screaming, "My cell is all on fire!—Murder! murder!—O, *do* let me out!—O, God, have mercy on me." It was startling. Seeing the danger they were in, their fears were wrought to the highest pitch; and anticipating certain death, they became almost frantic.

A singular, indescribable, multifarious, confused uproar, was the result of pounding, yelling, begging, groaning, the crackling of the flames, the crash of falling floors and timbers, the running, commanding, answering, and inquiring of those engaged about the fire. Some of the prisoners, with their broken bedsteads, dug through the brick wall, and came out. In our cell no noise was heard.

When the building was mostly consumed, the prisoners were let out for a short time, and then locked up again in the cells most distant from the fire. From four to six or eight were in a cell. There we all remained till morning. It was a desolate sight. The inside of the building, with most of its contents, was now in ashes —for "riches certainly take to themselves wings; they fly away as an eagle toward heaven."

That day (Saturday), we spent mostly in our cell, reading, while others were engaged wheeling away the ruins. Also on the Sabbath, numbers were at work in the same way! Thus the officers seemed to defy the Almighty to do his worst. Some who called on God so earnestly for mercy in their trouble, when they saw the danger past, were ashamed of their prayers, thus evincing their heartlessness. 'Twas now cold weather, and many of the mechanics were thrown out of work. They mourned the occurrence, not for the loss, but because they would be obliged to labor in the cold, having no shop.

On Monday morning, we were all collected and formed into a ring in the middle of which stood Capt. G. After making a speech, he called on all who would henceforth behave themselves, to step forward—all advanced. Said he, "This is a place of REFORMATION!" The reader will keep this in mind, and connect it with my past accounts. Remember it is a place of *reformation*. I told you a little about the teachers and the scholars, but you must form a more intimate acquaintance with this school.

CHAPTER III.

LETTER—EXTRACT.

Penitentiary, Dec. 5, 1841.

"DEAR FRIEND:

"Truly God's ways are not our ways, nor his thoughts, our thoughts." But may it ever be our delight to yield up ours, and cheerfully acquiesce in *His* ways, and thoughts toward us. May we always feel that they are wise and kind and good, nor for one moment give way to unbelief, but trust in Him, and experience the blessedness of his promises. *Ps.* xxvii. 14; xxxi. 19–24; xxxiv. 8, 22; xxxvii. 3, 40; cxii. 7, 8; *Lam.* iii. 25–27, 31–33; 1st. *Pet.* v. 7. Can you in view of all that is past and to come, adopt the language of the poet:

I.
"'Tis my happiness below,
Not to live without the cross;
But the Savior's power to know,
Sanctifying every loss.

II.
"Trials must and will befall—
But with humble faith to see
Love inscribed upon them all,
This is happiness to me.

III.
"Did I meet no trials here,
No chastisement by the way,
Might I not with reason fear
I should be 'a cast away?'

IV.

" Trials make the promise sweet ;
Trials give new life to prayer ;
Bring me to my Savior's feet,
Lay me low, and keep me there."

My feelings heartily respond to the above, and my whole
soul cries " Amen." Though our way be dark and
thorny, trying to flesh, and faith too, I can, with an unwavering confidence, joyfully trust all with my blessed
Savior ; and respond to the hymn in the Lyre,

" Although the vine its fruit deny," &c.

Should you at any time, feel anxious about me, just
say to your heart,

I.

" Be still, my heart, these anxious cares;
To thee are burdens, thorns and snares ;
They cast dishonor on thy Lord,
And contradict his gracious word.

II.

" Brought safely by his hand, thus far,
Why wilt thou now give place to fear ?
How *canst* thou want if He provide ?
Or lose thy way with such a guide '

III.

" When first before his mercy-seat,
Thou didst to Him thy all commit ;
He gave thee warrant from that hour,
To trust his wisdom, love, and power.

IV.

" Did ever trouble yet befall,
And He refuse to hear thy call ?
And has He not his promise passed,
That thou shalt overcome at last.

V.

" Though rough and thorny be the road,
It leads thee home apace, to God :
Then count thy present trials small,
For heaven will make amends for all."

Regard what Paul says in 1 *Cor.* iv. 5, and let us
continually endeavor in all things to be conformed to the
will of Christ. Though my circumstances are so dif-

ferent from yours, yet I am happy. The Lord blesses
my soul. I do not get much time to read, during the
week, but it is sweet to *think* of my Savior's words.

GEORGE."

The above is but a note to a friend, appended to the
letter—but this has been torn off, and is all I have. The
letter more particularly expressed our feelings.

After the fire, the carpenters had a room prepared in
the city, where they worked. There, James could talk
freely,—a guard only being with them, who would
often join in their discussions. Practical religion, and
frequently, abolition, were the topics of conversation.
In the same building, I worked at lathing, and could
converse without much restraint.

While we were there at work, a citizen asked permission to speak with James, and was refused. However he contrived to communicate with us through another prisoner, who was allowed to run about where he
chose, and we in the same manner sent word to him.
At one time he wrote a letter, enclosing paper on which
we could answer it, sending it to us through the same
medium.

He expressed himself as a warm friend, his abhorrence
of slavery, and belief that it could not continue long.
Spoke of the abominable injustice we had received, and
gave us assurance of his sympathy and prayers, advised
us to be faithful, &c.

We answered the letter, nailed it between two chips,
and threw it to him, as he came near, one day. In this
kind of correspondence, we did not much allow ourselves.
Connected with it was much danger to us, to the one
conveying the letter, and to the man who wrote to us.
Had it been discovered, we should have been severely
punished, as also the conveyer, and the citizen would
have been fined. And in trusting a fellow-prisoner, we
ran much risk of being betrayed.

AN EXAMPLE.

A *Trustee* (as those are called, who are allowed to go
out alone), with great professions of friendship offered

to get paper, pen and ink, for another, to write a letter
to his friends, and promised to put the letter in the office
for him. The man, confiding in him, wrote the letter,
and gave it into his hands. Soon he was called into the
guard-room, before the officers.—" Do you know that
letter ?" holding before him the letter he had just written.
The man was punished.

And this reminds me of another trait in the character
of prisoners; which is,

TREACHERY.

Situated as they are, one would suppose they would
feel a common interest—a general sympathy. It is not
so. There are a few, who would be whipped to death,
before they would betray trust, or get a fellow-prisoner
punished. But the mass will do anything to gratify
their own revengeful spirit, and procure the favor of the
officers. See the example above. The favor of the
officers was his whole object. When they thus betray
a fellow-prisoner, it has an appearance of regard for the
interest of the officer—and generally, by so doing, they
gain the confidence and favor of the officers, at the expense of their injured fellow-prisoners. For the officers
are so perfectly duped, they cannot see that one who
will betray his *fellow*, will betray *them*, just as soon as
he thinks he can reap advantage by so doing.

Many, by the fore-mentioned means and in similar
ways, have acquired the confidence of the officers—been
faithful trustees, and seemed to be very much interested
in the welfare of the officers—how long? Why, till
they could make all needful preparations for an effectual
escape—and they are gone.

Others have been very eager in espying out the faults
of prisoners and running to the officers with every little
thing—very much concerned for their interest—would
traduce and belie their fellows—work and " fly around"
nights and Sundays—how long, and for what? Till
they had so acquired the confidence of the officers as
not to be watched closely; when lo! some one privy to

7

their plans has betrayed *them* (to get favor, mark), and they have been found just ready to *scale the wall ! ! !*

One will betray others; then some one will betray him; next, he is betrayed by another; and so on, all for the same thing—favor of officers!

Two men, to gain favor, professed to be converted, and won the confidence of the overseer, who was a Christian. He trusted them out alone. Soon they backslid, (?) and were more wicked than before; yet he trusted them. One even assisted in taking some runaways, and thus gained confidence greatly. What next? *They* ran away.

I told the overseer, " you might have known that since they had proved false to God they would betray *your* trust."

One more case. Two men took a skiff to go after a paddle that had fallen overboard, but instead of coming back, plied their oars for liberty. A guard with two other prisoners was sent after them, in another skiff. These trustees were faithful till they were far enough away, then threw the guard into the water to get home as he could, and followed on to join their companions.

But enough of this though examples might be multiplied.

About the middle of December I stopped work ten days, being unwell; not confined to my bed, but unable to work. My time was principally spent in reading my Bible, now and then exercising lightly, and dieting on mush.

CHAIN OFF—TRUSTEE.

On the seventeenth of December my chain was taken off. I had carried it two and a half months. When I first attempted to walk I could scarcely keep my balance, but with a little practice I soon learned to walk again.

The next day I was sent out alone to procure materials to fill our bed. My feelings were very peculiar, and my heart involuntarily broke forth in thanksgiving to God, as I walked by the way, for his goodness. Af-

ter being under guard and in chains five months, it was
inexpressibly sweet and delightful to walk at liberty and
alone.

As I looked behind me, and saw no man with his musket following me, sensations were produced in my soul,
of which those who have not been captives can know
nothing. To the "good hand of our God" all this
must be attributed. A few days after I went out all alone,
to gather me some herbs—and again, was sent to the
woods to get elm bark for the sick. At other times I
was sent on errands (when in the woods and in the city,
at work), to get water, fire, &c. Other instances I shall
hereafter notice.

This surely was " the good hand of God." To what
else can such treatment be ascribed ? Look at it, reader. Not only a convict, but a hated abolitionist, among
enemies, in a slave state, in the penitentiary for twelve
years—and such confidence, on so short an acquaintance,
reposed in him !

This would be indeed surprising, did we not remember that the hearts of wicked men even, are in the
hands of God—and also recall his promise, " Verily I
will cause the enemy to treat thee well in the time of
evil." This explains the whole, and to God be all the
praise. Though they so vilified us at first, it was soon
evident we had their confidence—that they looked upon
us as honest men, who would be faithful to the trust
committed to them.

THE LORD'S SUPPER.

On the nineteenth of December, after preaching, we
obtained permission and spoke with the chaplain. He
was very kind, and gave us gospel instruction and comfort. His was the first Christian's hand we had pressed
since our arrival here, and the short interview made our
souls rejoice.

We told him our feelings; how long we had been
barred from the table of our Lord, and desired him to
break unto us the emblems of our Savior's broken body.*

* With my present light, I could not receive the Sacrament from a slave-

He saw no impropriety in the thing, and promised to attend to it the next time he came.

But in two or three weeks he came again, and said he had " consulted with his *brethren*, and they thought it would not be proper !—that we had forfeited the right to such a privilege—were considered as outcasts—and we had better wait till we were free !"   We could but submit and say, " the will of the Lord be done ;" yet we felt disappointed.   Truly this is strange reasoning for a Christian !   What will not " the fear of man" do ? Probably his " brethren" thought it would have too much the appearance of friendship for our principles, and render him unpopular !   " Father forgive them, for they know not what they do."

Feeling that our master's command was binding on all his people, and as much on us here, in prison, as any where, we anxiously desired to " show forth his death," and " remember" Him in his own appointed ordinance.

But what could we do?   Already we had been refused by our minister, and who should visit us in prison to break unto us the sacred emblems of his broken body ? We thought; we talked together; we prayed; and sought direction from above, and became settled in the conviction that it was the duty of all Christians to obey the command, " Do this in remembrance of me:" if they had no regularly authorized person to administer it to them, that they should administer it among themselves : if a certain kind of bread and wine and dishes could not be procured, that they should make use of such as they had ; and to God it would be acceptable, " according to what a man hath, and not according to what he hath not."

With these feelings we determined to obey the dying charge of our Savior, and administer the emblems to one another.

Accordingly we made choice of bread and water—the staff of natural life—the nourishment of the body—as fit emblems of the body and blood of Jesus—the sup-

---

holder, nor from one (like our Chaplain) who gives his countenance to the " sum of all villanies."

port of spiritual life—the strength and nourishment of the soul.

Gathered around our little table, we read, and sang, and convèrsed of the sufferings of our Lord. In our humble manner we prayed, and partook of the symbols of his broken body and shed blood—and our souls were feasted with love divine. Jesus was with us, and made it a precious season. From that time we continued to observe it, in this manner. Such seasons were generally much blessed to our spiritual comfort and peace. And at various times when thus gathered around our simple board, have we experienced a joy, and satisfaction, and *rapture* of soul, unspeakable, and far beyond anything we ever felt while enjoying liberty. Of some of these seasons, I shall hereafter speak, in their order : but here I will insert a hymn, which I composed expressly for those seasons, and which we often sang.

"DO THIS IN REMEMBRANCE OF ME."

I.

Dear Savior, now enthroned on high,
Who gav'st thyself for us to die—
And lest we ever should forget,
Thy dying groans, and bloody sweat,
Didst charge thy followers bond and free,
" This do in memory of me."

II

Thy dying charge we will obey,
In this our simple, humble way :
O ! let us each thy love partake,
While now thy death we celebrate ,
From sin's dominion set us free,
And help us to remember thee.

III.

Thou art the " true and living bread,"
O ! may our souls with thee be fed ;
As water makes our bodies clean,
Thy blood shall cleanse our souls from sin ;
Thy fair example let us see,
For Lord we would remember thee.

IV.

Thy spotless life we call to mind—
With all thy treatment so unkind ;

The garden, judgment hall, and thorns,
The nails, the spear, and impious scorns—
While each can say, " Twas all for *me*"—
O! Lord, we *do* remember thee.

V.

Our cov'nant vows, we now renew,
Thy will to suffer, or to do ;
Give us thy Spirit for our guide,
That we may never turn aside.
See now thy little children, see,
Henceforth, we will remember thee.

On the twenty-fifth of December, a gentleman from my father's neighborhood called to see me, with whom I conversed, in the presence of the officers. I told him to tell my parents that I was contented and happy, in my new situation.

Speaking of letters, Capt. Burch said, " Many letters come here, which the prisoners do not receive—and they write many which are not sent." This was very true. They were read by the officers, and if there was any expression they did not like, or if they had a spite at the prisoner, the letter was destroyed. While at work out-side, one day, I picked up a piece of paper which looked much like a torn letter—when in my cell, I placed the parts together, and lo, it was a letter to a prisoner, who had been anxiously expecting, and waiting for a letter from his wife and friends. It did not suit Capt. B., and was destroyed. However I told the man the substance of his letter. These few words may suffice to magnify the great goodness of God to us, in this respect. I think the reader will join me in saying, " It is the Lord," when he sees how freely we were allowed to correspond with our friends. Why, if all our letters were collected they would make a pile a foot high. I think I never, in any previous five years, wrote so many letters as during the five years in prison ! How was this? Others were not allowed this privilege. With a few exceptions they were not permitted to write. How was it then? " It was the Lord." Situated as we were, this was a great blessing. Communion with friends is sweet while at liberty, but a thousand fold

more so when we are confined in prison. O, how re
viving !

CONVERSATION.

Though all conversation was strictly forbidden, yet it
was common among the prisoners. Some guards would
suffer it, while others would eagerly watch and report
the first offence, and punishment succeeded. We made
it a matter of conscience to talk with our fellow prisoners as opportunity offered, and feel that it was not in
vain. They evidently felt our influence. We reproved
them for profane or filthy language, and many would ab-
stain in our presence. We recommended to them that
religion which we found so precious in all our afflictions,
and most were ready to confess their guilt. Some would
freely weep as we presented Christ to them, while
others would only mock and sneer.

In our evening labors, we had more opportunity to
converse with them about their souls, and endeavored to
improve it. Why not? The wicked took the privilege
of talking for Satan, and why should not we stand up
for God? We felt that we were his " witnesses," and
that we were bound to let our light shine.

DEATH OF ELLEN.

On the thirteenth of January, 1842, Alanson received
a letter from his wife; it was like cold water to our
thirsty souls, though it brought the news of the death of
his youngest child Ellen. She grieved herself to death
(so her mother thought) for her father, shortly after we
came to Jefferson. She was about three or four years
old—a lovely child. And who can deny that our persecutors will have to answer for her blood at the day of
impartial reckoning?

The following was suggested to my mind, when mus-
ing on the death of Ellen. I thought of not inserting
it, but others advised me to do it.

I.

Ellen, where art thou, my dear?
  I thy form no longer see;
Now thy voice I cannot hear,
  Say, my child, where can'st thou be?

II.

Mother, see on Jesus' breast;
  In my Savior's arms who died:
Nothing now can me molest,
  For He keeps me near his side.

III.

Ellen, why so soon removed?
  Was not I a mother kind?
Have I not thy sorrows soothed?
  Comforts sought for thee to find?

IV.

Mother, you were kind to me,
  And your voice I loved to hear;
Always loved with you to be,
  All your lonely hours to cheer.

V.

Had you not a father dear?
  Loved he not your fond embrace?
Loved he not to wipe the tear,
  Trickling down your tender face?

VI.

Yes, my mother—but in chains!—
  He could not come home at all;
He could not relieve my pains,
  Could not answer to my call!

VII.

Ellen. why for this depart?
  Why not stay and cheer me still?
Stay, and sooth my aching heart?
  Was not this thy Savior's will?

VIII.

Mother, Jesus saw 'twas best,
  To remove me to this place
In his will, O let us rest,
  Trust Him for all needed grace.

IX.

Ellen, sing your Maker's praise,
  With the saints around the throne;
Tune your sweet and heavenly lays
  To the Father, Spirit, Son.

X.

Mother, can't you come to me ?
  Better place than earth is this ;
O ! what beauties here you'll see !—
  Dwell in everlasting bliss.

XI.

Ellen, wait, till Jesus speaks,
  Saying to your Mother, Come :
Then with you I'll walk the streets
  Of the new Jerusalem.

XII.

Mother, will my father come ?
Brothers dear, and sisters too ?
Ellen, yes, we'll come as *one*,
  And for ever dwell with you.

My poetic musings were principally while at my work
—sometimes while on my bed.

SLAVEHOLDERS' CONSCIENCES QUIETED.

On the fourteenth of January I received a letter from
a friend who viewed our conduct in a different light from
what we did. It censured me pretty severely, calling
the act contrary to the example of Christ and the Apostles, and exhorting me to repentance. But truly we did
not know how, nor of what to repent, having a "conscience void of offence." We felt more like praying
that God would open his eyes, and bring him to repentance for having given such encouragement to slaveholders. For they were so pleased with the letter, that they
wore it nearly out, in circulating and reading it. After
I had read it, the warden called for it, and months passed away before I could get it again. As it was handed
to me, he remarked that it had been lent considerably.
And more than three years afterwards, that letter was
thrown in my face, by a slaveholder, saying, " He gave
you good advice." We were grieved to see such occasion given to the enemy, but we could only pray. If
in any letter, we had justified our course, it would not
have been sent ; therefore we had to be silent, and
acquaint our friends of our true feelings, by giving
7*

references to passages of Scripture expressive of our feelings. In this way we often wrote on subjects which our officers knew nothing about; for they would not spend time to look out our references, which were many. Our friends wrote to us in like manner. In this way we could express ourselves understandingly on almost any subject. We could exhort our friends to more earnestness in pleading for the oppressed—or they could tell us about the success of the cause—how many slaves ran away, &c. An example of the latter:—in 1 *Samuel*, xxv. 10, are the words, " There be many ser vants, now-a-days, that break away every man from his master." We all knew where this passage was. So that when our friends wished to tell us that any certain number had escaped, the understanding was that they should quote 1st *Samuel*, xxv., and give the verse that expressed the number of slaves—if three, it would be 1st *Samuel*, xxv. 3, and so on. If we wished them to circulate petitions, or write to the Governor, or come unto us with all speed, we had references suitable. If we wished to inform them of our circumstances more particularly than we could in words, we had appropri- ate references. In this way, while our officers were perfectly in the dark, we walked and rejoiced in the light of abolition news.

RUNAWAYS.

The two painters were accustomed to go to the city alone, to work. When they went to the gate with their paint kegs, the guard was wont to let them out, without asking any questions, supposing they had been sent by the overseer. One day, they went as usual, but did not return. After a few days, they were discovered in Ar- kansas. An attempt was made to take them, and one of them was shot dead; the other wounded, and brought back to serve his time out. When thus brought back, they were generally severely whipped; one side, or the whole of their head shaved with a razor; and heavy chains put on them. Many times they underwent great suffering.

On the evening of the 2nd of February, we were at work as usual, when suddenly there was a great excitement and confusion among the guards and officers. Quickly the bell rang, and orders were given, "Go, to your cell —go to your cell quick." Officers and guards were running to and fro, with pistols and muskets cocked, crying to every prisoner they saw, "Go to your cell quick." Slam, slam, slam, went the iron doors, and soon we were all safe. What was the matter, we knew not till the next morning, when we learned that one of the blacksmiths had made a key, opened the two large gates, and taken out with him three others. Two of them were brought back in a day or two, and dreadfully punished. One cried "murder," very loud, and was ordered to stop. "I can't help it," he replied. Excessively large chains were put upon them. One of the other two was brought back about five months afterwards. The other escaped.

During the winter, a number ran away. The history of their exposures and adventures, as I had it from their own mouths, would make a volume that would be read with great interest; but I have no room to insert them.

Before the second of February, I had asked Capt. G. to let me learn the wagon maker's trade. He answered very jocosely, "What do you want of a trade? You will go right to preaching when you get out." "Yes sir, but I wish I to teach the heathen how to work, as well as pray." "Well, I'll see about it." On the fourth of February, I was put at the turning business, of which I have before spoken. While standing at my lathe, I have had precious seasons, singing, and preaching to myself.

CHAPTER IV.

A MAN KILLED.

During the winter about twenty of the prisoners were taken six or eight miles to chop wood. They encamped on the ground, coming home once in two weeks for clean clothes. On the 8th of February, a tree fell on one, and killed him. He was brought here in his blood —wrapped as he was in a cotton sheet, placed in a rough coffin, and buried. I assisted in carrying him to the grave. It was an open, exposed place, near by, where other prisoners had been laid.

Two days after, one of our number was hung, outside the wall. He was charged with murdering the overseer —which took place a short time before we came. On the gallows he professed to be prepared to die, but persisted in his innocency of the horrid deed. We endeavored to improve these events for the good of some of the prisoners, but the effect soon wore away.

There are no funeral sermons here (one, afterwards of which I shall afterwards speak). Those who die, are nailed up in a rough box, and placed beneath the ground, with much less ceremony than many make over a dumb brute. When Capt. Gordon's dog died, he had a nice coffin made, and fine *grave-stones* out, with a splendid inscription, " My dog Trip," &c., &c. A fine specimen, by the by, of the value which slaveholders place upon a dumb brute over a MAN, if he chances to to be poor, or despised, or tinged.

But surely, if there is any place where funeral ser mons are needed, it is such a place as this. If there is in them any solemnity, any tendency to affect the heart, and rouse the careless from their death-like stupidity, then they are much called for in a penitentiary. We plead for the officers to send for a minister, but in vain.

On the twenty-fifth of February, James received a letter from Brother Seymour, which filled us with great joy. Nothing but the hand of God upon them, made them give it to us, for it was strongly tinctured with abolition. But our Father knew it would comfort, and encourage us, and suffered them not to withhold it. It was through the intercession of Capt. G.'s eldest son that we received it. He was always very kind to the prisoners, and to him generally they went for favors. Through him chiefly our letters passed. He said to James, " Tell your friends not to write any more abolition, for, if they do, you will not be able to get the letters." I would gladly give extracts, but I have none to give.

SECOND LETTER TO MY PARENTS.

DEAR PARENTS:

I received yours with great pleasure—the more so, because I have not heard a word from you, since I was taken prisoner. Circumstanced as we are, it is more than ever delightful to hear from Christian friends. It makes me more contented with my situation—not that I am *dis*-contented—far from it. I am happy. But shut out as we are from Christian society, and the courts of God's house, it is unspeakably sweet and refreshing, to receive the breathings of a Christian's soul, though on paper. But should I be deprived of even this privilege, still with my bible I should be happy. In this I can listen to the words of Prophets and wise men—yea, sit at the blessed Savior's feet, and listen to his " gracious words." I can be instructed and comforted by the apostles, and feast upon the promises which fill the " book of books." But should *this* be taken away, still there remains a source of happiness, which men cannot cut off—which the world knows not, nor can take away. Need I tell you what this is? I trust that you also drink of this spring, and know the sweetness of its waters. It is holding communion with heaven, and having " fellowship with the Father, and his Son Jesus Christ." Prevent this men cannot. In every place and condition

can lift my heart to God, and feel that He who " stick-
eth closer than a brother" is my " friend," ever near to
impart all the comforts I need and can receive. I never
knew how to prize the Bible, nor understood as much of
its meaning as I now do. It is exceedingly sweet to
my soul.

My mother, so far from murmuring at my lot, I can already bless the hand of God, and kiss the rod. " It is
good that I have been afflicted."

Granting that this is a punishment for my sins, as some
say, then surely we should rejoice, and bless the Lord
for it ; He does it in love, even as a tender father cor-
rects his child, and as you often corrected me, for my
good. Our sins are our worst enemies ; shall we repine
at that which separates us from them ? Should we refuse or murmur to bear pain a very short time, when
great and unending happiness is thereby brought to us ?
Ah, no. Better be deprived of all earthly comforts and
joys, and secure the favor of God and heaven, than enjoy all that earth can afford, and lose the smiles of the
Redeemer one moment—much more for ever.

Dear mother, " only believe," and you will be happy.
" Faith in God will quell every fear, and fill the soul
with light, joy, and peace. Unbelief will fill it with
gloominess and continual disquietude. Faith lets the
Savior into our hearts. Unbelief shuts Him and all comforts of His grace and salvation out of our souls. Faith
is all light, unbelief all darkness.

> " Have faith in God," the Savior cries,
>   Nor fear what feeble man can do ;
> Though clouds and darkness veil your skies,
>   All, all shall work for good to you.
>
> " Have faith in God,"—though tempests blow,
>   And billows like huge mountains swell ;
> Though every surge should overflow,
>   Have faith in God, and " all is well."

Dear parents when I gave myself to God, I surrender-
ed *all* to Him and His cause, to be used by Him in His
own way. I have often prayed that He would send me
where He saw best—make me useful in the way He saw

fit—continue me in the vineyard—call me away when and as He saw would most glorify His name. This is still my prayer. It is not for me to say when, where, nor how long I shall labor. I lay myself upon the altar, a whole, a "living sacrifice." If His will is that I should labor here, I am willing to do it faithfully, so long as He sees best, should it be my whole life. What pleases my Savior, shall please me. If I am to meet no more with the dear people of God on earth, I expect soon to meet with a larger and better company than earth can afford. Is it possible that Elias (my youngest brother), has again grieved the Spirit, and hardened his heart against God? O, that he would submit. Dear brother, every moment you continue in sin, you are heaping up to yourself that of which you will one day repent, and it may be when it is too late! Read *Prov.* i. 20–33.

We live on prophet's food, only a greater variety.

To close, how great the privilege of prayer! That such worms as we can approach the Majesty of heaven —the Maker of millions of worlds, the Ruler of the universe, and hold converse with Him as with a father, a friend, a brother! O, let us love the Mercy Seat.

Your son and brother,
GEORGE.

JOYFUL DISCOVERY.

We had supposed that we were the only ones in the prison who bore the name of Christ, for in all our converse with them, we found none who even pretended to be Christians. Some were old backsliders, but a "kindred spirit" we did not find till March 13, 1842. While working in the evening with W. G., I talked with him, and found him quite seriously disposed. This encouraged me, and that evening I told my companions that I had once more enjoyed the privilege of giving instruction to an anxious soul. He was naturally quite diffident, and being unacquainted with us, did not let his feelings be known hastily. In a previous conversation I learned that he was a murderer. He felt and conf

ed it a great crime against God and man. Being much
interested in his case, on the morning of the thirteenth,
I whispered to him, "Read the 51st Psalm to-day."
He read it, and when we were let out again towards night,
he said to James, " Tell Thompson that not the 51st
Psalm, but the 56th and 57th Psalms are suitable to my
case, and express my feelings."

We read them with eagerness—being anxious to become more acquainted with him.   And no one who has
not experienced something of the same, can even imagine what were our feelings, when we read those Psalms,
and saw there the expressions of a decided Christian.
Our hearts leaped for joy—we shouted and praised the
Lord.

But still we were solicitous for a further acquaintance,
and it being difficult to find opportunity to talk with him,
we had further recourse to the language of books, as our
medium of conveying ideas.   I selected the 360th and
412th Village Hymns, requesting that he would let us
know whether he could fully adopt the sentiments there
expressed.   On the next Sabbath he returned the book
saying, " They do not express my feelings," and a short
time after, selected others himself, as descriptive of his
feelings—such as the 145th, 155th, and 415th of the same
book—and gave to us.   We were now satisfied that he
was indeed a *brother*, and we could but shout " hosanna!
glory to God."   We were filled with comfort and joy-
fulness.   It gave new life to our devotions, and lightened the burthens and trials of the day.   He had been so
long alone, in the midst of such awful cruelty and wickedness, ignorant and weak, that he was nearly buried beneath the rubbish, and his light shone very dimly.

But he now began to be " dug out" a little—his spirit revived as he heard us sing and pray (he celled opposite us), and his strength began to increase.   From that
time till his death, he grew stronger and stronger—mounted higher and higher, and shone brighter and brighter.

THAT " SALT" AGAIN.

Not far from this time, a slave was put in here for

punishment. This slave was a Christian, could read, and loved his Bible. He has a family. He soon found us out, and was eager for conversation—said he saw us when we came—knew what we came for, &c. He wanted a " *writing*"—we told him we could not, in our circumstances, give one—but we placed the " salt" be. fore him. We told him of Canada—we told him of —— where he would find friends—and assisted to plan for getting his family away. We heard no more of him for years, and supposed he had gone—but latterly we have seen him here again. His family probably hindered his going—for slaves love their wives and children, as well as pale faces.

But what I am at is this :—Suppose that this man had made his escape. Suppose that others, here, before whom we have placed the " *salt*," make their escape— what then? Why, according to the decision of a Missouri court, we *stole* those men while here locked up in the Penitentiary! We placed the " *salt*" before them—we told them of *liberty*—and this was decided to be *stealing!* They sent us here to keep us from stealing their slaves—but it seems we can steal them *here*, as well as in Illinois, or any other State. If a man who is travelling, leave a book or tract, which makes known that England has no slaves, or that slaves are free in Canada—and a slave learning this fact, escapes, why then the book pedler *stole* him!

EXTRACT FROM A LETTER TO A FRIEND.

" It is unspeakably sweet to hear from dear Christian friends. It lightens our toils, sweetens our labors, cheers and strengthens our hearts, makes time roll more delightfully away, and stimulates us to labor more faithfully in behalf of those (the slaves), for whom we are engaged. By this do not understand that we could not, without such letters, labor cheerfully and happily ; for we do work as cheerfully as the man who gets great wages, and with more delight and satisfaction than he who receives his three, five, or ten dollars per day. I need not tell you why or how we can labor so happily here.

Jesus is our friend, and ever near. Though shut out from religious privileges, yet with our precious Bible and locked within our little Bethel, we are more happy .han the king on his throne. From this we learn the way.to be happy anywhere, to "rejoice always," to have the mind kept in "perfect peace," and to be like Jesus. O! with this fountain of knowledge shall we not be happy and rejoice?

The letter to which this was an answer was withheld from us more than a month, but in due time God caused them to give it up.

SHAVING ON THE SABBATH.—ALANSON WHIPPED.

It was the custom to have all the shaving done on the Sabbath, because they could not spend time on a week day—so much gained, they thought! We felt that the practice was very wicked—endeavored to leave no means untried to be shaved on a week day—talked with wardens and overseers—besought and plead, but in vain. We talked and prayed together about it in our cell. On the third of April, Alanson refused to leave the cell and go down to be shaved. A great stir followed. A guard came and said, "Work, why don't you come down to be shaved?" "I feel that it would be wrong." The over-seer came, threatened and coaxed—now flashing with rage, then speaking kindly. Capt. B. was quickly present, fiery and raging—his eyes flashing fury—he threatened, commanded, and stormed—"Do you not know the rules?" "I feel that I ought to obey God," "Well, put him in the dark cell, and see if that will be obeying God!" Alanson was then taken from us and put alone in a dark cell. The next morning one side of his head was shaved with a razor, and a heavy chain fastened to his leg. That evening he was summoned before the grand council, questioned and insulted, but not injured. The next morning early Alanson was brought back to us, and all hands kept in their cells that day. A general inquisition was held, and all were ex-amined and questioned, which occupied most of the day.

We spent our time in reading and prayer, not knowing what was before us.

When I was called to the guard-room, among many other things I was asked, " Has there not been an agreement between you that Work should refuse to be shaved ?" " No sir." " Did he not try to persuade you to join with him ?" " No sir. We talked and prayed about it, and each did as he thought best." Eager to find some fig-leaf with which they might hide their wickedness and ease their troubled consciences, Capt. Burch began to question me about this one and that one with whom I was acquainted—" Is not he in the habit of shaving Sundays ?" What could I say ? Speak the truth I must. But what occasion and advantage was this giving the enemy ! How did it strengthen them ! Again : " Do not farmers generally, where you are acquainted, shave on Sundays ?" O that I could have answered boldly—No. But I could not. O ! did Christians know the evil influence they are exerting by thus desecrating God's holy day, surely they would desist at once. May the Lord open their eyes to see their sin. Had it not been for the wicked example of professors, behind which these men tried to hide themselves, who knows but I should have utterly confounded them ? " O that they would consider !"

The next Sabbath Alanson was called to the guard-room ; and while James and myself were on our knees, beseeching heaven in his behalf, we were interrupted by the sound of the whip—upon whose naked flesh we well knew. Our own flesh quivered. He received ten strokes, inflicted by the overseer, John Fulkerson. Capt. Gordon gave the sentence, with the charge to the overseer, " And double the dose every time he refuses to be shaved," and other very insulting remarks. As Alanson arose, he said to them, " May the Lord forgive you." It was comforting at that time to call to mind— " Some had trials of cruel scourgings." " This is thankworthy, if a man for conscience toward God endure grief, suffering wrongfully." " If when ye do well and suffer for it, ye take it patiently, this is acceptable with

God." "Rejoice and be exceeding glad." "It is enough for the disciple that he be as his Lord," &c.

As a farther punishment, Alanson was kept from us till the last day of May. When he returned, we united in heart-felt thanks to God for his goodness, in permitting us once more to unite our hearts and voices before the throne. While thus separated, he wrote to us on a piece of his sand paper with his pencil, saying that he felt the need and worth of social intercourse—that it was "good to be afflicted," &c. I wrote to him in the same manner. Afterwards he felt that as he had solemnly protested against the procedure, and sustained his protest by suffering, the whole responsibility of the matter lay with them, and that if they persisted in their course he would not be held guilty. We did not feel that the act was ours, and the wicked wardens themselves confessed "You can't help it, Thompson; if there is any wrong about it we shall have to bear the blame."

THE PLEASING SIGHT.

For some months we had all worked within the walls, and were thus excluded from the beauties of spring. The spring of 1842 was very forward. On the twenty-first of April, I worked in the city. And what a scene now burst upon the sight! The earth clothed in green —the air perfumed with sweetness—the trees waving in blooming colors, and loaded with green fruit—while all nature rejoiced in the goodness of its Creator! It was delightful. Our Father's garden, thus variegated with richness and beauty, was well calculated to fill the soul with admiration, wonder, and love.

Could a blind man suddenly have his eyes opened to see the wonders of nature, in vernal bloom, how would he be filled with rapture and amazement! What words could he find to give vent to the fulness of his soul? If he were a Christian, how would he adore and praise his Maker for his wonderful goodness to man!

Imagine, then, what were the feelings of my soul,

when I was taken from the dungeon, and suddenly placed in the midst of such a bright display of heavenly wisdom, goodness, and love.

Those who carefully watch the opening spring in its gradual advances from step to step till it puts on its perfect dress, can form but a faint conception of the impression made on the mind of one, before whose eyes such inimitable richness and beauty is suddenly spread.

It was not merely that I might gaze and feast upon his wonderful works, that God so unexpectedly sent me to the city to work, but to see a friend and fellow-laborer in his cause. While there employed, a fellow-student came from the Institute, bringing news from the brethren. He called, and talked but a few minutes, as the boat would soon start. It was reviving to see the face, and hear the voice of one with whom we oft had united our prayers and labors for the oppressed, in the social circle, and in the sanctuary. He brought us letters, which were a rich feast to our souls.

EXTRACT FROM MY ANSWER.

"Heaven will make amends for all these days of trial; but should I get no other reward than what I get every day in my own soul, I shall feel abundantly repaid for all these deprivations. Just let the child of God believe the Bible, and what can make him unhappy? Will afflictions—will persecutions—will tribulations, or distress, or anguish of body—will the scoffs, and reproaches, and threats of earth and hell combined—will imprisonment—will the famine or the pestilence discompose him? Will death terrify him? Will anything— *can* anything cause him to be anxious and unhappy, while he rests on the eternal truth of God? I tell you nay. He stands upon an eternal *Rock*, and nothing in earth or hell can destroy his peace, but his own sin. He is more than a conqueror."

OUR CHARACTER GOOD IN MISSOURI.

On the twenty-eighth of May, a man who has been a

7*

legislator here, came to see us. He was quite familiar,
and spoke very frankly.

He enquired concerning Alanson's family, and promised to write to them. Said he, " There is *no imputation* against your characters; but the excitement against
your doctrine is increasing, and all the sympathy there
is for *you*, is on account of your family."

To James, he said, "You [all three] have a good
character here—you have a good name all over the
country. We have nothing against your characters—it
is only against your doctrine."

To me, he said, " The officers give you a good name,
and say you have behaved well. I hope you all will
learn to mind your own business, when you get out of
this place," &c.

REFLECTIONS.

Has a murderer—a thief—a robber—a kidnapper, a
good character" in community? Is there " no imputation" against them? Then what mean the above confessions from a Missouri statesman? Do they not plainly
declare, that the people did not believe what they
charged against us? That they did not try, sentence,
and imprison us as State felons, but as *abolitionists?*
That it is not because we have violated their *laws*, but
because our *views* are diverse from theirs? Because our
consciences have not yet been warped, our eyes blinded,
and our tongues tied by slavery? For these reasons,
we are here placed, and here held—as will appear more
fully as we advance.

SLAVES ESCAPING.

As we were not allowed to write on abolition—consequently could know but little of what was going on,
the Lord sent a man one hundred miles to tell us that
the slaves were escaping very fast, and they were able
to retake but few of them. I was taken aside by Capt.
G., with him and other strangers, where I was questioned
as to the " *slave route.*" Said Capt. G., " There is a

regular stage route, and he can tell you all about it if he will." I replied, " There is such a route, but I do not know it, but a short distance."

The man said that three slaves had gone to Canada from ———, and that an anonymous letter had been sent to the master, from Quincy, stating that his slaves were safe in Canada. He wished me to promise that I would give him the name of the author, should I know the hand writing—that the person might be taken. Said he would send the letter, but I never saw it.

The assurance that the oppressed were being delivered, by our coming here, made us clap our hands for joy. We felt more willing to labor for them twelve years—" thanked God and took courage."

The man said that when we left Palmyra, it was the determination of the people to raise a petition for Work, in a year, and get him out. But when the guard came back, and reported that he was unyielding in his principles, they all said, " If *that* is the way he talks, let him stay."

THE POLYGLOTT BIBLE.

While James and myself were working in the city, old Mrs. Hart passed by, frequently, and looked with pity upon us. She said to James, as he was near the fence, " Would you like a volume of bound tracts ?' He replied, " I do not know as I should be allowed to have them, but we would be very glad if you would get us a Polyglott Bible." She quickly obtained a very neat one, and together with her daughter-in-law, after pleading a long time with Capt. G., prevailed on him to let us have it. Reader, his objection to our having it, was, " I don't want to teach them *another Religion !*" We consider it a rich treasure—a choice companion. This good old lady afterwards sent us divers little comforts, tracts, books, &c.

On the thirteenth of June, I received a letter from home, bringing the news of the conversion of my youngest brother.

AN EXTRACT, IN REPLY.

BELOVED PARENTS :

When I read your letter, I could scarce contain myself. My soul was filled to overflowing with joy and gratitude. "I have all and abound,"—"my cup runneth over,"—I feast on the heavenly manna—the life-giving fruit that grows on the banks of Canaan's river.

Dear Brother, you have now sworn eternal allegiance to the Savior. The heathen are dying. I am shut up, and at present, cannot go to them. And in the name of my Master, I charge *you* to step up immediately, fill my place, and hasten to those who are perishing."

"ABOLITION ALL THE TIME."

As James was at work, outside, with two others, on the Fourth of July, a slave watching his opportunity, when James was alone, asked, "Are you one of the three abolitionists who came here last fall?" "I am." "Are you *abolition* ALL THE TIME?"—meaning if he still continued to be an abolitionist, though in prison and suffering on account of it. James answered, "I *am* abolition all the time." Then came up another prisoner, and asked the slave, "Why are you not keeping *Fourth of July?*" The slave, very beautifully and expressively answered, "Ah, when I am FREE, I will keep Fourth of July—I'll keep it then, Sundays, and *all* days."

Though he was a slave, he understood the nature of *Liberty*, and clearly saw the palpable inconsistency of our Fourth of July celebrations, while in our land, Liberty is but an empty sound,—a mockery. Let this *shame* the thousands who are so enthusiastic in celebrating this day, in honor of *liberty*, while millions are groaning in chains and cruel bondage, from childhood to death.

And "they are contented," are they? So ardently did this slave long for liberty, and so highly prize the blessing, that could he obtain it, he would hold a *continual* celebration, and make *every* day a day of gladness and rejoicing, on account of it; thus proving the barefaced *falsity* of the declaration of slaveholders—" they would not be free if they could." And this slave, probably, was " *treated kindly*," not " worked hard," and allowed many privileges. He belonged to a Methodist class-leader.

THE HARVEST FIELD.

During haying and harvest, I worked in the field, swinging the scythe and cradle. James assisted a few days, in the latter part of haying. This was hard but pleasant work. It did not seem much like being in the penitentiary—except that the guard, with his musket, was following us around. The grain was about four miles distant. To and from our work we walked every day—carrying our provision and tools, which was the hardest part. Frequently, after walking home at night, I would be so completely exhausted I could not eat. The view of the stone wall, as we returned, after a hard day's work, was cheering; and almost involuntarily I would break forth with " Home, home, sweet home." I longed for a place to rest my weary limbs. In the field, and by the way, we could generally converse freely.

At this time, Capt. G.'s oldest son was sick. The prisoners were much attached to him, as he was always kind to them. I asked the old man if I could go up and see him. He turned me out alone, and I went and conversed with him, about his soul, and the importance of being prepared to die. The family received me kindly. This we looked upon as an advance in the opening for usefulness, which we gladly improved, blessing the Lord.

A MAN HUNG.

Adjoining the hay field was the public gallows. On the eighth of July, a man who had poisoned his wife in the city, was hung. As it was near, Capt. G. allowed us all to go to the place. A large concourse assembled. A document of his own was read, in which he confessed the crime; as also his repentance, pardon, peace, and hope of happiness. He warned the multitude to learn

wisdom from his example. The most of that day, I was
without a guard, with two others.

OUR FRIENDS.

On the ninth, being unwell, I abstained from work, to
rest and recruit a little. And this sickness was very
providential—for on that morning Mrs. Work and my
aunt came to see us, so that I had an opportunity to
converse with them, which I should not have enjoyed
had I been well. Thus " All things work together for
good."

We were allowed to converse with our friends separately, a short time, which was a great feast to our souls.
The next day (Sabbath), they came to our cell a few
minutes—but Capt. B. was present, and we could say
but little. However, for the privilege of seeing them,
we felt grateful. They brought us letters, which we
answered. They brought us two Polyglott Bibles, my
Greek Testament, Saint's Rest, and Christian Instructor.
This was a valuable accession to our Library. They
brought my Webster's Dictionary, but this Capt. B.
would not let me have. Why, I cannot tell, only he
said we did not need one.

Mrs. W. brought two children with her. They were
treated kindly and with attention, by the officers—treated as no other convict's wife or friends were treated. The
sight of them awakened the sympathies of some, and
their visit deposited a leaven which continues to work.

They went to see Gov. Reynolds, but he refused to
do anything for them. He told Mrs. W. he did not
blame abolitionists for helping slaves *after* they were in
a free state—it was right enough.

Previous to this, a petition from Connecticut came to
the Governor, for Alanson. He refused to grant it, and
wrote a long piece against letting us out. And the great
reason was, " because he still persists in the same sentiments,"—not because he had broken any law, but because he will not renounce his sentiments. That is it,
reader.

A man asked Alanson's little son his name. He answered—"Edwin Lovejoy Work,"—and the babe was named Alanson. Learning these names, a citizen re- marked, " He ought to stay there every day of his time, (why ?) for naming his children after such men !" Pa- rents, be careful what names you give your children, lest you get into the penitentiary. O ! what will not slavery do ! It was not because they were named after some noted infidel, or robber, or murderer, or pirate, or tyrant—then it would all have been well enough—but an abolitionist ! this is insupportable !

" RELIEVING THE NIGGERS."

On one Sabbath Capt. B. came to our cell with three strangers. As he opened the door, and they looked in, one exclaimed, " Ah ! these are the men who have placed themselves in this condition to relieve the niggers ! Well, there are but few of them in a worse condition." This taunt may have two meanings either of which is true.

1st. That our object was benevolent—" to relieve the niggers"—" to relieve" those who are trodden down by the cruel oppressor—" to relieve" our brother, robbed and spoiled of all that is dear in life.

2nd. That our coming here would have a tendency to relieve the poor slaves from their suffering, and hasten the day when every chain shall be broken and all shall be free. That this has been the case, there can be no doubt ; and this is one source of our contentment. We have felt that not one stroke should be in vain—that all would tell on the demolishment of the great American dragon—and it has been our constant prayer that God would give all our earnings to the slave—put all to the account of the widow and fatherless, and not let the op- pressor have one cent.

Of the multitudes who came to gaze on us, some manifested in their countenances a feeling of sympathy others seemed to feel highly gratified at our suffering. The sight of us, under such circumstances, seemed to feast their malice and spite, while their looks plainly said, " Aha, so would we have it." Frequently the in-

quiry was heard, " Where are the abolitionists ?"   And
then, " This is one of them."

THE NEW CELL.

On the eighteenth of July, we were removed from the
cell which had been our home for nine and a half months,
to one much more retired, and more desirable on several
accounts.

1st. It was so far from the guard-room that we were
not disturbed and continually annoyed by the whipping,
except when the cries were very loud.   This was a
great blessing.

2d. There we were overheard so easily that we felt a restraint in conversation, and frequently in prayer and praise.
Here, we could converse freely, and sing and pray as
heartily as we pleased.   Though we were never once reproved for talking in our cell, when it was known by all
that we did talk, and talk about slavery and abolition
too.

3d. Being so far from " head quarters," we had more
opportunity to converse with our fellow prisoners, &c.

On taking possession, we kneeled down and unitedly
consecrated it to be " HOLINESS TO THE LORD ;" to be
the " house of God, and the gate of heaven" to our souls;
not imagining that it would prove thus to so many others
as it has.   It is emphatically " the hallowed cell ;" hallowed not only by consecration, but also by the glorious
display of God's saving grace in converting sinners,
and comforting and establishing saints.   But I am anticipating ; after a little you shall hear more about the
" hallowed cell."

As yet, the windows of the " new cells" were fastened down, which made them extremely warm and oppressive in the summer.   Capt. G. refused to let them be
opened.   But at our request, granted us the privilege ;
as also to have the little door left open, so that we enjoyed the free circulation of fresh air, of which others
were deprived.   Thus was the " good hand of our God
upon us."

"THE PREACHERS."

This is the appellation by which we have most commonly been designated, by prisoners and visitors. If they wished to speak of our cell, it was "the preachers' cell." And many a time have we heard the remark, when locked up, and officers were passing around—"this is the preacher's cell."

Frequently, as the guard went round on Sabbath afternoons, to let out the brick yard hands and others, when they came to our door, would say—"The preachers' cell is there; you need not look; they don't go." No. God kept them from even asking us.

At one time, there was some disturbance, and we were all sent in haste to our cells. We heard the officers going from cell to cell, for a long time, searching them. As they came to ours, Capt. B. remarked—"This is the preachers' cell; you need not look here;" and passed to the next. What was the matter? Two muskets were suddenly missed, and it was supposed some prisoner had hid them in his cell; but they did not even suspect that the persons whom they had charged as being "worse than murderers, and meaner than chicken thieves," would do such a thing!

CHAPTER V.

BEGINNING OF REVIVAL—DEATH-BED SCENES, &c.

THE FIRST CONVERT.

For some time we had observed E. R., and now and then spoken a few words to him. Finding him quite sociable, well informed, and familiar with the scriptures, we were soon interested in his case. He also became attached to us, and took pleasure in our company. Find-

ing him to erably sound on anti-slavery, we took more
interest in drawing out his feelings. He was particularly kind to us; and as he was allowed to go where he
chose, he received many little favors from persons outside, which he gladly divided with us; thus bringing
us apples, peaches, tomatoes, grapes, &c. By him persons would frequently send us favors, thereby manifest-
ing their regard for the three abolitionists.

About the middle of August, E. R. was evidently in
a serious state of mind, and searched for the truth with
an eagerness that indicated the workings of his soul,
and the influences of the spirit. As his mind was a
little confused on the subject of future punishment, we
gave him the Christian Instructor to read, directing him
to the chapter on this point. He read it with attention;
his eyes were opened; he saw his danger and lost condition; and betook himself to pleading with God for
mercy. The contest within was strong—whether
Christ or Satan should rule over him—but grace tri-
umphed, and he threw himself at the Savior's feet—a sub-
dued child.

During the afternoon of the twenty-first (Sabbath),
he came to our door, and looking in, with a smile, said,
" I have had a hard struggle to-day—I have overcome the
wicked spirit." " Have you given your heart to God ?"
" I have, and I feel his love in my soul." With the angels we rejoiced, and cried, " Glory to God." We were
encouraged to pray, and watch for opportunities to speak
" a word in season." We pursued our toils with glad
and light hearts. At evening, he would frequently come,
a few minutes, just before we were locked up, and tell
us how he prospered; what temptations, difficulties and
trials he encountered ; and with what feelings he met
and endured them. This gave us opportunity to counsel, encourage, and strengthen him. His work, usually,
was such as kept him outside till the rest were shut up, then
he would come softly to our cell, and talk till the guard
came to lock him up. Thus we fed him, as a lamb, and
" strengthened his hands in God." Here he would
come, and hear us sing and pray, when he could not

get in to join his voice with ours. Frequently, as we
we were at our devotions, we would hear his gentle
footsteps, coming to unite his heart with ours. At one
time he said, " I have had a severe trial, last night and to-
day. I have been tempted to turn back, but I keep good
courage." At another time, " Go as it may with me,
you have done me no harm, but much good." Jesus
shall have all the praise. He talked with his cell-mate,
and obtained his consent to let him pray with him, but
could not get him to pray for himself. But I shall have
occasion to speak of him again.

FIRST DEATH-BED SCENE.

On the twelfth of August, about midnight, the overseer came and called,—" George Thompson." "What is
is wanting, sir ?" " I want you to get up a little while,
to go and see Richards. We think he won't live long.
Take your books and read and pray with him. It can't
do him any hurt, and it may do him good." I was quickly ready. In the guard room I saw Pope Gorden, son
of Capt. G., who said, " Ask him if he wishes to send
any word to his friends—and he may wish to confess
something to you about the Bullard scrape"—(the murder of the former overseer). I went to his cell, but already was he beyond the power of utterance, and sinking in the arms of death. The short breath, the fixed
and glassy eye, and the gnashing teeth, showed that he
had but a short time to stay. He soon expired, and it is
to be feared he exchanged this for the gloomy prison of eternity. We laid him out, and four of us remained there the rest of the night. I endeavored to improve the event for their good. The next day he was
buried. The effect on the minds of the prisoners, was
transient. This man had been tried on the charge of
murder, above mentioned, and acquitted. His disease,
I believe, was that mentioned in *Prov.* v. 11.

FRUIT, SABBATH, ETC.

During peach time, bushels were brought in, and divided among the prisoners. Though confined in prison,

we were not deprived of all the luxuries of nature. On the third of September, I obtained permission and went alone to the woods for pawpaws—and afterwards, in like manner, for grapes. At these times, I enjoyed the inestimable luxury of prayer, alone, in the grove, "Where none but God could hear." Others would go out on the Sabbath, and gather grapes, nuts, &c., and divide them among the prisoners. When offered to us, we refused, telling them we could not receive things which were obtained by breaking the Sabbath. The rebuke was felt by prisoners and officers, and the "prison was shaken" morally. But what if we had quickly received all they brought, disregarding the manner in which it was obtained? Of course they would have been encouraged. Can a man, with any consistency, say unto a thief, "thou shalt not steal," when he is ready to share with him the stolen property? So neither could we, with any propriety or efficacy, have opened our mouth for the Sabbath, had we given our sanction to their wickedness, by being participants of the ill-gotten articles. And so of any other sin. If we would reprove with any effect, we must not be "partakers of other men's sins." The same principle applies to slavery, and slave produce.

PREACHING AGAIN.

We had been without preaching about four months, when, on September 4th, a large number of Methodist ministers attended, and preached for us twice, a thing not done before. Conference was sitting in the city, and many came to see and do the prisoners good. Then, for the first time, about half the prisoners were assembled in one of the shops, while the rest sat as usual at their doors. The speaker, standing in a door, was easily heard both ways by all. It was a rich feast, once more to listen to the glad tidings of salvation. Never did a famishing man receive food with more eagerness and pleasure, than we the words of eternal life, after so long a famine.

It was also a solemn time. Some, speaking of it af-

terwards, said that it made them think more seriously about their souls, than they ever in their life
had done.   We strongly desired to express our feelings
—E. R. likewise.   I asked one of the ministers to give
the privilege in the afternoon.   He consulted with Capt.
B., who refused to grant it.   But, at the close of the
sermon, my soul was full almost to bursting, and I felt I
must call on my fellows to come to Christ.   I arose—
said " I should like to say a few words to my fellow
prisoners, if it would not be out of order," and began,
when Capt. Burch cried out, " It's out of order, Thompson, take your seat."   His wife, who was present, on
hearing this, burst into tears.   I took my seat—but the
privilege of a social prayer-meeting then appeared more
precious than ever !   O, what would we not have given
for the opportunity of giving vent to our almost bursting
hearts, in exhorting sinners, and in testifying to the
goodness' of God !   But this was denied us, and we
" withheld our tongue even from speaking good, because
the Lord did it."

REFLECTION.

Ah ! how little do they know what they do, who wilfully neglect the place of prayer !—or who, when there,
are backward, and even refuse to speak or pray !   How
little do they value that which is of such inestimable
worth !   Yea, how would they prize and desire what
they now so lightly esteem, were they once wholly deprived of it, as we are !   Reader, I hope it may not be
necessary for God to send you to a Penitentiary, to
make you prize and improve your high privileges.
Then take a prisoner's advice, and be " ready to every
good word and work." '
    For thus attempting to speak " in the name of Jesus,"
I was called before the " Grand Council," which consisted of the wardens, overseer, all the guards, &c.—a
room full.   Capt. Burch was the " speaker."   I was
" questioned in many things," but " finding nothing how
they might punish me," I was, for this grievous crime,
sentenced to wear a heavy chain.   I " departed from the
8*

council, rejoicing that I was counted worthy to suffer shame for the name of Jesus." My chain I carried about with me, as my constant and precious companion, for ten days, at which time Capt. G. ordered it off. I rejoiced in being able to tread so much more nearly in in the steps of Paul. The day after it was put on me, a wicked man remarked to his cell-mate, "Now you see if some judgment don't happen to Capt. B. for putting that chain on Thompson." And so it was, for the Lord killed his horse; and unless he repents, that chain will appear against him at the judgment. Think not, reader, that we did, or do, feel a spirit of revenge towards Capt. B., or the most bitter enemy we may have. No, far from it. We heartily forgive, as we hope to be forgiven of God; and we would rejoice to manifest our forgiveness by acts of benevolence to them.

THE DOOR OPENING.

About this time, W. G. expressed a wish to be baptized, and wished counsel. While I was conversing with him one day on the subject, as we walked across the yard, the overseer suddenly came round the corner of a building, and called out "What is the chat, Thompson?" I told him plainly. "Has G. any serious thoughts about Religion?" "He has, sir." "Well if you and he, or any other one, wish to converse on *that* subject, come to me, and I will gladly hear what you have to say. If any one wishes to converse with you about their souls, ask me, and you shall have the privilege; for I am favorable to religion and have respect for it." Here, it will be noticed, is an *advance* in opening the door for our usefulness. We rejoiced in the prospect, and " took courage."

We informed the seriously disposed of what the overseer said, and advised them to get permission, and come to our cell, expecting, of course, that he would be present to hear every thing. But as God always goes before his people, exceeding their petitions, and granting what they neither asked, nor had faith to hope for, so *it was in* the present case.

On Sabbath morning, the eleventh of September, Capt. Gorden came to our cell, bringing W. G. and G. G., saying, " Here is G. G., he wishes to learn to read. I turn him over to you to instruct on the Sabbath. Also instill into him christianity. As for W. G., he can read, and can speak for himself, and tell you what he wants." He left them with us, and departed. E. R. also came, and we spent the day together. Then we felt that " God had done great things for us." What a door was now opened! How gradually, and yet how *rapidly* did circumstances combine to bring about this event! And to what can we ascribe it, but to the " good hand of our God upon us ?"

After prayer, we entered upon our work. Said W. G., " I *know* I have been ' born of the Spirit,' but the *water* is yet wanting." We then explained the nature, design, and mode of baptism—leaving him to satisfy his own conscience as to the form. And as he felt he ought to be immersed, we did not attempt to argue him out of his opinion.

G. G. was impenitent. We taught him to read and exhorted him to repentance. He tried to play the hypocrite, and came a few Sabbaths, but the fire was *too hot* for him, and he ceased coming. The other two continued to attend. We all studied the Bible together, sang praises, and then for the first time, for more than a year, united with *others* in social prayer to God, and listened to supplicating voices we never before had heard.

Oh, how did our souls rejoice—our bones fatten, and our tongues praise the Lord! It was far beyond our faith or our hope, and rebuked our unbelief. We could but exclaim, " What hath God wrought!" " Halleluia!" " Not unto us, O Lord, not unto us, but to Thy name give glory."

The two brethren " grew in grace," and increased in " knowledge and utterance." At first, W. G. was diffident and confused—could say but little—but by *going forward*, trusting in God, he gained the victory, and mounted up as on wings of eagles.

THE METHODIST PREACHERS.

On the twelfth, we were pointed out to companies of
the ministers, who came to have a view of the three abolitionists. They gazed and looked—and looked and
gazed—surveyed us on every side, and some seemed
to *pity*—but we could not speak. We desired to
ask, " Watchman, what of the night ?" but had to
content ourselves with praying, that they might open
their mouths for the oppressed. " We are a spectacle
unto the world, to angels, and unto men !" When we
were pointed out to strangers, every eye would be fixed
upon us, marking every turn, viewing every feature, our
stature, and form, as if to ascertain whether we *were*
really human beings, or such *fiends* incarnate, as we had
been represented to be.

SECOND DEATH-BED SCENE.

On the eighteenth of September (Sabbath), as we were
engaged in our social exercises, a guard came and called
for me to go and talk with a sick man. He had been
sick about two weeks—we had talked some to him, and
saw that he was fast verging towards his end. As I approached the bed, it was evident he had but a short time
to remain—what was to be done must be done quickly,
or not at all. He called me by name, but could only
articulate faintly. His eyes sunken, his breath short and
difficult, he was gradually sinking into the arms of death
—sensible of his condition, but unprepared to die. Do
you think you shall die ? " Yes." Do you feel ready ?
" No." Are you willing to die ? " No." Do you feel
that you are a great sinner ? " Yes." I spoke of the
Savior to him—what he had done—his willingness to
pardon, even him, if he would now truly repent, and
cast himself upon him for mercy. I spoke of the thief
on the cross—reminded him of his own condition, and
asked, can you not look to Jesus, and now cast yourself
upon Him ? " I *don't know*—Lord have mercy on me,"
said he, and continued to sink in death.
    I knelt by him, and prayed. Many others were in the

room—some standing—others kneeling—some weeping, and others careless. I spoke a few words to those around, warning them against a sick-bed repentance. He expired, leaving us to fear that he also had exchanged this for the prison-house of eternity.

We used our endeavors to have a funeral sermon, but to no effect. It will be observed in this instance, that the door was opened wider, than at any previous time. Notice further advances. Keeping in mind the character of our officers—the strict rules, and the odious name we bore, how plain is the " good hand of our God !"

THE CLOSING YEAR.

Just fifty-two weeks had passed away, when we were permitted to witness a very interesting scene. After preaching, W. G. was called forth by the minister (an Episcopalian), and questioned respecting his desire for baptism. Many of the prisoners accompanied him to the river—and a crowd of citizens was present to witness the ceremony.

As we stood upon the shore, while the sun was sending forth its last rays, from the West—there to unite in solemn prayer and praise to the Redeemer, and behold a dear brother publicly covenant to be the Lord's—to crucify the flesh—to resist the devil, and live only for the Savior. O! it was delightful ! Who can imagine our joy, and exultation, as we returned to our " hallowed cell," to render thanksgiving to God for the wonderful things He had shown us in the penitentiary during the year that was then closing ? In looking back, and viewing our Father's hand at *every step*, we " thanked God, and took courage"—hoping and praying for still greater blessings, which were abundantly bestowed in the succeeding year.

THE SLEEPING GUARD.

James, with myself, and one other, were at work in the city—our guard went to sleep—he was reported to Capt. G., who accosted him about it, and said to him, " These men do not *need* any one to guard them—but

when I hire a guard, I want him to pay attention to his
business, and do his *duty*."   Reader, what think you?
" When a man's ways please the Lord, He maketh even
his enemies to be at peace with him"—so we found it.

Oct. 15.   A prisoner, who ate his dinner as usual, was
taken with convulsive fits, and narrowly escaped with
his life.

Oct. 17.   An old man died, who had been sick a long
time.   We had no opportunity of conversing with him.
He was a Catholic.

Oct. 19.   I obtained permission of Pope G., to go
out and get some grapes, while my lathe was occupied
by another.   On my way, I met Capt. G. " Which way,
Thompson?"   " I was going to get some grapes, sir,
while my lathe is occupied."   " Ah, Thompson, that
won't *count*.   I can find something for you to do."   I
returned with him, but God recompensed his covetous-
ness a hundred fold; for on that same day, three valuable hands ran away!

Thus whenever they have attempted to afflict and
oppress us, the hand of the Lord, in some judgment, has
fallen heavily upon them!

THIRD DEATH-BED SCENE.

Alanson's shop-mate had been unable to work, for a
long time, and about the middle of October was confined
to his bed, from which he never arose.   He all the time
had his reason, failed gradually, and sank in death.   On
the twentieth Alanson talked with him.   He expressed
no fears of death, but did not wish to *die in a penitentiary!*   As if it would be thrown up to him in the eternal world—even in heaven!   And this is the feeling of
most here—that it is a great disgrace to themselves and
their friends, to have it said of them, " He died in a
penitentiary!"   And the same objection they have to
getting religion here—put it off, promising to attend to
it when they get free!   But the monster needs none of
these objections and excuses.   He *comes*, and with re-
lentless grasp lays his cold hand upon them—

> " Pursues them close, thro' every lane of life;
> Nor misses once the track; but presses on,
> Till, forc'd at last to the tremendous verge,
> At once they *sink* • • • • • *p*"

During the day, James went in to see him. Another prisoner, a physician, was standing by. The sick man looked on them and said, " one a physician of the body ; the other, of the soul." That night, James and myself sat up with him. I asked, is Jesus near? " I hope so." Is he precious? " Yes." Are you willing to die? " Yes ; but I would like to see my wife and child." He then gave me a message to send to his wife, which I gave to Pope Gorden. Capt. Burch had just been to see him—left and went to the guard room; called out a number of prisoners; and while the long, mournful groans of the dying man were ringing through the hollow-sounding hall, at THE SAME TIME, were mingled with them the noise of the strap and paddle joined to the shrieks and cries for mercy, of another fellow-prisoner, beneath the torture!!

O! it was an awful mingling of strange and discordant sounds!

But such is the hardening influence of *slavery*, SLAVERY, SLAVERY!

The poor man died at half past nine. We laid him out, and staid with him the rest of the night, busying ourselves in reading.

The death of this man caused some solemnity among the officers, for they thought much of him. It was also a loud call to Alanson, as he was taken from his side, and from before his face.

The whole business of chair-making now devolved on Alanson, bringing with it a weight of responsibility and care. It also brought him more into notice, and afforded him more frequent opportunities of speaking a word for the honor of his Master.

EXPERIENCE MEETING.

Nov. 6. After shaving, the usual three were locked up with us to study the Bible, sing and pray. We then had an experience-telling exercise, which was very interesting and profitable, as it made us better acquainted with each other's souls.

W. G., before he committed the crime for which he came here, had been anxious for his soul, and felt the importance of being a genuine Christian. But a neighbor of his had threatened his life, and was watching for an opportunity to shoot him; so that he was in constant fear, day and night. He was much agitated. He felt he was not in a proper state of mind to repent, as he would be liable to be influenced only by fear; and his mind was so confused he could not bring it to bear upon the subject long enough to accomplish the work. He was in great distress lest he should be killed and go to hell. And under this excited state of mind he was influenced to take the life of his enemy, not because he hated the man, nor because the man had injured him, nor merely to save his own life, but that he might have an opportunity to repent of his sins in a proper frame of mind.! He felt that the act was very wrong, but felt impelled to do it, rather than be killed himself and go to hell. He was apprehended and put in prison to await trial. As he was on his way to the jail, he yielded his heart to God, while riding along the road; light and peace broke in upon his mind, and he was happy.* Everything appeared new; he felt himself a *new man*, but was doubtful whether this was religion. (For the man was very ignorant, and learned to read in jail.) He talked with one of the guard, who was a baptist professor, who told him his experience, and began to speak of his hope. This was too dry for the new-born soul; he broke out, " My religion is better than that; it is stronger than a *hope ;* I feel that I have it in *possession.*"

In jail, he read his Bible from morning till night, with much prayer, and was filled with joy and peace unutterable.

Then he could look at death and rejoice. He was

* It should be understood, that some considerable time elapsed after the commission of the crime, before his arrest.

tried, and sentenced to be hung; the day of execution came; his funeral sermon was preached on the gallows-stand; the sheriff showed him his watch and said, "You have six minutes, sir, to live." During all this, his mind remained calm and unruffled; "none of these things moved him;" his wife and children he had committed to God; himself, resigned to his will, he felt ready and longed "to depart and be with Christ." But before the time had expired, a reprieve from the Governor came, saving his life, and sentencing him for ten years to the penitentiary. Said he, "When the reprieve was read to me, I felt really disappointed. I felt that it would be better to die, than suffer the imprisonment." He seems to be fast ripening, either for some station of usefulness, or for heaven. He is willing to do anything for his Master. There dwells within him a warm heart —a choice spirit—a noble soul.

In the afternoon we had preaching—after which, I again requested the minister to administer the Lord's supper, not only to us, but to the other two brethren.* He acknowledged the propriety of the thing, and promised to consult with the wardens, but we heard no more of it. I continued to administer the ordinance myself to the brethren.

CHAPTER VI.

PRISON SCENES—VISITS—REFLECTIONS, ETC.

THE STRONGEST TEXT.

November 12th was quite cold. W. G. had come to our cell as usual. Our clothing being thin, our blankets few, and our bed broad, we all crowded therein, with our heads raised so that we could read, and thus we studied

* See note on pp. 147, 148.

the Bible, fed the lamb, and strengthened each other.
While we were engaged in this manner, Capt. Burch and
a Senator came into the cell. I arose, but the others
clung to their warm nest. Capt. B. began—" G., what
is their strongest text to support their doctrine ?"—(abolition.) G. not comprehending his meaning, and being
confused, we replied, we do not teach any particular
doctrine, except that a man repent of his sins, and love
God. We can fellowship all who give evidence of being Christians. " But how will you judge ?" By the
Bible, sir. " But the Universalists and others take the
Bible." Yes, but " by their fruits shall ye know them."
Capt. B. still wished to enquire of G. about the doctrine
we taught. We said, we have not attempted to instil
abolition into the mind of G., as that subject is not
allowed here. He replied, " But placed as you are here,
you can't help talking—and having so good an opportunity, you must converse on the subject. I know that
the prisoners talk; I know that I give rules which are
not kept fifteen minutes, and I don't expect they will be
kept when I give them." But we have the fear of God
before our eyes, said James. "And so do I have the
fear of God before *me*," replied the scorched and fiery
drunkard. Then turning to the Senator, he said, " Their
doctrine is a reasonable one—that 'all men are born free
and equal.' I agree with them in the theory, but when
it comes to the practice of it, I can't go with them."
The Senator asked, " Is there no way for the men to
keep warm on the Sabbath ?" " No other than that you
see," said Capt. B , pointing to those in the bed.

Nov. 30. Mr. Slocumb, a Presbyterian minister, and
Hinton, a Baptist, came to talk with us. They were
very friendly, gave cheering consolation, and argued the
subject of abolition. They said to me—" You are a
professor of religion I suppose ?" Yes, sir. " You
think you enjoy yourself here ?" I know I do—I am
contented and happy.

The next Sabbath, Mr. S. preached for us ; and then,
for the first time, all the prisoners were assembled in
one room—the carpenter's shop. A Methodist minister,

from town, came with him; and after preaching, they both, with Pope G., came to our cell.

MESSRS. SLOCUMB AND CHANDLER.

Mr. S. made many inquiries about us—names, residence, sentence, &c. Said he, "It is hard, is it not?" No sir, it is good to be here, I replied. Alanson said, it is not pleasant to the flesh, but the confidence that it will work for good makes us happy. He was very anxious to try and do something "to bring us out of this place;" and as the giving up of our principles seemed to be the pivot on which our deliverance turned, he was anxious to convince us of our error, as he called it, and bring us to look at the subject in its *true* light. "For, until you can see and say that you have done wrong, and will do so no more, I feel that all I can do for you here, with this people will be of little avail." Accordingly they tried their reasoning faculties, to convince us that what we did was legally and morally wrong, bringing the old illustrations of the sheep, horse, salt, &c. The same kind of strange infatuation, and blind, mock reasoning, we had heard so often, that it was disgusting to us. We told them plainly, that we could conceive of no such thing as the slave being comparable to a horse —that we could not admit the principle of property in man. We contended, "The slave is a *man*, and as such has an indisputable right to himself, to his earnings, and to his liberty (unless forfeited by crime), and it is but just and right to use any lawful means to aid him in obtaining that of which he has been so unjustly and inhumanly deprived." Mr. S. confessed that if he was in a free state, and a slave should ask his assistance, he would help him—not as a slave, but as he would any other man. Said he, "I would ask no questions—I would not stop him." Mr. Chandler said, "We will allow our abolition friends to go thus far—they may help them after they get into a free state. They need not stop return them, but assist them if they choose." He acknowledged, "We ought to obey God rather t man"—that where human laws clashed with the divi we ought to refuse allegiance to the former, even unto death. And again, he said, "I see no reason why the whites should not be slaves, as well as the blacks."

REFLECTIONS.

They both contended that it would be larceny to deprive the owner of his slave, whether by enticing, threatening, forcing, or any other way, while he is in a slave state; but that it would be just and right to help him after he had escaped! What logic! How perfectly does slavery blind the eyes and pervert the mind and reason of those under its influence! According to their doctrine, one man may help a slave across the river; another may take him to Canada. The former is guilty of grand larceny, the latter " has done that which is just and right."

The very men who charge us with breaking the laws of God and man, in our attempt to aid a poor slave, on one side of the river, say they would help him, if he was on the other side !

If a man comes into Missouri, and steals a horse—takes him into a free state, and delivers him up to another, the latter is not justified, but considered just as guilty as the former. But according to the reasoning of Missouri moralists, he should be fully acquitted. The slave is property—the horse is property; both are taken from Missouri to a free State, and delivered up to another—parallel cases. But here they are not so fond of their *horse illustrations.* They are unwilling to carry out their principles. The man who helps away the property of another, after his comrade has brought it across the river *is* accessory to the crime, and as guilty as the principal—so pronounced by the laws of God and man. Now mark—if the slave is property while west of the Mississippi river, he is when east of it; for certainly the bare crossing a river cannot change a chattel into a man—cannot deprive of legal ownership—cannot destroy the right to recover that which has escaped; and if it is property, whether horse or slave, that has crossed into a free State, then to assist that property in escaping from its owner—to prevent his recovering what is legally his own, is evidently wrong. But slaveholders tell us we may help the slaves, after they get into a free state—we may assist them in their struggles for "liberty and the pursuit of happiness." So said Gov. Reynolds, so say the clergymen of Missouri, and so say we.

And when they have granted this, they have virtually said what we affirmed, that the slave is not property. As I said one day to Dr. Moore, so long as the slave is possessed of a rational mind—an immortal soul, it is out of the power of any or all human legislation, to change him into a piece of property. Rob him of these grand distinctions, and his body may be made a chattel, but not till then. After all the legislation, he is still a man ; and the laws of sympathy, of kindness, of humanity, and of God, are as binding upon us respecting him in his low, suffering condition, as in reference to any other man in afflictive circumstances. In view of the foregoing, then, our enemies themselves being Judges, when brought to the bar of reason, it is right to help the slave in a free state—thereby depriving them of what they call property—but which has been shown from their own concessions, not to be property—otherwise it would be wrong to deprive them of it.

GIVING UP OUR PRINCIPLES.

Dec. 18. Mr. Slocumb again preached for us, and came again to our cell for further conversation. He said he had talked with the Governor about us, who thought we might do much good if we would correspond with our friends, and entreat them to desist from their exciting work. "If this can be stopped, and you are willing to use your influence to accomplish the work, then he (the Governor), may do something for you. But if you persist in your course, and maintain your principles, you will have to stay your whole time out. You could have much influence with your friends, if you would only give up, make it known to them, and beg them to refrain and be quiet. You suffer on account of what they do, and you will have to stay your whole twelve years, unless your friends stop." How clear that it is not felony, but doctrine, that locks the doors upon us. If we are willing to renounce our principles, and manifest the sincerity of our abjuration, by persuading our friends to do the same, or to hold their peace, and not speak against slavery, then the Governor will begin to think about letting us go!

There is a something sweeter to us than liberty—namely, a clear conscience and our principles respecting "human rights." Liberty! It is but TRASH when put up as a price for the renunciation of those great principles, founded on that immoveable basis—the word of God. Yes, when we deem them too dear to be bought or bribed away from us by life, even much less by what is called liberty!

THE LEGISLATORS.

During the sitting of the legislature, we were often visited by crowds of the members, who would inquire, dodge, and look, to get a view of the abolitionists, and then gaze and stare, more like idiots than statesmen!

On the 25th of December (Sabbath), four of them came to our cell to "gratify their curiosity," and learn our principles respecting helping the poor.

They inquired how we felt about the deed which brought us here. We answered, " We feel that we acted imprudently, but that we did not sin." They confessed that slavery was wrong; " But how shall we do? Our legislative bodies know not what course to adopt." Said I, " send your statesmen to me, I can tell them what to do, very quick." " Well, here are four legislators, you can tell us." " Why just stop doing wrong. Abolish your wicked oppressive laws, and at once enact those which are just and righteous. Just take your foot off the neck of the slave and let him get up ; and no longer rob, spoil, whip, and oppress him."

" O! if we do that, they will cut their masters' throats, and raise insurrections !"

Sirs, which is most calculated to exasperate them to

such desperation, robbing them of everything that is dear in life, and acting the part of a cruel tyrant towards them —or paying them for their work, and treating them kindly? If they do not rise up and cut your throats when you are heaping all manner of abuse and outrage upon them, is it at all according to reason, observation, or good sense, that they will be thus enraged because you come to them in the spirit of kindness, and say, "I have been treating you wrongfully; I am sorry for it, I will do so no more. You are all FREE MEN; and now if you will work for me, I will pay you your wages." Is it the nature of kindness to provoke? They could not get over it.

I appealed to the Bible in support of my positions. He replied, " I do not pretend to be a religious man, who takes the Bible for his guide." Suffice it to say, we gave them a compendium of abolitionism, which was not very palatable. And we rejoiced in having the privilege of lecturing boldly in the centre of Missouri. Here we may preach the strongest anti-slavery to ministers and statesmen, and no man dare lay his hands on us. Here we can pray and "cry aloud," with no fear of molestation! Behold the wisdom of God.

RENUNCIATION AGAIN.

While pursuing our avocations, we were all three called for to go to the guard room, where we found Mr. Slocumb and James Gallaher waiting for an interview with us. Mr. S. was very anxious to induce us to concede, so far as to secure executive clemency, in our behalf, as also Mr. G.

Mr. S. " Can you not feel and say that you have done *wrong*—that your views were mistaken and unsound? How far can you, in conscience, renounce them? I may secure the influence and talent of the Legislators in your favor. If you continue to persist, and refuse to yield and confess publicly, there is NO HOPE of doing anything for you. Petitions will be of no avail, and all that I or any other man can say in your behalf will be in vain so long as you remain inflexible on this subject.

I have talked with the members respecting your case; and the other evening I met a large room full of them, to whom I mentioned the subject of your deliverance. Those who were from the interior and back parts of the state, who had heard and felt but little of the excitement, would con·erse with calmness, and reason upon the subject; but those from the eastern borders would take fire in an instant at the mention of the thing, and were so excited that they could not speak of it but in very harsh language.

He spoke of the increasing excitement in the community, and said, "If this state of things continues, it will tear us all to pieces as a nation, and fill our land with carnage and blood; but if you will only renounce your views, it will have a tendency to quell the excitement and cool down the abolition fever."

Mr. Gallaher also said—"I have no doubt that if it was known to the people of Missouri that you had given up your principles, they would very soon be reconciled and willing to sign a petition for your release. If the exciting cause could be removed they would easily forgive and forget, and you would be delivered. But so long as that remains which caused the irritation,—hatred and prejudice,—any effort for your deliverance will be useless."

As Mr. S. wished some answer, full and definite, and not having sufficient time then, I proposed writing out our views and feelings, frankly and fully, that it might be known just where we stood—what we could do, and what we could not do. They wished it written in such a manner that it could be published (hoping it would be of such a character as would please slaveholders), so that the people might be induced to act for us. I accordingly wrote; and as the letter cannot be obtained, I will give the substance of what we addressed "To the Governor and Legislature of Missouri,—Men, brethren, and fathers," &c. We stated how long we had been here—how cheerfully we had toiled, and contented and happy we had been, amid all our sufferings—the thing we attempted to do, namely, to help a poor man across the river, who asked for our assistance, and the feeling which prompted us, pure love —that we had no other feeling than *love*, toward those who had been most active in sending and holding us here—that we would as soon help the most bitter ene- my we had as the most wretched slave living—that we should remain cheerfully and work faithfully, just so long as they saw proper to hold us. We stated plainly how far we could go, and how far we could not go, that we could not refuse to " open our mouth for the dumb," for God had *commanded* it—that we must " cry aloud, and spare not, and show the people their sins," for it was heaven's injunction—that we could not assist to re- turn, or stop their slaves who escaped, for God had said, " Thou shalt NOT deliver unto his master, the servant that is escaped," and wo to those do it—that we could not say we would not *help* them on their way, for this was commanded by God—that we could not give up one single principle which we conceived to be truth, and founded on the word of God, for liberty, or life itself— that much as we valued the blessings of freedom, of Christian society, and the house of God, and ardently as we longed to be preaching the gospel to those in mid- night darkness, we could not, on any conditions, purchase these privileges, by any act, which we should lament on a death bed, or at the day of judgment. That if they wished us to say, we would not come to this State, to help slaves away, so far we could promise, and no fur- ther (not because it would be sinful so to do, but unsafe) —that our writing to our friends would not stop the ex- citement; for it was their *putting us here* that caused, and their holding us here, that continued the excitement, and all they could do or say, while they held us, would oily be pouring oil on the fire—that if they wished to stop the excitement, they must *let us go*. We informed them that in sending us here, they had confined three men, who could not say or do much, any how; but in consequence, THOUSANDS had arisen, and would rise up in their stead, who *could* speak, write, and act with effi-

9

ciency and power—that though we had been, by an earthly tribunal, condemned, we had taken an appeal to the court of the *universe*, which was recorded—that there we were sure of being acquitted, for Jesus Himself, would be our advocate and Judge.

We reminded them of the tears, groans, and prayers of the widow and fatherless (Mrs. Work and family) which they must meet at the last day, and other things not now recollected. What was the effect, perhaps will not be known till it is divulged to an assembled world. We followed it with many prayers, but heard nothing of it, till about four months afterwards. Mr. Gallaher called again—said he saw it at the office of the Governor, " but it was rather too *high toned* to suit."

REFLECTIONS.

From the foregoing (as also from more that will come hereafter) what can be more evident, than the fact before affirmed, that it is our *sentiments respecting slavery*, that placed and detain us here in the penitentiary? And that too, in a land of liberty! where freedom of thought is allowed, and liberty of expression tolerated! Yes, it is clear, " Put a gag in your mouth—wear our slavery goggles—sear your conscience—harden your heart—stop your ' ears against the cry of the poor'—stupify and destroy your moral sensibility, so that you can connive at slavery, then we will sign a petition, and use our utmost endeavors to have you speedily set at liberty !" Such is the plain English of their propositions and actions. " Doctrine ! doctrine !" Yes, blessed be God, that it *is* doctrine, and not *crime*. For our *doctrine* we rejoice to suffer, and to lay down our *lives*, if need be.

CLOTHING DURING THE WINTER OF '42 and '43.

As the conduct of Capts. B. and G., had been such toward the prisoners, that they had little or no hope of being able to lease the establishment again, they were desirous to expend as little as possible, and make as much of what they had, as they could—and so did not buy any fresh supply of winter clothing; but arrayed

us in the *mock covering* of the patched rags, saved from
the fire, leaving many of the prisoners to suffer extremely, by day and night. Some, who were more adept at
stealing, and " shirking for themselves," wore two pair
of summer pantaloons—others, and the majority, were
dressed in the *had-been* clothes. Many, during all the
severities of winter, had nothing but a shirt, a *once-was*
roundabout, a thread-bare cotton pair of trowsers, a pair
of shoes, and perhaps an old pair of socks, and perhaps
not. Neither was there a change of shirts, but if we
wished a clean one, we must go without, till it could be
washed and dried.

In this plight we were driven through wet and dry,
rain and snow, cold and heat. I myself, with others,
worked in town, on the top of buildings, in winter's
piercing days, with only my thin, ragged, cotton pantaloons to shield my body from the sleet and winds—chill-
ed from morning to night. But by most, the night was
more dreaded than the day—for instead of bringing them
release from their sufferings, it only added to them.
Their covering was so very insufficient, that they could
with difficulty keep from freezing. We know from our
own experience, what it was, though many were much
worse off than we. With many, getting warm in a cold
night, was altogether out of the question. And during
the latter part of the winter, the rags would scarcely
hang together. With numbers, they were not sufficient
to cover their nakedness, as legislators and others can
testify. _ Some were driven to such extremities, that
they were obliged to buckle their *blankets* about them, to
hide their naked bodies! O, we were a pitiable company indeed ! Our appearance, even, made the legislators
turn their heads, and draw their faces with scowls of pity.

Let no one think this is the language of murmuring
and complaint. We had better than we *deserved ;* and
felt that we received what infinite love, wisdom, and
goodness saw *best* for us. And from these trying circumstances we learned many important lessons. We
were reminded of thousands in a *worse* state. We
learned sympathy for the poor—" to feel another's

woes," to pray for the needy and destitute. As oui tribulation abounded, so our consolation abounded, " that we might be able to comfort them which are in any trouble, *by* the comfort wherewith we ourselves are comforted of God." We can testify to his faithfulness, in supporting and comforting his little ones, even in fiery trials and deep waters, if they will only trust in Him. We can testify to the sufficiency of religion, to make its possessors happy, in the absence of outward comforts— in the midst of deprivations, hunger, cold, and nakedness —in sickness, poverty, and reproach—in prisons, chains, and weariness. O, it was *then*, that religion was *sweet* to our souls, and seemed more lovely than ever.

TREATMENT OF THE SICK UNDER G. AND B.

It was their language to the prisoners, " We don't wish any man to work, who is sick," but their *actions*, which spoke louder than their words, were quite different. Men *did* have to work when they were sick, and scarcely able to walk. And I have seen the poor sufferers driven like beasts, to labor in piercing cold weather, when they were shaken like an aspen leaf, with the ague —others that could with difficulty walk straight, ordered to their " burdens"—others who could hardly hold up their heads, compelled to continue their work, and others were driven till they could go no longer, and fell to the ground in a *swoon !*

I was not thus with *all*—there were some *favorites*, to whom they paid more regard. The diet of the sick was almost uniformly, a little mush and molasses. Those who were not able to be about some business, were frequently locked in their cold cells, not even allowed to come to the fire—and that too, in severe winter weather. But this was not always the case.

If a man was sick on the *Sabbath*, it was all well enough—but if on a week day, a storm of oaths and curses, complaints, and lies, might be looked for, from the officers. The Doctor came two or three times a week—and when he was here, it would remind one of the sick, halt, maimed, and blind, at the pool of Bethesua, awaiting a cure—to see them linger around the door, each waiting his turn to be called before him. It mattered not much what the complaint was, a dose of *pills* was the usual medicine, to be swallowed with cold water. We have great reason for gratitude, that we had not much need of his services. And when they were confined to their beds of straw, or hard boards, they had no soothing voice, to cheer and comfort them—no angel-hand to minister to their necessities—but it was roughness, indifference and neglect. One man, who was sick and confined to his cell for two weeks, had no one to sit up with him, nor even a *light*, till the night he died.

Toward the latter part of the time of these wardens, the sick, who were confined to their beds, had a little better attendance—some one to wait on them a little during the day, and to sit up with them at night.

Now to what shall we trace the *cause* of this inhumanity, this driving, this indifference to another's woes? Is it thus in *civilized* countries? Are the sick thus treated in prisons, where slavery does not exist? It is a well known fact that *slaves* are treated similarly, and worse—half-naked, half-starved, driven early and late, urged on by the lash, their aches and pains disregarded, and when they can *go no longer*, cursed, because they can't work.

Yes, to the influence of slavery in hardening the heart, and creating a *habit* of treading down the poor, must be ascribed the reason of this barbarity.

O, slavery, thou cruel monster! when will thy death-knell be proclaimed, and from thy curse, my countrymen and brethren be redeemed?

CHAPTER VII.

TERM OF CAPTS. GORDEN AND BURCH CLOSING

PRAYER FOR THE CONVERSION OF THE WORLD.

JANUARY 1st, 1843, we observed as a day of fasting and prayer, for the conversion of the world. Though shut up in prison, we could not feel ourselves *released* from obligation to those who sit in the " region and shadow of death." And though by providence prevented from going to them—from calling on the servants of God to awake—from uniting vocally with the thousands of Israel—yet in *heart* we rejoiced to unite in seeking Zion's welfare, by beseeching her King to extend and multiply her victories, till the nations should cheerfully submit to his sway. Placed as we were, we knew comparatively little respecting the state of the Church, and the world—the position the two contending armies maintained in relation to each other, consequently we could not pray so definitely as others—yet we had the great directory, the prophecies and promises of our Lord; and on his faithfulness, we could cast ourselves, and plead their speedy fulfilment.

Frequently we were favored with the perusal of various newspapers, from which we kept a general idea of the condition of the world. At times we have been constrained to shout aloud, by the intelligence of the onward march of truth and liberty! And we have been encouraged to pray that God would " overturn, overturn, overturn," till the kingdoms of this world should become the kingdoms of our Lord, and his Christ"—that he might " reign for ever and ever."

By law, we were forbidden " to receive any periodical." How did we get them? The *Lord* sent them. His wisdom and power, found ways enough to convey to us such intelligence, respecting his cause, as we most needed, and *at the time* we were in the greatest want of it, thus cheering our souls, and increasing our faith. If we were praying for the Jews, and ardently wishing to know what was the prospect of their return and conversion, a paper or a piece of one has fallen in our way, giving us the desired knowledge, which we received as from God.

If we were imploring the blessing of heaven on the representatives of our nation assembled at the Capitol, in due time, God has sent us the intelligence, that taught us *how*, and *what* to pray for in their behalf—that they might repeal all unholy and oppressive laws—" executive judgment"—" break every yoke," and " let the oppressed go free." To the distant rumblings of the chariot, we have listened with attention, marked the movements of providence, and the signs of the times," watching for the dawning of that day, when " the wickedness of the wicked shall come to an end," and the earth be filled with the glory of God.

Thus our heavenly Father has been faithful to send us *just* the things we needed, and we have " lacked *no good thing.*"

Jan. 2. While a number of prisoners were at work about seven miles distant, one was taken unwell, quit work, became speechless, and died in a short time. He was a wicked man—was brought here and buried.

THE SYMPATHIZING GUARD.

About the middle of January, James, myself, and three others, were finishing off a house in town. By the fire, I talked considerably with the guard. Among other things, he said " There are *many* who sympathize with you ; and if you conduct yourselves as you have thus far, you will not stay your time out. The *Book* tells us " that all things work for good to them who love God" —not a *part*, but ALL THINGS—and this dispensation, undoubtedly will be for your *best good*," &c. So we believe, felt, and *knew*, for He cannot lie that has promised."

Jan. 26. 1 went to the cell of W. S., who was very sick with pleurisy, to converse about his soul. I asked, are you ready to die? He replied, " Yes, long ago." Do you think you would be happy? " Yes." Are you willing to die? " Yes." Can you commit your family to God, and trust Him to take care of them? " I can; I leave them with him. If it is his will, that I should die now, I am satisfied." I then prayed with him. Hereafter, it will be observed, we were with the sick considerably. To enjoy the privilege of talking and praying with them, we esteemed an invaluable blessing. And I wonder, Christians are not more anxious to get around the beds of the sick, and dying. It is so profitable to the sick and well—the dying, and the living! Why is it, they are so backward? Is it because they do not like to be so forcibly reminded of their own destiny? Of this, we cannot think too much ; nor be too well prepared, to " depart, and be with Christ."

FOURTH DEATH-BED SCENE.

C. was a cripple, in his hands and legs; and had endured a great amount of suffering in his time. As he could not *work*, he had been the principal one to sit up with, and wait on the sick, for some time. He had attended on a number, till their spirits took their flight. He was present at the second and third death-bed scene. But now (February), *his* time came to be waited upon, and ministered unto. James was with him one night— Alanson two, and myself five nights. At these times another sat up with us, thus giving us an opportunity to converse freely with them, which we endeavored to improve. During the three last nights I was with him, and had frequent occasions to speak a word for my Master, as many came in to see him. At one time, I talked with the overseer, who came in, and remarked, " Oh ! it would be better for him to die, if he was prepared—that he might be freed from his troubles, and sufferings." I spoke of the *importance* of being *ready to die*, at any time—and mentioned the case of Moses Hunter, who said, on his dying bed, " My work of preparation for death, was done *years ago*." He listened attentively, and seriously. On the night of the eleventh, as the sick man appeared rational, I asked, Do you feel that your sins are forgiven? He replied, "Yes." It you should die now, do you expect to be happy? "Yes." Are you willing to die? "Yes." Shall I pray with you? "Yes." I did so. At one time, he seemed very earnest in prayer himself. I could not understand all he said, but he closed distinctly, "for Jesus' sake, Amen." He soon died, and was buried as a brute is buried. I was fearful he was trusting to his *morality*, but the judgment will show.

VARIOUS INCIDENTS.

Many of the prisoners come here, dressed in the highest style, expecting to have their clothes again, when they go out into the world. The *law* also makes such provision. But the best of the clothes were taken by the officers, and sold—the proceeds of which, they put into their *own pockets*—thus as really STEALING, and ROBBING, as did the thieves who wore them here!

Frequently prisoners brought money with them which was never returned. And when men had served their time out, they were put off with some ordinary, half-worn, and perhaps patched suit of clothes; with, it may be, one dollar; some, fifty cents; some, one shilling; and some, nothing, to go forth into a strange and hostile world; thus, as it were, driven, or at least tempted to steal again, the first opportunity.

And the most of the remaining clothes which were worn here were given to the men inside, to cover their nakedness during their last winter, and worn out, to save them from buying any new supply!

Such was the honesty of men placed over thieves to reform them!

ARDENT SPIRITS.

Many of the prisoners have frankly confessed—"It was whisky that brought me here. Had it not been for whisky, I should never have been here," &c. With many it has been the immediate cause of their coming

9*

here, and with others the remote. The immediate is where they have committed the crime under the influence of liquor. This class is numerous. Again, by drinking they have been led into bad company, and thus tempted to do what they would not have done under other circumstances. Of this class there are many.

A case of the remote cause. C. lived in N. Y., and was much given to drinking. At a time when there was a demand for soldiers in the west, he enlisted when he was drunk, was shipped to New Orleans, and from there up the Missouri river, to one of the forts. After a time he deserted, stole a skiff, and was coming down the river, when a colored man asked the privilege of riding with him. He took him in ; but at St. Charles was arrested, put in jail, tried for *stealing a slave*, and sentenced here for seven years. Though years intervened between his being drunk and his coming to the penitentiary, yet how obvious is it that whisky was the cause. He felt so.

P. R. cannot read. He was drunk, and traveling to a certain place. A slave with whom he was acquainted had stolen two of his master's horses, overtook R., and asked him to ride, saying, "I am going to the same place." He mounted the horse, but when he became a little sober he learned that the slave was running away ; divulged the fact at a tavern; was arrested ; charged with stealing the slave, and sent here for two years.

I might trace some causes even more remotely. Many are here for stealing, stabbing, murdering, &c., in a fit of intoxication. Others, who never stole or did any flagrant crime, by drinking, have associated with thieves and such characters, have been taken up on suspicion and sent here. And were the real truth known, doubtless it would appear that *alcoholic drinks* have been the proximate or remote cause of three fourths of the prisoners coming here. O! the misery, despair, and death of the intoxicating glass !

J. J. is a free colored man. A slave girl, in or near St. Louis, had an iron yoke on her neck, which, she complained was choking her. He took a file and cut it off. For this he was arrested, charged with stealing the girl, and sent here for three and a half years, which he faithfully served! What will they not make out "stealing" next? This is only a specimen of -slave-holding justice. Truly a man must be careful how he *looks* at a slave, lest his pity should move!

J. J. took it very cheerfully, felt that he was suffering in a good cause, and would do the same again if occasion required.

THE HYPOCRITE!

J. C. was a very intelligent, loquacious man. He soon attracted our notice, and was very free to tell us his history at different times.

I lent him a short but very pointed tract. When I questioned him about it, he replied, " I thought when I got to the *penitentiary* I should not be troubled with appeals to the conscience, on the subject of religion : but I find *they follow me here.*" Poor man! For many years he was one of the most active and zealous members of the Church in Philadelphia—engaged in Sabbath schools, bible classes, prayer meetings, in destitute portions of the city—missionary and Bible societies, &c., but he frankly confessed, "It was all to secure the favor and influence of certain rich merchants in the Church, who, I hoped, would take notice of me and *set me up in business ! !*" For a long time he professed to desire to study for the ministry, and plead with different ministers to aid him, but says, " my whole motive was selfishness—a *popular education !*" He was one who assisted in burning the Pennsylvania Hall—came to St. Louis— was clerk in a store—stole some thousands of dollars from his employer, and was sent here, for four years. Are not the motives of many in the Church similar? " Search me, O God, and know my heart ; try me, and know my thoughts."

In conversation with gamblers and highway robbers, who have had many thousands of dollars at a time, they have confessed, " It did me no good. All that I ever got in that way never did me any good. The thought

of how it was obtained would spoil all my enjoyment."
This was the confession of Elijah P. Lovejoy's murderer, of whom I shall speak hereafter.   Said T. J., " All
that I ever procured in that way never benefited me any.
I never derived any profit from it.   Somehow it would
slip away as easily as it came."   And he has handled
much.   W. W. confessed, " In all my scenes of mirth,
riot, and wickedness, I never knew what real happiness
was; never felt anything worthy the name of happiness."   Mark ! these are not the words of converted
men, but of those who continued to cleave to their folly.
Many have confessed similar things.   " There is no
peace to the wicked."

W. P. was born and brought up in New York.   Said
he, " Many a time has my mother got up at twelve and
one o'clock at night and gone to the city (a half mile),
to hunt for me, found me at the *card table,* and led me
home."   When grown up and in business the habit
followed him.   By gambling he lost his property.   He
" could not dig, and to beg he was ashamed."   The next
step was to rob some one, for money he must have.
Then conscience would trouble him ; and to drown its
whispers, free use was made of the bowl.   Whenever
he reflected, and called to mind his old mother he was
miserable, and would rush to the tavern or grog-shop to
drown his feelings.   Thus from step to step, he advanced,
till he landed *here,* for ten years, charged with highway
robbery !   Said he, " I *deserve* every moment of my time
in this place."   He promised an amendment, and swore
entire abstinence from liquor, for ever.

In giving this sketch of his case, I draw the picture
of very many here.   They have pious parents, brothers
and sisters ; but liquor has led them to the card table, the
gambling shop and " the way to hell ;" this company has
led them on to new scenes of wickedness ; and thus
proceeding, they have hardened their hearts, and seared
their consciences, till they have " sold themselves to
work wickedness," with all their might.

SATISFACTION.

A number here who confessed themselves guilty of what they were sent here for, told me, " I will never give another man whom I rob, the opportunity to appear against me in court"—meaning they would kill him on the spot.

And a great many talk about getting " satisfaction," when they get out—some by killing their prosecutors, or those who appeared against them in court; some, by flogging; and others by stealing from them! They say, " I must have pay for all the time I spend here," by stealing and robbing whom and where they can. If one gets into difficulty there are generally enough to step forward and swear him innocent.

A highway robber told me all about the circumstances of his knocking a man down and robbing him ; and yet, in court he had three witnesses to swear he was in bed at the time the deed was done! That is the way they do it.

Another, who ran away, said, " I had three men who swore I had been sick in bed five weeks in St. Louis, when I had been but three weeks from the penitentiary!" What is an oath!

THE WONDER!

I confess I never before knew what an amount of wickedness there is in the world—that every town and city, river and railroad, steamboat and stage is infested by such connected gangs of thieves, and robbers, and murderers, who are disciplined and taught the art from childhood; and who make it their only business to go from place to-place, dressed in the garb of gentlemen, to lay hands on everything they can, not caring for tears, groans, nor life even, if they may but succeed! But very little do we yet know. Still there is an eye which sees the whole, and will one day bring it all to light.

O! what a sight will be presented before the universe!

REFLECTIONS ON THE FOREGOING PAGES.

Keep in mind the character of the men, we, to this time, had been under—slaveholders, profane, blasphemous, sabbath-breakers, God-hating, and enemies to all good;—connect with this the treatment we have received, the privileges enjoyed, the opportunities of usefulness granted, liberty to write and receive freely on the subject of religion, to sing, read, and pray as heartily as we chose, and to converse with our fellow prisoners—and how manifest to every one is the *hand of the Lord.*

Such things could not, humanly speaking, have been looked for, or hoped for.

But "It is the Lord." "He hath done all things well." If this truth is evident from the foregoing, much more will it appear from what is to come. Reader, "Because I have said these things, do you believe" that God will take care of his own in every situation? Follow, and "thou shalt see and hear greater things than these."

PART THIRD.

CHAPTER I.

TERM OF CAPTAIN RICHMOND AND JUDGE BROWN

NEW WARDENS.

By all the prisoners it was understood that at that session of the Legislature (February 1843), the penitentiary was to be sold, for ten years, to the highest bidder. In almost every bosom, there was an anxious solicitude as to *who* should be placed over us. A thousand inquiries were made, and reports were circulated, but " we gave ourselves to prayer," knowing that it was the Lord, who could raise up and cast down, and send us whom He chose.

Thus, by casting our care upon God, we were saved from the manifold anxieties, and gloomy forebodings which agitated the bosoms of the ungodly. They often thought of their sufferings, and cruel treatment, and had many apprehensions concerning the future. But with the settled assurance that the "Disposer of all events," would place over us just such men as would, on the whole, most glorify his name, we were composed—and feeling that the character of the men might depend on our prayers, we earnestly "besought the God of heaven," if it could be possible to give us men who would fear his name, and seek the spiritual good of the wretched prisoners. We knew, that no one could obtain the station without his consent, that our " good" was secured by eternal *promise*, and therefore we were satisfied.

On the 16th February 1843, the new Wardens took possession—giving security for the sum of fifty thousand dollars, for the use and profits of the prison for ten years.

The morning we spent principally by the stove reading, while the majority were locked in their cells. In the afternoon a committee from the Legislature, came to examine into the condition and circumstances of the prisoners. We were all assembled in the carpenter's shop, where we passed before the committee, one by one. The principal questions, were such as follows. " How long have you been here ?" " To stay ?" " Charge ?" " Guilty ?" " Enough to eat ?" " Comfortable clothing ?" " Work hard ?" " Work when sick ?" " Treatment when sick ?" " Read ?" " Write ?" " What your occupation before coming here ?" &c., &c. They wrote down the name, age, where born, whether he could read or write, occupation, &c., of each one. They listened to some pitiable tales indeed—for some of the prisoners had such an inveterate spite against G. and B., that they " brought out the whole budget"— stating what kind of food they had been obliged to eat —how they had suffered day and night with the cold— that they had not had a clean shirt for four, six, or eight weeks—being driven to work, with two large chains on, when they were so *sick* they could scarcely walk, &c.

Sometimes they would ask, " Are those all the clothes you have ?" " Yes sir"—which wrung a scowl and long sigh of pity, even from those wicked men. They manifested their enmity to us, Dr. Nelson, and the Mission Institute.

RECOMMENDATION TO THE WARDENS.

James was in the sick room, just above the guard-room, where he overheard the following, as the new officers were making many inquiries about the prisoners. " Well, what kind of persons are the abolitionists ?" Mr. B., an old guard, who was generally kind to us, replied, " O they are *first-rate* fellows—they will do no harm. I let them go just where they please. They would not run away, should the gate be left wide open. Without an honorable discharge they won't leave." He came into my cell, a day or two after, and said he had given us a good name to the officers, and wished us to conduct ourselves exemplarily, and we would fare well.

See here " the good hand of our God," in causing one who had long observed us, to speak a word in our favor, to those who knew us not, and were probably filled with prejudice against us! " Blessed are all they who put their trust in Him." Reader, try it.

The next morning we were all assembled ; and in the midst of the crowd, Judge B. mounted on a bench, read to us some *Rules*, with various remarks. Said if we behaved well, we should be treated well—but if any were lawless, means would be employed to *make* them obey.; when any were sick they should be well taken care of, &c. Reader, remember this promise. For a few days, very little was done, but to sit around the stoves. Soon they concocted their plans, and began to tear down the middle wall, which furnished work for some—but who should go ? For many had not clothes sufficient, to venture forth into the cold—and some had neither clothes nor shoes. We had opportunity to read considerably.

CHARACTER OF NEW OFFICERS.

Judge Brown is a member of the Presbyterian church, Capt. Richmond, of the Baptist, and the overseer, of the Presbyterian. At first, they all manifested much kindness toward the prisoners. They seemed to take an interest in their eternal welfare, as will shortly appear—but this feeling gradually wore away, and its place was supplied by a spirit of indifference, and contempt of a convict's welfare, as the reader will notice in the sequel. But many very important points were gained, under our new officers.

1. All chains were taken off, and every man placed on a *new probation*—the past was all overlooked, and opportunity given to each one to secure favor, by his good conduct.

2. Swearing was not only prohibited among prisoners, but there was a corresponding *example*, on the part of the officers.

3. All Sabbath-work was stopped, for about one year.

4. The shaving was changed from Sabbath to Satur day.

5. A Chaplain was appointed by the State—as also Inspectors.

6. We enjoyed free opportunity of talking with the prisoners—though it was forbidden, yet we were never reproved for so doing.

7. We had a godly overseer for one year, to whom we could go with freedom and confidence. He would listen to a prisoner's tale of grief, and try to comfort and relieve. He was remarkably kind and gentle.

. When the first Saturday came, with what anxiety did we watch the movement of things! And when we saw the men being shaved, and found ourselves without a beard before the Sabbath, and saw them cutting wood enough to last till Monday—O, how our hearts leaped for joy! How did we bless and praise the Lord, that our eyes were permitted to see such a change! Then we perceived it was not in vain to pray—for with joy we beheld an answer to our many and oft repeated supplications. The blessing, so long implored, was unspeakably sweet and precious. We had very many times, "in our hallowed cell," plead with God to send us a man, fearing him and loving souls—to bring an end to Sabbath shaving. And to see these blessings granted —to feel that they came from God in answer to prayer, was cheering to our souls, reviving to our faith, and encouraging to our hearts. We felt almost as if we were in a new world.

We were, by all the officers, treated with more kindness and respect than we could have expected, and allowed to cell together, as formerly.

HEART-HARDENING INFLUENCE OF POWER.

For some time our officers were kind, and made many promises of what they would do in future. For example, the wardens, overseer, and Capt. R.'s son, time and again, promised us a Sabbath School. Said J. R. (the son), "When we get our Sabbath School in operation. you will have an opportunity to do good to your fellow prisoners by teaching them." This was glad news, indeed. Capt. R. said, " we shall have a Sunday School, and shall set you to teaching the prisoners. We intend to give all who wish an opportunity to learn to read and write, and endeavor to send them forth into the world, honest and useful citizens. These and many similar promises greatly rejoiced and elated our hearts. For these things we had been praying again and again; we spoke to them about it, but they " said and did not." No Sabbath School came—nor were any taught to read or write, though many ardently desired it. Our entreaties and arguments were all ineffectual.

They solemnly promised that they would keep no guard who would use profane language before the prisoners. After a few months guards were heard to swear unblushingly. I went to the officers time and again about it. " O, we can't help it. It can't always be avoided," was the reply—and a guard could swear as much as he pleased. I was telling J. R. how much I had been annoyed by profane guards, previously. He remarked, " I am not a Christian. I sometimes swear, myself, but I will not do it in the presence of any one whose feelings I know it will wound." This respect for a prisoner's feelings did not last long. He also stated, " We mean to do all we can to make the prisoners happy and contented with their lot. ' It is bad enough at the best, and we wish to regard their feelings, and consult their comfort and happiness. 1 shall treat every one kindly, and I am determined that no one shall hear an unkind word from me so long as I stay here."

But his professions were not carried out, though he always treated us kindly. Use and authority soon hardened his heart, so that like Hazael, he could perform deeds of cruelty and barbarity, the thought of which, a short time before, was revolting to his mind. Though he remained here only a little more than a year, he became a perfect tyrant to the prisoners generally.

Capt. R. professed to feel for the prisoners, and did treat them kindly for a time, but *his* heart also soon became unfeeling, so that he could disregard and contemn

a prisoner's sufferings, to a degree that was shocking.
He came to the cell of one who was unwell one morning, and had not yet got out of his bed, and said, " W.,
why are you not at work? Get right up, and come out
here quick, and go along to your work, or I'll flog you
like a dog. Come, be quick." Another had made repeated applications to stop, because he was sick. I
saw him—I worked with him—I heard him complain—
I saw his swollen legs, upon which he could scarcely
stand, frequently having to lie down. He was driven
on until he suddenly fell to the ground in a fit!

I have seen Capt. R., again and again, walk up to
a prisoner, and with his hickory cane repeatedly try his
strength over the head and shoulders of the sufferer,
who dared not resist, and that too, when there was no
occasion for it.

Judge B., who was so gentle and kind, at first, has
hardened with an amazing rapidity, so that a prisoner's
comfort and happiness, health and life, are regarded with
shocking indifference, neglect, and even contempt.

All this tenderness, and sympathy, and attention to
the happiness of the prisoners, by degrees passed away,
and a want of feeling for another's woes, was exhibited,
that was truly awful. And about in proportion as the
press of business increased, did this disregard of the
pains and ills of the sufferers increase. So true is it, that
people do not know themselves until they are brought
to the test. Such is the deceptive nature, the hardening
effect, and the too common fruits of power, when not
under the influence and government of religious principle, of holy love, of enlarged philanthropy.

Poor, ragged, ignorant back-woodsmen, come here
and hire out for guard, and they soon seem more lordly
and of greater consequence than monarchs. It is laugh-
able and disgusting to see them.

PARTIALITY.

Soon after the change of officers, one of the guard-
rooms was set apart as a hospital, to which the sick were
removed. James, being sick, was taken there. We had

free access to him, and to all in the hospital—to talk and pray with them.

Also we were permitted to remain there, by the fire, Sabbath days, while the other prisoners were locked up in their cold cells. There we read, sang, and prayed with all who came—and enjoyed some precious seasons. Our kind and good overseer, would come in and talk freely with us—tell us his experience, sing, bring us religious newspapers,—in short, he seemed not so much like an overseer, as a *brother*, who delighted in the image of Christ wherever found—in high or low, bond or free —though in a despised *convict !*

In the time of G. and B., we were not allowed to lend our books—but these men came to us and said, " You must lend your books to the prisoners, till we get some—and do them good in this way." We rejoiced to do so.

The prisoners finding that the officers would let them write letters, many made application—soon an order was given that no prisoner should have more than a half sheet at a time, but they always, with one or two exceptions, gave *us* a whole one, and as often as we desired, for the first two years. A frequent objection to our letters was, " They are *too long.*" Now, while we were under G. and B., those extremely wicked men, that objection was never mentioned to me, though I always interlined, and filled my sheet—but so soon as covetous professors of religion take their place, they can't spend time to read such long letters ! It is very strange, yet such is the truth. However, they sent our letters, for which they have our thanks.

I also was privileged to write letters for other prisoners, who could not write ; and for numbers who could write, because they thought I could do it better. In this way I preached the gospel to many a far off—to wives, mothers, children, friends—to the widow and fatherless —the bond and free—directing them to Jesus, for comfort, amid their sorrows—to the widow's God, and the " Father of the fatherless," for support and defence, while the husband, father or son, was shut up in prison.

And often, while reading to the old gray headed father, what I had written to his children, would the tears abundantly flow—and the eyes of the son, would pour forth a flood, as he heard what I said in his name, to the old father, or widowed mother, from whom he had run away. And then to read the *answers* to some of these letters, in which were the rejoicings of the aged widow, united with those of brothers and sisters, over a " son that was lost, but now found," was truly cheering, and abundantly repaid me for all my trouble.   For some seemed almost to overlook the crime, the suffering, and the disgrace— so great was their joy to hear that their son or brother was yet alive, that their many prayers were answered, in their conversion to God, though by means so different from what they had marked out.   Again, and again, have they sent their thanks to me, from distant States, free and slave, for the interest I had taken in the welfare of their unfortunate children or brothers.

OUR WORK.

Alanson continued as before, at his chair making, with the addition of spinning wheels, large and small— having frequent opportunity to converse with customers, about their souls, or concerning the news of the day. No one to hurry him, or find any fault with his work, he did much as he chose, taking care, however, not to give prisoners or officers, occasion to complain of him.   He was faithful to his trust.   At one time he said, " Sometimes I am tempted to be lazy, as no one looks after me, to see whether I do little or much; but then I think, that the angels and God, are looking at me—our friends, and the anti-slavery world are watching eagerly to see if we will work cheerfully and faithfully for the poor slave, and at my work I go with new resolution, and vigor." So we all felt.

James continued his carpentering, when he could work (being sick much of the time), for nearly a year. The cause of change I shall mention in its place.   I worked at turning awhile—then carpentering sometime —then spinning bale-rope about four months—then weaving bagging about one year and a half—lastly in the wagon shop, sixteen months, including about four months of sickness. At times, I worked a few days at other things, but such was my general employment—pursued with much pleasure, while I felt that all was foi the cause of humanity.

Our food continued much as before—generally, corn bread and bacon—now and then, some potatoes or turnips, hommony, or beans.

· In the spring, a long table was prepared, in one of the halls, and all ate together at breakfast and dinner—having our corn bread, in our cells at night. With this arrangement, our overseer, introduced into the prison, for the first time since its commencement, the practice of publicly seeking from God a blessing on our food. This was new to the prisoners, and made many of them very angry. Frequently the victuals would be very poor, then to hear a blessing asked over "*such*" food would make them curse Christians and their God. The overseer often called on Alanson, James, myself, or W. G. And when he was absent, one of us was always spoken to. This state of things continued only during the time of this overseer.

For some months, the sick were treated with a good degree of attention. The officers would come to see them, and find out their wants—but this, as I have already intimated, soon passed away, and the sick have been left to suffer unaccountably. The young, inexperienced, ignorant, unfeeling *doctor*, was the cause of more cruelty towards the sick, probably, than all the officers together—for he had the *power* to see that they were *well* taken care of—but he was bribed by the officers, and sought not the good of the prisoners, but the favor of his employers. But facts, hereafter shall speak for themselves.

PREACHING.

The first two Sabbaths we had no preaching. As we were in the hospital, on the next Sabbath, reading and praying, the overseer came in, and said, " We have been talking below, and I have come up to see if you will preach for us this afternoon, if the minister does not come." I told him I was willing so to do. But the chaplain came, and preached to us his first sermon. He is a warm hearted, zealous Methodist preacher—generally very earnest in his exhortations to saints and sinners, and helped us to do good.

After sermon, he called on me to pray. This was another new thing which caused much talk among the prisoners. We felt that God was fast opening " a great and effectual door" of usefulness, for which we desired to be prepared. We had long been praying, and looking, and waiting, but now we saw the clouds dispersing; the sun began to shine, and we could see our way more clearly. We were greatly encouraged to look up, and ask for "great things"—to " open our mouths wide," and to " commit our way unto the Lord."

SING US ONE OF THE SONGS OF ZION.

March 12. We had spent our Sabbath in the hospital as usual, with James, who was there sick. Alanson and myself had retired to bed, but soon a guard came for me, saying, " I want you to come into the hospital and sing for us." So of old, " They that carried us away captive, required of us a song"—but, blessed be God, that we were not obliged, through grief and sorrow of heart, to say, "How can we sing the Lord's song in a strange land ?" With joyful hearts we arose and went. The guards, five or six, were assembled, and we sang some of our favorite pieces for them.

OUR FIRST PRAYER MEETING.

19. After preaching, I went to Capt. R., and asked permission for a few of us to have a season of prayer together in the Hospital. It was granted. We assembled—eight in number—sang, prayed, and exhorted. In addition to our usual praying number, J. D., our colored brother was present. He had frequently conversed with us on the subject of his soul's salvation, but this was the first opportunity we had of praying with him. He

v.as considerably broken and confused, but in earnest.
An old man who was present and heard him pray, said,
"I did not know as old J. had got along so far as that."
He confounded the wicked.

W. S. was sick in the Hospital.   After we had sung
and prayed, he broke forth as follows, "I feel the love of
God in my soul.   Jesus is precious.   He is very sensi-
bly and feelingly near.   O, if I had a tongue, I would
persuade all to go to glory with me, but I am too weak."
It was a precious little season to us, and a commencement of a series of meetings never to be forgotten.
True, our number was small, yet we were enough to
claim the promise, " Where two or three are assembled
together in my name"—no matter where, though in a
prison, enclosed by high walls, secured by locks, and iron
gates, or in a dungeon, or a cave—"there am I in the
midst of them."

CHAPTER II.

PRAYER MEETINGS—CONVERSION OF SINNERS, &c.

THE REVIVAL.

MARCH 25.   I had considerable conversation with J. R.
about the spiritual wants of the prison, and begged the
privilege of a stated prayer meeting, every Sabbath
morning, promising that I would hold myself responsible
for any misconduct that might occur in meeting.   He
spoke favorably, and said, "I will talk with my father,
and let you know."   Accordingly, the next morning
(Sabbath), I was called down to the guard room, where
were Capt. R. and others.   He said, " We have concluded to grant you that privilege, and you can have your
meetings in the hospital."   O, what glad tidings were
these to our thirsty souls !   Our hearts leaped for joy at

10

the prospect of again exhorting sinners to "flee from the wrath to come," and pointing them to the Lamb of God. The thoughts of our prayer meeting, during the week, would lighten our toils, and sweeten all our cares and pains. We saw clearly that God "had not despised the affliction of the afflicted," nor withheld any good.

At our next meeting, about a dozen were present, and interest was manifest. The number continued to increase. The attention of the impenitent was arrested. The Lord heard prayer and blessed his own truth, so that while some came from novelty, others evidently had an arrow in their hearts.

In our exhortations, singing, and prayers, we aimed at the immediate conversion of sinners—beseeching them to come to the Savior tearing away their excuses—and, from our own experience, testifying to the excellency of religion, and to its power to support and cheer, even in these trying circumstances.

We soon had evidence that the Spirit was in our midst, seconding our feeble endeavors, and pressing sinners to forsake their evil ways.

We had a few meetings when one with whom we had frequently conversed, cried aloud for mercy. This not only encouraged us, but it affected the wicked, and a "shaking among the dry bones" was observable. Some mocked and ridiculed, while others became more serious, and anxious to attend the meeting. They tried to harass and vex the convert, but he bore it with patience, and continued to pray with us.

Soon another was anxious to know what he must do to be saved. We talked with him privately, and he made up his mind fully and deliberately to serve the Lord. Though both were extremely ignorant, being scarcely able to read intelligibly, yet it was exceedingly interesting to hear them pray. Their broken and half choked words,—disconnected sentences and ideas were "music to our ears." One of them in prayer, used this language, "O Lord we are here in this dreadful house of bondage, I thank Thee for the privilege of praying together in this little cell.   I never expected such a great privilege," &c.

April 9.   Attended the communion, inviting W. G. to unite with us.   At the first suggestion he was pleased with the idea ; but soon expressed doubts as to the propriety of the thing without a regular minister.   We reasoned the case with him—showed the general nature of the command, explained the design of the ordinance, and gave him what light we could.   A few days after, he came and said, " I have been studying and praying over that thing, to know my duty, and I have come to the conclusion that it is right for me to unite with you."   He came, and for the first time, obeyed the dying command of our Lord.   He was much blessed, and greatly strengthened by the occasion.   It was sweet to feed this lovely lamb. O, how eagerly he would drink in the truth !

April 14.   W. F. P. came to my cell, with whom I conversed and prayed.   He says, " I feel that I am forgiven of the past, and am now determined to live for God the rest of my time."   Bless the Lord !

A DREAM INTERPRETED.

With H. B. I had frequently conversed, when at work—he always acknowledged the necessity of a change—knew his duty, but said, " I am so wicked, it seems like I could not bring my mind to the subject. Sometimes I feel as if I could forgive my enemies, then again I am full of revenge."   One morning he told me his dream, which I interpreted, according to the event, though it did not come to pass, for perhaps six months. The dream—" I saw a very beautiful bird of exquisitely fine colors, beyond anything I ever saw, or can describe. It was called the King Bird of Paradise.   I pursued it through thickets and thorns, over stones and logs—amid many difficulties, falls, and bruises, but finally I *caught* it, and it was the most delightful creature I ever saw in all my life."

The interpretation. —" The King Bird of Paradise' is the *Savior*, the " chiefest among ten thousand, and al together lovely."   The " thorns, logs, rocks, bruises

falls," &c., are the trials and sufferings through which
you are now passing. And happy indeed would you be
amid them all, if by these afflictions you should behold.
and embrace the blessed Savior.

He afterwards acknowledged the interpretation abund-
an·ly true—frequently blessed the Lord for all these afflictions, which had been the means of leading him to
Jesus, and in strong terms expressed his peace and happiness, as far beyond everything he ever experienced
while at liberty.

He came to our prayer meetings, became interested
for his soul's salvation, and would freely weep, while I
presented Jesus before him, with entreaties to repent
and accept of his salvation. I conversed with him privately, urging him to immediate submission.

His wife came to see him. After she left, I asked
him, "Have you given your heart to God and determined to serve Him?" "Yes, I have resolved to serve
God, and do right the rest of the time I have to live."
"Did you tell your wife so?" "Yes, and she smiled,
and said, I think we shall see happy days togethei
yet." He came out a burning Christian.

Many things in his case would be interesting to the
reader, but should I mention half the particulars during
the revival, they would swell this volume to an immode-
rate size. An *outline* is all I can present. But I will
mention one thing about H. B. When he was converted,
he was a perfect slave to *tobacco*—it had been all his
comfort. Before he came to prison, he was a " great
drinker" too. But mark, when he submitted to God,
and turned enemy to his sins, he " swept the board"—
swore eternal abstinence from liquor, and cast away his
tobacco pouch, to touch it no more. The habit was
strong, but he cried to God, to subdue the desire and in
less than a week, he was a *free man*, though in prison.
O that his example might *shame* any of my readers who
may use this " abominable thing."

The interest increased, and we multiplied our meetings
—not that we trusted in them, but so great was the
wickedness here—anxious sinners confined with the

vile who did all they could to turn them away, and there being no place of retirement, almost the only hope seemed to be, to get them alone, or in a meeting and press them to submission on the spot.

The sick increasing in the hospital, and some of them being low, we met in our cell, which accommodates about thirty persons. It was soon crowded—we preached Christ, and invited weeping sinners to Jesus. The Lord blessed the truth, and to all it was evident " Truly God is in this place." We felt it and rejoiced.

Perhaps I cannot better give the reader an idea of these scenes than by quoting from my journal, where I recorded circumstances, and the spontaneous overflowings of my soul, as they occurred.

I had informed the Chaplain of the state of feeling, and advised him to call the anxious forward. The next Sabbath is described in my journal as follows.

April 30. " Alleluia!" Salvation has come with power. Prayer meeting in the morning; after which, when we were locked up, I preached in my cell to six brethren, fellow prisoners, from *Acts* ix. 16. New-born souls rejoicing! Prayer meeting again after dinner; deep interest. The Chaplain brought with him another brother, who preached from *Heb.* iii. 13, a very searching sermon, and cutting appeals concerning the " deceitfulness of sin." The anxious were called for; eight rushed forward, dropped on their knees and begged for mercy, sobbing and groaning aloud. The Chaplain prayed and called for others to follow;—James and myself did so. It was an awfully solemn scene. The mass of the prisoners crowded around to gaze. The officers were present.

After meeting I led them to my cell, and O! what a sight! Here were the murderer, the highway robber, the profane, the unclean, the thief and gambler, prostrated, crying for mercy, and yielding themselves to God.

Glory! glory! glory! The tiger is changed into a lamb, the vulture to a dove. One cried, " I am lost, I am lost, I am so wicked." " Submit to God," I cried.

"I will," said he. Another—"I will go with you. I yield to God for ever, and will serve Him." Amen. Another—"I submit to God. I yield to Him body and spirit, to take me and do as He sees best." Hosanna! Another—"I will serve God." "When?" "Now. I will obey Him." O, reader, I cannot present this scene before you in words. Had you been here, you would have heard them bewailing before an offended God, their mountain-towering sins—seen them trembling with fear of being rejected and cast off, almost in despair—some calling for "mercy, mercy, mercy,"—others, "there is no hope for me, I have been such a great sinner; no hope," &c. We felt that it was a critical time with them, and pointed them to the Lamb of God," beseeching them to look, believe, submit, and yield their hearts to Him. It was solemn as death.

We almost forgot we were in prison, where the rules strictly forbade our speaking to a fellow prisoner. We could not hold our peace. Speak we must and speak we did, " no man forbidding."

We now saw a great work before us in watching over and instructing the lambs, searching out the anxious, and warning the careless. But blessed be God for our good overseer. His heart was also in the work. He conversed with prisoners about their souls, and allowed us to do the same with freedom.

May 2. Conversed with C. S. in my cell—a very interesting case. Said he, "They point at me, and laugh and make fun of me, but I am determined not to care for it." He is very decided. Prayed with me—the the first time he ever prayed in English. He is a Russian—talks well—is very forgiving toward enemies—and thanks God for sending him here.

3. Talked with J. M., but he did not submit.

4. Talked and prayed with him; he also prayed and signed his name to an article of entire consecration, which I drew up. He seemed to be in great distress—would give or suffer anything, if he could only feel that his sins were forgiven. When we arose from prayer, he looked round the cell and said, " Your cell is a palace,

and you are happy in it, but ⸏ am miserable." I reasoned and plead, but tremble for him.

5. Met, in F. D.'s cell, with three converts and an unbeliever—talked and prayed—a precious season—delightful to hear the babes pray and praise the Lord. The sinner would not bow. Glory to God! for sending me to a penitentiary to preach the gospel. Last night with the sick.

6. Saturday evening, prayer-meeting here with the converts, after they had finished their work. They are very anxious to get together—could not wait for the Sabbath. O! how " the good hand of our God is upon us!"

7. Glorious Sabbath! Murderers and thieves submitting to God—converts rejoicing and praising their King, and pleading for sinners who are trembling beneath the load of their guilt. Three prayer meetings to-day besides preaching. In one, the Chaplain was present, and heard them tell what God had done for them. In sermon he spoke of the prayer meeting, and urged all to attend—there is full liberty for all who wish to attend. I have all talk and pray who profess to be converted.

9. James with the sick—Alanson staying with S. to talk with him—J. S. and E. S. with me. Talked and prayed. They give good evidence of being truly converted.

12. W. B. with us—formerly an ignorant Catholic— has been very wild and profane—lived eighteen years without going into a meeting house—but truth reached his heart, and he trembled in view of his sins—now seems penitent, humble, decided, ready.

13. Saturday eve. Meeting full of interest and warm hearts.

14. The most glorious day I have seen! The power of God wonderfully displayed. In prayer meeting, four new cases of conversion; cell crowded to overflowing; converts mounting higher and growing stronger; while the long-hardened tremble like Belshazzar. Preached to twelve converts, in my cell, from *Luke* ix.

23. In the afternoon, a powerful sermon—six new ones came forward—I talked and prayed with them, " no man forbidding." Glory to God !

19. A. D. with us to stay all night—appears well.

20. A good prayer meeting this evening.

21. The work is rolling—glory to God! Two new cases in the prayer meeting. Preached to a crowded cell, from *Luke* xv. 26–33. O! what scenes! Hosanna! E. R. is overflowing. He talks and prays like a preacher. His whole soul is in the work. At one time he said, "I find that the more of the spirit of religion I possess, the more of an *abolitionist* I am !" This is good.

In the afternoon, divided our prayer meeting, and filled two cells—James and Alanson conducting one, and I the other. Glorious! glorious!

E. P. LOVEJOY'S MURDERER.

23. Last night, J. M. cut his throat—bled three quarts—still alive. This is all from UNBELIEF, which drove him to *despair*. Submission to God would have saved him all this. See May 3d and 4th.

Just here I will say what I have to say about this person. He came here on the night of the fire. I worked with him some time. He told me all about the Alton "scrape"—acknowledged he was one of the leaders of the mob, and was the man who fired the building. He and a young doctor (he would not give the name), swore to each other as follows, that he (J. M.) would ascend the ladder, and fire the building, if the doctor would *shoot* DEAD the first man who should come out of the door, to shoot him. E. P. Lovejoy was the first, and was shot dead, by the young doctor. J. M. was indicted and tried for arson. Mr. U. F. Linder, the ringleader of the mob, plead his cause, and he was cleared, but banished from the place. Subsequently he was engaged in house robbing, and an attempt to murder a woman—and came here for seventeen years. He is said to be guilty of various other murders.

He professed to be anxious about his soul, for a time

—became sullen and downcast—cut his throat, which was sewed up—two days after, he picked up a hand axe, and struck a prisoner on the head, hurting him severely. When asked *why* he did it—he repled, " I felt it my *duty* to kill somebody !" He was locked in his cell, where he tore his blanket into strips, and tried three times to hang himself from the iron bars of the window, but the string broke every time. He was chained to the floor—tore open his throat wound—wished the officers to give him a rope, and let him hang himself—then begged that he might drown himself, &c. A desperate character. He was one of Murrill's right hand men—and told me of many of his deeds of robbery, kidnapping, stabbing, knocking down, &c.

While working with him one day, he remarked, in the presence of the guard and myself—" There is a man in Ohio Penitentiary for *fifteen years*, for a crime which I committed myself. He is perfectly innocent, and knew nothing about it !"

Can nothing be done for that man's release ? There are also men in Missouri prison, for what others did ! One slaveholder served two years there for what his *slave did !*

28. Four new cases. Interesting prayer meeting, a bundle of tracts given to us, for which we are thankful.

June. 4. James quite sick—chaplain came to see him.

7. Last night staid with James, in the hospital—and drew up a temperance pledge—also an anti-tobacco pledge.

10. This morning seven prisoners made a break, by knocking down the gate keeper, and opening the gate. Two were soon taken—one was shot—four balls passing through the fleshy part of the arm, into his side. He came near dying several times, while the wound was being dressed. " The way of transgressors is hard" most certainly. Two others were drowned, one of them leaving a large family.

11. Very interesting prayer meeting. Preached to about twenty-five, from *Ex.* xxxii. 26. Said J. D.,

10*

" A *lazy* man cannot seek religion, nor be a Christian."
It is good to feed the lambs.

18. Preached to parents with respect to trusting their
wives and children with God—blessed time. In the
prayer meeting, J. D. full of the Spirit—the cell could
scarcely contain him—he jumped as if on springs—
clapped his hands, and shouted glory ! The old man
sixty-two years old pleading for mercy. Lord save him.

19. W. S. with us to receive instruction on baptism.
He is an old gray headed man, and appears of an excellent spirit.

22. H. B. with us, for instruction on baptism. He is
a lovely spirit.

25. An old Baptist man preached. After sermon,
those who wished to be immersed, came forward, and
were examined. Six were immersed.

EXTRACT OF A LETTER TO A FRIEND.

Through the goodness of God, we can yet exclaim,
with one of old, " *Ebenezer ;*" and call upon you all to
" magnify the Lord with us." I cannot describe to you
on paper, His wonderful works in our midst. The
number that now unite with us in prayer, and in telling
" what God has done for them, and how he has had compassion on them," is upwards of twenty. Give God the
praise. The work is His. In the converts, the turning
point with many was, forgiveness and love of enemies—
but God gave them no peace till they gave up all animo-
sity. Said one, " For three long years, I have lived with
bitter enmity in my heart against two men, on whom I
was determined to have revenge, when I left this place ;
but God told me I *must give it all up*, or He would not
hear one word to me, and now I feel to love them, and
find more happiness than in all my life before. You
must do as I did—forgive your enemies." I tell you
these scenes are glorious. The wicked, who surround,
mock, deride, and lie ; but in the face of all this, to see
men come out boldly on God's side makes our souls rejoice. I never saw men appear better than some of

these converts do. They just "*cast off* the works of darkness," and yield up to God.

Alanson says, " Tell my family to trust in God, and be patient; and all things will work together for the best." He is as happy as a king.

James has been sick, and nigh unto death. We did not much expect he would stay with us long—but through the mercy of God he has nearly recovered; he now wants bodily strength. He was in the hospital two weeks and a half—felt willing and ready to " depart and be with Christ, which is far better"—still thinks it doubtful whether he meets you all again, till we meet where sighing and sorrow are not known."

THE RECONCILIATION.

July 2. We had an interesting scene in the prayer meeting. H. B. and W. S. were sent here on the false testimony of G. S. They were perfectly innocent as to the thing charged against them. G. S. was hired to swear falsely, and they were sent here. Soon after G. S. stole, and came himself. The two former had cherished bitter feelings of revenge against the latter, and he knew it. But when they were converted, they went to him and told him they freely forgave him. He could hardly believe it. H. B. went to his cell, talked kindly, and assured him of his hearty forgiveness. G. S. melted into tears, confessed his guilt, and said, "I would be willing to do or suffer anything, if you could only be restored to your family." To-day they were all present in the prayer meeting. G. S. professed repentance, and a determination to serve God! I addressed the three. My heart was moved; and before all I asked, "H. B., do you freely and fully forgive G. S. ?" He frankly replied in the affirmative, arose, and gave him his hand in token of reconciliation. I turned to W. S., and asked the same question. He expressed his cheerful forgiveness, and gave his hand in token of friendship and love.

It was affecting. A little before they were at variance, and meditating each other's destruction, refusing to be reconciled; now, melted down, their enmity slain, and love filling their souls, they embraced each other, as brethren going to heaven together.

9. A good prayer meeting. Preached from 2 Cor. v. 17. In the afternoon, after sermon, the chaplain baptized four persons by pouring, which he thinks is the only proper mode.

23. Prayer meeting in the carpenter's shop. Many prisoners and the overseer attended. C. N. came to our cell—gave evidence of conversion—prayed and talked well. Two weeks ago, we were spinning together, and I reproved him for swearing. Said he, "From that time I began to pray, and ask for the forgiveness of my sins, and ceased not till I found relief." Ah, "a word in season, how good is it?"

28. Glorious Sabbath! Salvation and rejoicing! Interesting prayer meeting—excellent class meeting. Some new cases. J. P. said, "The thing which brought me here was forsaking Christ. I have a pious wife and children. It has been three years since I forsook God. First, I neglected secret prayer; second, family devotion; third, the house of God; now I am fully determined to be faithful." He prayed and wept freely. Just came last week.

W. W. very much broken down—wept like a child. He said, "I believe my coming here will be the means of saving my soul."

O, what God can do! "Is anything too hard for the Lord?" No preaching; no time to read; all day occupied in helping others; but praise to God for such a privilege.

Said one, "My first year here was one of misery and death. The second has been one of life and peace."

James in another cell laboring. He had a melting time. The Lord was present in power.

Aug. 7. Judge B. granted us the privilege of a lamp at night, so that we could improve our evenings by reading. O, what a great blessing! After being deprived of it more than two years, how sweet to enjoy again the bliss of reading God's word, after the toils of the day! O, how good is our Father! May we value and improve the privilege.

13. No preaching. After prayer meeting, went into another cell with four others. Had a precious time. They drank in the truth with eagerness.

14. Last night T. sent for me to sit up with him. He is quite sick—sees himself a great sinner.

20. After dinner, Judge B. came and called me out of my cell, and said that there had been a request that I might preach in the absence of the chaplain, who was sick. " I have no objections, and you can address them, or hold a prayer meeting. Just take your own course."

The prisoners were assembled, and with great delight I preached to them from *Ephesians* v. 14. Excellent attention. Judge B. and wife, overseer and others, present. Truly this is the hand of the Lord.

These quotations from my journal show pretty clearly the nature of the work, our circumstances, and the way we were occupied for about one year or more after the change of officers. Some general remarks about the revival, and I must leave it.

My usual course was to sing while they were collecting, which answered the purpose of a bell—for there was so much heart and life in the singing, that we could be heard all over prison. After two or three prayers, I read a portion of Scripture with remarks suitable to the occasion—warning sinners, and instructing converts in the various duties devolving upon them. And it was very gratifying to see with what eagerness they sought to know the will of God, receiving the truth with a relish that convinced us our " labor was not in vain in the Lord."

After I had talked, opportunity was given for any one to speak or pray, and it was expected that all would take a part. They were remarkably *ready* on all occasions, to go forward in any Christian duty, and many of them were bright examples of piety. Frequently they would be seen, coming to the prayer meeting leading the impenitent, with whom they had been talking, and whose conversion they particularly desired—a cell mate, or some fellow laborer. The obstacles in their way were many. The hardened ridiculed and mocked, but they bore it patiently, and the work rolled on. They all looked up to us, as children to a father. To us they came to make known their joys and sorrows, their temptations and their victories, their falls and uprisings, for instruction and counsel, for encouragement and help.

The responsibility of watching over, and feeding, of seeking out, and reclaiming this interesting flock, all rested on us. The chaplain rarely came to talk with any of them, except on the Sabbath. When he called for the anxious, we were privileged to talk and pray with them. During the week, we had to look after the lambs, who dwelt among wolves, and carry forward our labors also. If we wished to stay all night with any one, or have any one come and stay with us for conversation, it was only to *ask* and we received.

They loved the prayer meetings—and would remain from breakfast to dinner, without weariness. After dinner, again they assembled to praise and pray, reluctant to leave the place where God had so richly blessed their souls.

The work was so great, and important, that we ceased for a time to desire, or pray for liberty. We felt that this was the place for us. And we rejoiced to thrust in our sickles, and reap a rich harvest, "gathering fruit unto eternal life."

I.

I love in such a place to dwell,
These lambs to me, are dear,
Glory to Jesus, for my cell;
Hosannah, that I'm here.

II.

O! what is liberty to me,
Or friends, however dear—
Since scenes like these, I here can see,
And things like these can hear?

III.

Let those who wish, seek worldly fame,
And warriors wonders tell;
But give to me, reproach and shame,
With Jesus and my cell.

We saw here a flock of lambs, which, if we should go
away, would have no shepherd. They dwelt in the
midst of ravening wolves, and who should look after
them? Our wardens soon became indifferent, and cared
not for their souls. Our good overseer was occupied
with a multiplicity of other cares; and after a while was
turned away—his place occupied by an enemy of all
good—new wardens came in, who "feared not God, nor
regarded man"—our chaplain had other business, that
he thought more important, and who should look after
these precious souls? Who would care for a poor, despised convict? We felt our responsibility—we saw
their need of our help, and frequently heard them say,
"I don't know how we should get along, if you should
go away;" and, blessed be God, we rejoiced to stay and
do them good. To us they would listen—they felt a
confidence that as we were "tempted in all points" like
as they, we could enter into all their feelings, and sym-
pathise with them in all their temptations and trials—
that we would listen with patience to all their difficul-
tied and sorrows, and gladly "comfort them by the comfort wherewith we ourselves were comforted of God," in
"all our tribulation."

About forty professed to be converted. How many
were truly, in heart renovated, we cannot say. The
parable of the "sower, and the seed," is just as true
here as in places where liberty is enjoyed. Some "ran
well" for a time, and turned back—a number were
"stony ground hearers," who could not endure the
scorching rays of ridicule and persecution—of "thorny
ground hearers" there were but a few—of those who
"received the seed into good and honest hearts" there
were a goodly number. "How do you know?" How
do I know? How does the husbandman know that his
seed found a place in fertile soil? that his grain did not
all fall upon the rock—or that it was not all consumed
by the fowls, nor all choked by the thorns? How?
Why, he sees it spring up and *grow*—he sees it blossom
—he sees it ripen—he fills his garner—he *eats* thereof,
and is strengthened. How do I know? "By their *fruits*

ye shall know them." They gave every evidence that
can be desired. They brought forth *fruit*—they still
bring forth fruit; and we trust they will bring forth *more
abundantly*, when again restored to liberty. When we
see them so perfectly transformed in their characters,
minds, thoughts, words, actions, how can we doubt?
When we see them hating the things they loved, and
loving the things they hated—when we view the "old
things passed away, and all things become new "—when
the image of Satan is changed into the image of God;
and the spirit of heaven takes the place of the spirit of
hell, how can we but believe that they have "Christ in
them the hope of glory?" Their gentleness, docility,
and exemplary walk would shame multitudes of professors, who enjoy far superior advantages. And could
they have been present in our *convict* meetings, and witnessed the readiness and eagerness of these poor prisoners to give vent to the overflowing of their full and
warm hearts, in testifying to the love of God, the preciousness of the Savior, and the blessedness of His service, they surely would have blushed in view of their
own backwardness, and indifference. And to have witnessed those scenes, would have made the heart of any
Christian rejoice and praise the Lord. But I must not
fail to give the reader a glance at one scene, in our
"hallowed cell," which we shall ever remember with
joy.

THE PRISONER'S COMMUNION.

We plead again and again, with the Chaplain, to administer to us, and to the converts, the Sacrament*—but
in vain. We then concluded to invite a number of
the brethren to unite with us. During the week we
tried to show them the importance and nature of the ordinance. They obtained permission to remain in our
cell after the prayer meeting—at which time we endeavored to "remember our Savior" in His own appointed
ordinance. Five of the brethren were with us—making

* See note on page 147, 148.

eight in all.   Upon our little table was a cup of water, and a neat piece of corn bread, around which we were gathered.

In a few words I endeavored to give them proper views of the ordinance, and with what feelings it should be observed.   I tried to point out the *appropriateness* of the emblems, showing that as bread is the staff of natural life, so is Jesus the "bread of heaven"—"the living bread," upon which, by faith, our souls feed, and are strengthened.

As water cleanses our bodies from filth, so the blood of Christ cleanses the soul from sin—as without water, we should soon die, so without the application of the blood of atonement we should perish for ever—as receiving a draught of water quenches our thirst, so a draught by faith, from "the fountain opened to the house of David, and to the inhabitants of Jerusalem," quenches all our desire for sin, and the vanities of the world, &c.   I spoke of the love of our Savior—that we should remember Him, with penitence for sin, with gratitude, and a full consecration of all our powers to His service—that we should remember His life, His example, His promises, His sufferings, death, ascension, and His intercession in heaven for us.   Portions of the scripture were read—each one prayed, and all united in praise.   And while we partook of the simple emblems, the Master of the feast was present, to bless in a remarkable manner. Every soul was full, and all eyes "a fountain of tears," so that our little cell was truly "*Bochim.*"*   Such a scene I never witnessed.   It was a sweet, heart-melting, blessed season.   With four of them, it was their first approach to the Savior's table—and often have they spoken of that time.   We felt ourselves repaid a hundred fold, for twelve years' imprisonment.   O! "hallowed cell," how dear thou art!   With what rapturous delight shall we look back from the heights of Zion, to this sacred place!   And when we sit down, with these little ones, "at the marriage supper of the Lamb,"

Judges II. 4, 5.

how shall we then praise His holy name, for a *Peniten-tiary!* To "Him who is our life," shall be all the glory.

We had many other precious seasons, but I cannot particularize. Thus, reader, I have given you a sketch of our prison revival—the details would interest any person, but my limits will not permit. In its order, I shall tell you a little about the *breaking up* of our class and prayer meetings by our wicked officers.

CHAPTER III.

LETTERS—SICK-BED REPENTANCE, &c.

EXTRACT OF A LETTER.

BELOVED PARENTS:

AGAIN let me assure you that "*all is well.*" "The Lord reigns." "He doeth his will in the armies of heaven, and among the inhabitants of this lower world, and none can stay his hand, or say unto Him, what doest thou?" Nor should we wish for a moment to "stay His hand," or alter His course in anything—for all His ways are in infinite wisdom and love, and *always* for the present and eternal good of his children.

My prison proves more than a palace—"it is *good* to be here." Worlds on worlds could not purchase from me what I have here obtained. It is more precious than rubies, and infinitely above silver, or the most fine gold. I do and will rejoice. I kiss the rod and bless the hand that applies it. O, rejoice with me! Let no one weep on my account. There is no cause for weeping. It is joy—joy unspeakable and full of glory, that fills my soul. Peace, like a river from heaven's eternal ocean of love, rolls in upon me. I have cause to rejoice. We have long prayed; the Lord has answered our prayers, and gone far beyond our feeble faith and hope. The Lord has opened a great and effectual door of usefulness before us, and we expect to see a great work here. My privileges are too great for words to express.

I rejoice to labor among these dying sinners, and exhibit to them the gospel of Jesus. And if only one soul is made for ever happy in heaven, through our instrumentality, shall we not be abundantly paid for all we have suffered, or may yet be called upon to endure? O, rejoice that I am placed here. Do not say that I could have done more somewhere else. God is wise. This is just where he has put me, and therefore I know it is where I can do the most good. O, it is inexpressibly sweet and glorious to lie quiet in his hands, and believe his promises! Blessed is the man that trusteth in Him. I *know* it. GEORGE.

THE SICK MAN'S RESOLUTION.

McM. was very sick in the hospital. I was with him two nights. We talked with him about his soul, and urged him to repentance. The overseer did the same, and warned him of his danger. He was so full of pains, and in such distress, that he said, " I can not attend to the subject now as I should, I have so much else to think about. If I should repent now, I should be liable to be actuated by wrong motives—fear of death and hell, rather than hatred to sin and love to God. I feel that a sick bed is a poor place to prepare to die, and if the Lord will spare my life and raise me up, I will then attend to the subject."

He recovered, but did not repent. We reminded him of his promise, and plead with him to be a Christian. He said he would serve God, but meant to do it secretly, without any noise or show, without making a profession of religion. " I will live a sober, upright life, while here, will not join with the wicked, and when I get my liberty I will connect myself with some society." Thus the devil deluded him, and I fear obtained his purpose—the ruin of his soul. How many such !

THE SICK-BED REPENTANCE.

L. H. was a young man—a mere boy in years, but old in sin. He was taken down with pleurisy, and sent for me before day-light, to come and see him. I found him very sick and shuddering at death. He said, "You are the first pious man, George, I ever sent for to see me, but I feel that I need the instruction and help of some one, for I can't live long." "You now feel the need of the consolations of religion." "Yes, I *do*, George. I feel that I need it, and if I ever get well, I will live a different life, and be a Christian." "But you may die now." "Then I'm *lost*." I exhorted him to repent, and look to Jesus for mercy, casting himself upon Him, and he should find pardon. That night I sat up with him. He soon asked me to read and pray. "Do you feel that you are a sinner?" "Yes, the greatest in the penitentiary, and need God's grace as much. I have been viewing my past life to-day, and my sins pressed on my head like seas." "Have you repented and confessed them to God?" "Yes, I have. I think I have truly from the heart, repented, and turned from all my evil ways." "Some promise God on a sick bed, they will serve Him."—"It makes no difference with me. I don't ask God that I may get well. Here am I, do as seemeth Thee good. I am willing to die, George, if it is God's will. I have felt a change of some kind, to-day, I know not what it is, but I feel that in my bosom, for which I would not take a world of gold and silver. I feel contented and happy." "Do you feel willing that the world should know all your crimes?" "Yes, I am willing that everybody should know them. I think I can make reparation in all cases but one." (Probably murder). "Do you wish to talk with and warn your evil companions?" "Yes, I have done it to-day, though they made sport of me—but I did not mind that." "Well, what do you wish me to pray for?" "That God will forgive my sins, and give me grace to serve Him, and that I may truly repent." While I prayed, he seemed to unite heartily, and to be much affected,

frequently adding with emphasis, "Amen, Lord have
mercy on my soul." I said, " We need not fear to die, if
Jesus is our friend." " I feel that He is my friend," he
replied, " I have made my first prayer to-day." "Look
to God to help you to stand fast, and cleave to Him."
" I know I can do nothing without Him, and on Him I
depend for strength." "How do you feel towards
Christians?" "I once hated them, but now I love
them better than I do my own life. And I have often
cursed you, George, when I have heard you pray on
Sundays ; but I do ask you to forgive me, for God has.
I was plunging into all manner of vice and sin, never
thinking I had a Supreme Master, or that there was any
hereafter—but I feel that God has afflicted me, to bring me
to consider and see my sins. I was blind this morning,
but now I see where I was, and through the blood of
Jesus Christ I hope to be saved. It was the happiest
day that ever happened to me, when I came here. I
had a good mother, but she spoiled me by humoring
me."* He also confessed his true name.

On the Sabbath, Alanson was with him all day. He
warned his evil associates of their danger, and exhorted
them to repent and forsake their evil ways. One replied,
" I can't." Said he, " You can, if you will. You must
bring yourself to say, '*I will.*'"

James was with him one night. He was restless, but
seemed much interested in James' prayer, and often
cried aloud, " Amen, Amen."

At evening, I called to see him. " How do you feel,
L.?" " I'm gone! I'm gone! George." " Submit to
God, and put your trust in Him." And while I held
his hand, he prayed that God would have mercy on him,
forgive his transgressions, grant him grace, as he needed,
&c., " for the Redeemer's sake, Amen." Again, when
he was worse, I said, " Commit yourself to God." " I
have—I have. Let Him do what he sees best. His
will, not mine, be done."

Again, Alanson said to him, " Be patient, and in the

* Mothers, will you learn a lesson from this prisoner's confession?

spirit of a little child yield to the Lord." He replied with emphasis, " I *do* yield." Alanson repeated, " And let this feeble body fail," &c. He exclaimed, " O, may I be of that happy company."

The foregoing is the substance of our conversations with him ; and should no more be said, it might be inferred that his repentance was genuine. So we hoped, and watched with trembling every symptom for good or ill, till he recovered ; but we were disappointed. As he became better in body, he grew worse in spirit, and could soon curse and swear freely.

I have been thus particular with his case for various reasons.

1. To verify the truth of God's word, " In trouble men call upon God." " In their affliction they will seek me early."

2. In health, men can despise religion, blaspheme God and curse Christians ; but when death stares them in the face, they desire the consolations of that very religion—will call those same Christians to pray for them, and beg God for mercy.

3. See how perfectly a man may be deluded by Satan, even on a dying bed—willing to die, full of expectation of happiness, yet unprepared. Had he died, instead of getting well, we should have had hope. Do not multitudes die in this way ? O ! a death bed repentance !

4. How manifest the folly and danger of putting off repentance to a sick bed. True, many on a sick bed do repent, but not because they hate sin or are sorry they have offended God, or because the love of God has melted their hearts—they *do repent*, but it is from fear, a servile, slavish dread of hell. And being conscious of *a repentance* they think God is reconciled, their sins forgiven, and they prepared for heaven.

5. How important that those who converse with persons on a sick bed should be faithful in probing them to the bottom—in showing them the true character of God, and what it is to repent and love Him. We tried to do so in this case, yet see the result.

6. From both the preceding cases, learn the secret of

the ephemeral peculiarity, so common to a sick bed repentance. They are influenced only by fear, and when the cause of that fear is removed, their religion vanishes. For they love *sin* just as much as ever. They have no true love to God because He is holy and hates sin, but because they know he will punish sin—and when the prospect of life is again restored, this kind of fear departs—and having no decision, no principle, the heart remaining unbroken, they are led captive by Satan at his will. O! a death bed repentance! Beware!

As a candle appears most brilliant in dark places, so true religion shines with clearest lustre in dark dispensations, but with greatest brightness in the gloom of death. When all men forsake it, it stands by its possessor and is more precious than ever. When earthly prospects are all blasted, it opens a door of hope, an assurance of immortal riches and glory. When trials and sufferings combine to crush, it comforts and supports, so that " we glory in tribulation," " rejoice in our sufferings," " and reckon them not comparable with the glory that shall be revealed." But O, in death, when riches cannot profit, honors cannot relieve, friends cannot help, and everything earthly fails—when nature is sinking, and our clay tenement crumbling —when earth fades away, and eternity opens upon our view—while the cold waves of death dash over us, who can tell the worth of religion then ? It lights the dark valley, dries up the deep waters, quenches the raging flame, so that the last moments are the most delightful of the whole life.

As its possessor draws near his heavenly home, and more clearly beholds the blissful company, he leaps for joy at the prospect of meeting his Father and Elder Brother—of " sitting down with Abraham, Isaac, and Jacob, and all the prophets, in the kingdom of God," to be " for ever with the Lord."

O! blessed religion! What would this prison be without its comforts! What a prison would this world be, were it not for its blessed influences! How unspeakably foolish are they who reject its easy yoke! How cruel they who would exterminate it from the earth! And how inexcusable are all who do not rejoice in its life and peace giving power!

We add our testimony—that no place, no troubles, no circumstances, no calumny, NOTHING can deprive its pos-sessor of the comfort and joy it affords, so long as he *trusts in God.* "*Perfect peace*" is his portion.*

AN EXTRACT OF A LETTER,

Written in the time of the revival, will show our feelings.

"Beloved, this is a delightful place to me. These walls are sacred, these cells are hallowed *palaces*, and the rattle of bars, bolts, and locks, sweet music in our ears. Believe me when I say, a more soul-cheering, blessed place than this same "hallowed cell," I never dwelt in. I had almost ceased to pray for any other field of labor—as to anxiety, I have none. Such scenes as I have here witnessed, I never saw, in all the pro-tracted meetings, or in all the anxious rooms, or prayer-meetings I ever attended. I am in a penitentiary, but it is *here* I have seen the power of God—the long-harden-ed, cut down by the two-edged sword, prostrate before the Lord, and begging for mercy, in accents almost startling—yea, *here*, I have seen those same persons sit-ting at the feet of Jesus, clothed and in their right mind, "praising and glorifying God" for what He has done.

O, how they sing! how they pray! how they do bless God for a penitentiary! "My soul doth magnify the Lord, and my spirit rejoices in God my Savior." When I see the tiger take the disposition of a lamb—the vul-ture become a dove—obscenity turn to purity—curses to prayer and praise—hatred to love, and hell to hea-ven, I must acknowledge the hand of God, and rejoice,

Some of the hardest, and those least expected, have bowed, while the self-righteous moralist stands aloof.

Our days are so occupied with work, and our Sabbaths in laboring with sinners and feeding the lambs, that we get but little time reading; but we cheerfully forego this privilege, for the sake of doing others good. We

---

* Written, while sitting up with a sick man one night.

adopt the language of one of old,* "I have learned to see a *need* of everything that God gives, and to need no-thing that God denies me. There is no dispensation, though cross and afflictive, but either in or after, I find I could not be without it, and nothing that I am without, whether taken from me, or not given to me, but sooner or later, God quiets me in Himself without it. I cast all my care on the Lord, and live securely on the wisdom and care of my heavenly Father. I find that when *faith* is steady, nothing can disquiet me—and when faith tot-ters, nothing can establish me."

GEORGE.

JAMES, OUTSIDE.

About the middle of July, as James was recovering from a severe fit of sickness, Judge B. granted him the liberty of going outside for his health, to breathe the fresh air, eat at his house, hoe in the garden, &c. Thus, without any guard he went out when he wished, to bathe, gather Nature's spontaneous productions, assist Mrs. B. about the house, read, meditate and pray in the grove, " where none but God could hear," and drink in the pure air of fragrant Nature.

He had free access to Judge B.'s library, from which we had many valuable books. This liberty was very reviving to James' system.

About the last of August he was very sick again. He was taken in the night, so that we had to knock on our door, for the guard, who called up the hospital steward, and came with some medicine. We felt that he could not last long, but the Lord raised him up. In the fore-part of September, I was taken down for some days. Having no physician—no helper but Jesus, it was sweet to go to Him.

SCARCITY OF FOOD.

Sept. 24. Sabbath. Two men worked most of the forenoon to dig potatoes enough for a scanty dinner, and for supper we had *nothing*. Food for the body, and

---

* John Elliot.

temporal comforts may fail, but glory to God! for the fountain, *ever* flowing, and the loaded tables of rich provisions, for the *soul*, to which we may at all times freely come—no man having power to prevent, and no condition or place being able to bar us from the rich repast.

Oct. 3, 1843. · Now entering upon our third year. How short the time! How varied the scenes, trials, and circumstances! How many and trying the temptations! How glorious the victories! How multiplied and imminent the dangers, and how striking the deliverances! What favors and blessings unspeakable, unnumbered, and ever memorable! To God be glory, and praise for ever.

THE BUFFALO ROBES.

Oct. 14. This evening, Judge B. went round, and left a buffalo robe for each cell, which is a great comfort in our circumstances. How much have we suffered from the cold nights! But now we shall be comfortable —for the first time, in a cold night, since we came here. May we be thankful.

By our scarcity of bedding, we have learned to " remember the *poor*." How many have neither shelter nor covering! But we can assure them that Jesus will warm the *soul* with his love, while the *body* may suffer.

KNITTING.

After we obtained our lamp, the evening and the cold cell were welcomed with great delight, that we might refresh our minds, from the fountain of truth.

After devotions, Alanson and James would knit, while I read to them aloud. In this way, and when they were unwell, Alanson knit for himself two pairs of socks, and James knit for himself one pair. For so covetous was Mrs. B., that she influenced her husband not to *buy* socks for all the men, but made many of them *knit their own*, before they could have any. In this way, many went with cold feet, a long time, till, in their slow way, by knitting Sundays, and all their spare time, they provided themselves. And from this cause numbers suffered most of the winter. I did not learn to knit. For the most part I wore my own stockings.

***

CHAPTER IV.

VISITS—FAVORS SHOWN—LETTERS, &c,

"IN PRISON AND YE CAME UNTO ME."

ON the morning of the 21st of October, Mrs. Work, with three of her children, W. L. A., and M. C. (now my wife), arrived at our habitation. They called on the Chaplain, who accompanied them to the prison. Judge B. came in with him and said to us, "Wash yourselves, get shaved, put on clean clothes and prepare to go out and see them." We all went out into Capt. R.'s parlor, where we once more beheld the faces of those we loved. Mrs. R. and the Chaplain were present, but we could converse freely. It was a happy meeting. Mrs. R. was *very kind* to them. We conversed as long as we chose, and came back to our work, after being assured that they could come in and see us, at our room, and on the Sabbath. They ate their meal, and came in. As they came to my room, the first words of M. C. were, "I am *glad* you came here—there are so many slaves getting away, in consequence." Cheering. We quit work and came to our cell, where we all spent most of the day, in free conversation and prayer. Thus to unite our hearts and voices, was beyond expression delightful. How oft had we imagined such a scene! How frequently talked about it, and besought the Lord for the blessing. And yet we never really expected *so great* a favor in a penitentiary where the rules are so strict.

THE RULES.

" Every visitor shall be accompanied by the overseer,

or some one of the guard, and shall, under no pretence whatever, be allowed to speak to any of the convicts, without the written permission of one of the inspectors."

They had no such permission, nor had they seen the inspectors.

Again, " No person, when on a visit to the penitentiary, shall be permitted to remain here longer than one hour." They staid a week.

Again, " No person shall speak to, or hold any conversation with any of the convicts, unless by the express permission of the lessees, and then only in the presence of some one of the guard or overseers ?"

Now, reader, keep these printed rules in mind, as I tell you of the blessings we enjoyed, so that, with us, you may "magnify the Lord," for the remarkable manifestations of his great mercy to us. Generally, prison rules are very strict, and sometimes, almost like the laws of the Medes and Persians. Yet here, in a slave state, almost everything like a rule is set aside to show favor to the despised abolitionists and their friends. Who ever heard of such a thing ? No other prisoners or their friends are thus treated. Well, it is no more than equitable. In our conviction, they entirely set aside law ; and why not now disregard their rules, and show us favor ? But to proceed. The first day we were by ourselves, and could converse about what, and as we pleased, no man forbidding.

At night, Mrs. R. would have us come out, and all eat supper with her. That evening, Judge B. asked Alanson and myself to go outside, and spend the evening with them. Alanson went, and spent the whole evening with his family alone. I chose to stay with James, and read letters, which they brought—some of which passed through the officers' hands, and some did not. O, what a feast ! They also brought us books—Holy War, H. Page, Christian Lyre, Dying Thoughts, Life of Payson —and winter clothing, quilts, flannels, stockings, two or three quires of writing paper, steel pens, and other articles, all of which Judge B. allowed us to have, without once looking at them. This was perfectly contrary to their laws.

Convicts permitted to have their pen, ink, and paper, to write when, what, and as much as they please! Such was, and is the simple fact of the case. Well, "It is just like God," and in accordance with his pro- mise—"I will cause the enemy to entreat thee well, in the day of evil."

On another evening, Alanson went out, and was alone with his family. He sang and prayed with them, gave them counsel, and encouraged them to trust in the Lord. Was ever convict treated thus! See how the hearts of men are in the hands of the Lord.

After reading the letters, I wrote the following in my journal.

Glory to God, for such inestimable blessings. Ho- sannah, that the wheels are rolling, the light spreading, the old fabric tottering, and the cause advancing, though many rise up in violent opposition. Yes, glory to God that I am here!—that he will take such feeble worms as we, to accomplish such wonderful results. His be the praise. O, how my soul leaps within me with re- joicing, to hear of the progress of the glorious cause! Most cheerfully will I spend my days in prison, if such may be the blessed effects. The cause is God's and must prevail. Vain are threats and violence; they are but oil to the fire; stop the work they cannot. No, let earth and hell unite their force and rage, the Mighty Conqueror will tread them beneath his feet. The ban- ner of Liberty shall be unfurled, and the trumpet blown through all the land. Arise, ye brave; unite your pow- ers, and enlist with your Captain. Wield manfully the "sword of the Spirit," relying on God, and victory is yours. Be valiant. Fear not. Regard not fines, me- naces, prisons, death.

Ride on thou Mighty Conqueror—triumphantly ride, till all our land submit to thy peaceful sway—till "op- pression shall cease," and violence and spoil "be no more heard in our borders."

That such as the following should be permitted to come to us, is remarkable.

DEAR BRETHREN :

The cause for which you suffer is on the advance through the country. I have also been called to suffer in the cause, which has not been in vain. That such a cause can be advanced without suffering and sacrifice, is utterly impossible ; and we ought to be willing to lay down our lives if necessary. Community are opening their eyes. The lover of liberty has more friends—the outcast finds a hiding place—the oppressed are delivered—light is breaking in—and the whole land feels a tremendous agitation. "May God speed the work," is the prayer of thousands in our country ; and there is good evidence that the prayer is heard and answered. The field is great and white to the harvest. The north star shines as brightly as ever, and is directing many to the land of the free.

R. EELLS.

THE ANSWER.

BELOVED BRO. E. :

We could not help shouting and praising God, when we read your epistle. We hail you as a fellow-sufferer, yea, *conqueror*, in the cause of bleeding humanity. Do you not feel that it is good to suffer for the slave, who has suffered so much and sweat so profusely for you. I am heartily willing ; yea, I rejoice to be "bound with him ;" yea, more, to lay down my life for the cause in which I am now toiling. Our work shall not be in vain. God will bless and give effect to every stroke, in pulling down the pillars on which the temple rests. Our prayers will come up before the mercy seat, and prevail. The groans and tears of the widow and fatherless shall be regarded and avenged. Be of good courage. Fear not what man can do unto you. Work with all your might. Rouse up all who feel for the slave to a united onset, and storm the enemy's camp. Face opposition, trust in God, and glorious will be the achievement.   GEORGE.

On Sabbath morning, our friends came in and attended our prayer meeting, and assisted us by exhortation and prayer.   We again had opportunity to converse with them.

In the afternoon, they came in with J. R. to the guard room, where we spent some time in singing the " songs of Zion ;" while the prisoners, astonished and delighted, gathered around the door and window to listen.   Also at preaching they were present, and took a part in the exercises.

THE PETITION.

During the week, they circulated a petition in the city for Alanson, which, with one Mrs. W. brought from Palmyra, they presented to Gov. Reynolds.   He refused to grant their request.   The wife plead for her husband—" No."   Our sister entreated—" No."   The children, with tears, besought their father's restoration to them,—" Can't you let my father go home with me ?" " No, my child, I cannot."   To Mrs. W. he said, " So long as the abolitionists keep up such an excitement, I cannot let your husband go." Many sympathized while others mocked.

THE PRIVILEGE.

From day to day our friends were allowed to come in without any officer, when they chose, and converse with us, at our work or in our cell.   And what is the more remarkable, while we were at preaching, a number ran away from the brick yard, where they were at work; and the next day a " break" was made from the rope walk, in which upwards of a dozen ran away.   These things produced very great excitement in prison and in the city, yet our friends were allowed to come in as if nothing had happened.   Thus we had abundant opportunity to say to them all that we wished.

On the next Sabbath, they came to our cell, and spent
the day with us.   It was a "high day."   Here we
sweetly united our hearts and voices, in prayer and
praise, before the Lord.   Then was the feast richer than
ever.   After being so long,

"'Mid scenes of confusion and creature complaints,
How sweet to our souls was communion with saints."

It was delightful, and God shall have the glory.
They staid and ate dinner with us, partaking of our
coarse prison fare, with their fingers (as yet, we ate our
Sabbath dinner in our cell), thus, learning a little how to
sympathize with poor prisoners—for, only by entering
into the circumstances of others are we prepared to weep
or rejoice with them; and the more this is done in *ima-
gination*, the better can we sympathize with, and administer comfort to the afflicted.
Alanson's little boy slept with us several nights.

THE LETTERS.

We wrote many letters to send by them, to our friends
who could not come.   The preceding letter from Dr. E.
and the answer may be considered as a specimen of many
we received and wrote at that time, which passed not
through the officers' hands.   And why should they be
examined by the officers?   Already they had granted
full liberty to talk what we pleased without their presence.   They had given us paper, pen, ink, and opportunity to write what we pleased—and what else could be
expected, but that we should improve so favorable an
occasion for pouring out the fulness of our almost bursting hearts, to stir up and quicken the friends of humanity?
Again, I gave Judge B. a bundle of eight or ten to
examine, and he gave them back to me, to hand to our
friends myself.   From the appearance of the bundle it
was manifest he had not opened it, to read a single letter.
And a short time before this, he gave me a letter from
home, without breaking the seal.   Certainly this was as
much as to say, " Write what you please."

THE DEPARTURE.

On Monday morning they came again to our cell. We kneeled down, while I returned thanks to God for the rich displays of his mercy towards us, and commended them to his protection and guidance during their journey home.

We then bade each other farewell, with as much cheerfulness and composure as though to be separated but a few weeks.

JUDGE B.'S HOSPITALITY.

When our friends arrived at Jefferson, their money was spent, except enough to pay ferriage home. They were hospitably entertained, apparently as cordially as though they had been possessed of thousands of dollars. Their carriage broke, which he repaired gratuitously. The bill for their horse-keeping was five dollars—this Judge B. paid, refusing to receive recompense. And then we sent various articles of our manufacture to our friends, with his consent. When severely censured, in the papers, for treating the abolitionists with such kindness and partiality, he replied, " So long as they conduct themselves as they have thus far, I shall not regard such things at all." And when we thanked him for his kindness, he answered, " I have done no more than I felt it my *duty* to do." " I want no compensation," &c. The Lord reward him.

In view of all these things, my journal says—" The past week has been a memorable one indeed—a week of wonders, considering our circumstances. ' The good hand of our God upon us,' has been wonderful to us and to our fellow prisoners. They never saw such treatment of visitors or prisoners before. And where is the man who ever did?

" It seems as if I could not cease thanking my Savior for the great favor shown us on this happy occasion. Everlasting praise be to his name."

Their presence here caused much talk, spread much light, and awakened an interest in many minds favorable

11*

to anti-slavery. After their departure, many came in to
see the persons, about whom so much was said ; and the
countenances of many exhibited an unusual appearance
of pity, which seemed to say—" I wish they were out of
this place." Well, we shall go out, in God's own time
which is the best. Till then we rejoice to wait.

CHAPTER V.

LICENTIOUSNESS OF THE SOUTH—LETTERS, &c.

CRUEL DEATH.

B. V. had been here more than a year. He was in a
diseased state, most of the time, and was shamefully
imposed upon by the officers, and Dr. Moore. He was
sick, and unable to work, yet but little was done for
him. He was taken with fits, and in great distress much
of the time. Through hard-heartedness, or ignorance,
the Dr. said to him, a little before his death, " there is
nothing the matter of you, and you must *go to work !*"
A fellow prisoner, who was a doctor, said, " with proper
attention, the man might have been cured." Be that as
it may, he did *not* have attention—and, no doubt, was
virtually *murdered.*

I had conversed with him some, but fear he was unprepared to die.

In the fore part of November, Alanson was unwell for
some days, but not confined to his bed, all the time.

WHY WAS HE PARDONED?

Dr. B., who had been here, but a few weeks, was
pardoned out, by Gov. Reynolds. Why? An *extensive
slaveholder*, with plenty of *money*, came from the South,
and undertook his case. To such a man, the Governor
would listen—when, if a *poor* man had come to plead for
his friend, probably it would have been of no avail, thus

clearly exemplifying *Prov.* xvii. 15, 23 ; *Is.* i. 23 ; v. 20, 23. There have been a number of such cases.

AMALGAMATION.

A guard, in conversation with Alanson, about abolition, amalgamation, &c., remarked, " probably *one half* of the white males in town, have unlawful intercourse with black women !" What a recommendation of the morality of a town, and of the healthful influence, and precious fruits of *Slavery !* Yet who can deny the truth of it, in slave states?

Slaveholders cry out against abolitionists, " Amalgamation !" But from what source, do our tawny population proceed? From abolitionists, or slaveholders? Doubtless the latter. *Facts* may speak, for they cannot be denied ? Where are mulattos the most numerous? In the South. Who are the most valued ? Fine mulattos. Whom do the *gentry* buy for their own unholy purposes ? Mulattos. What children do fathers most value ? Their mulatto children. On all these points, abundant testimony might be adduced, but why multiply words? Is there not ample *ocular demonstration*, that fathers and sons, lawyers* and statesmen,† rich and poor, in slave states, are engaged in this *abomination ?* " Mother of abominations !" O ! how it destroys the moral sensibilities, and changes men into brutes and *demons !*

But again, a slave overseer from the South, was knowing to the following. " In Adams County Mississippi, Abner Green, was a slaveholder. A Mr. Ford was his overseer. Maria was a slave girl, whom the overseer, with a cow-hide, whipped very hard *fifteen* times, for refusing to yield to his beastly desires !"

Again. " Children are very often destroyed in wells, and various other ways, by slave mothers, *hired* so to do, by white fathers, to prevent exposure !" " It is *common,*

* In Mississippi, the wife of a young lawyer shot herself, leaving a young child, because her husband had connection with the slaves.
† A vile woman in town, said, one day, " I can show as much money, as any other woman in town, during the sitting of *Legislature !*"

for masters, overseers, and young men to have inter-course with the slave women!"

"Men from the North, who have wives, frequently go South, and commingle freely with the slaves—their wives knowing nothing of it!"*

Daughters of the North, and of the church, what think you? Do you say, these are extreme cases? They are not so. They are common, every-day occurrences. I have it from witnesses, too numerous to be doubted—ear-witnesses, eye-witnesses, experimental witnesses—and everybody, who has lived long at the South, knows, and most are ready to own, that illicit intercourse with the slaves is as common as the shining of the sun. I might multiply *facts*, but will not defile my pages with such corruption.

Reader, what will you do, to put away this *abomination?*

THE FALSE TONGUE.

Several of the guards, whose hearts were opposed to good, endeavored to injure us, by exciting the preju-dices of the officers against us—vilifying us to them, and others, on account of our *principles*. This has been frequently tried, by wicked guards. But in the midst of the multitude of "false tongues" that surround, and are drawn against us, like "sharp swords," how has God wonderfully fulfilled His promise, *Job* v. 21; "thou shalt be *hid* from the scourge of the tongue"—also in *Ps.* xxxi. 19, 20. Thus, "He is faithful that promised." In spite of their envy, defamations, malice, and lies, our "heads are lifted up above our enemies"—"our cup runneth over," and no man has been allowed to "set on us to do us hurt." Verily He is a "shield and buck-ler, to all who trust Him." Malicious prisoners, have frequently tried the same thing, but God, as often, has "disappointed their crafty devices," and kept us securely.

* A gentleman, in Huron County, Ohio, who has lived some time in Slave States, also confirmed the truth of this statement—declared that he *knew* the practice to be common; and mentioned a number of his own acquaintance, who thus left their families, went South, and during their residence there, *lived with black women!*

THE INSPECTORS' FIRST EXAMINATION.

It was the custom of the inspectors, to have all the prisoners separately brought before them, about once a year ; at which time, each one had the privilege of making ar y complaint against the officer, respecting food, clothing, work, punishment, or any injustice—respecting all these things they were questioned—and the inspectors listened to many sorrowful tales and bitter complaints—some of which were true, some exaggerated, and some without any foundation. As they had confidence that *we* would speak only the truth, they were generally very particular in their inquiries of us, respecting the officers, treatment of prisoners, sick, meetings, chaplain, &c. &c. We endeavored to tell them the truth, cut where it would. They treated us with great respect, and allowed us to come near to them.

At their first sitting, among many other things, they asked if we thought the preaching did good—if it was spirited, pointed, and arousing—if the chaplain did his duty in efforts to reform the prisoners. To the last I was obliged to answer somewhat in the negative, as he rarely came during the week, except when called here by business.

Our prayer meeting was freely talked about, and no objection whatever made to it. One proposed, and all thought it would be an excellent plan, that I should address all the prisoners on Sabbath morning—promised to converse with the officers, and if they were willing, have arrangements made. On Saturday, General B. said, "I will go right out and have arrangements made for to-morrow." I told him I should consider it one of the greatest favors they could bestow upon me, as my desire was to be useful in every possible way, to my fellow prisoners. But I suppose the officers were afraid of public odium and censure, should they grant the abolitionists such privileges—indeed, they have expressed the same to me, themselves. I was not called on—though the inspectors thought the influence would be good on the prisoners, and were desirous to bring it about.

As their printed rules forbade our talking any, I asked the privilege of conversing with my fellow prisoners about their souls, (though I had all along taken it). They replied, " We have agreed to let you preach on Sabbath mornings; and we grant you the same opportunity that we do the chaplain !" I asked for the Missionary Herald—they granted it—though the law forbids any periodical being sent to a prisoner! I asked for a work on the prophecies. They mentioned, and sent me, Isaac T. Hinton's " prophecies of Daniel and John"—then just published in St. Louis, in pamphlet form, ten numbers—which a fellow prisoner bound into a neat volume—a book we read with great interest.

They wished to have me steward of the hospital, that I might labor for the good of the sick, but I was too good a hand to work, for the officers to be willing to give me up. Money and not souls, was what they desired.

Reader, these inspectors were all wicked men, yet see how God turned their hearts towards us. What but the Almighty Spirit could induce those in authority, and who are not governed by his laws, to deal thus kindly with men, who are the *pests* of their community, and the *abomination* or slave States?

They manifested their good will, and said, " We grant you anything that will conduce to the reformation of the prisoners." Our worldly-seeking officers will be held responsible for all the good that might have been done by the carrying out of the Inspectors' plan.

OUR TEXTS—CORRESPONDENCE WITH THE CHAPLAIN.

With the chaplain I had frequently conversed on the subject of slavery. He said he was opposed to the system—never did, and never would hold a slave, but could not approbate our course. He requested me to write down for him the passages of scripture, by which we justified ourselves in helping slaves. As I did not keep a copy of the letter, I can only give the reader the references, with some of the principal ideas.

In the commencement, I laid down the doctrine that "human legislation *cannot* unman the slave"—that

" man, born in the image of God, *is man*, of whatsoever.
color, rank, or condition"—that " there is no such thing
as *property in man*." Therefore, it being true that
the slave is a *man*, the commands respecting helping the
poor, relieving the distressed, &c., apply to him as our
" brother," our " neighbor," " bone of our bone, and
flesh of our flesh," as really as to any other class of poor
and needy.

I rejoiced to comply with his request, as it gave me
an opportunity of preaching the truth, backed up at
every step with a " Thus saith the Lord ;" to which he,
as Zion's Watchman, was bound to give heed and obey.

The references—*Luke* x. 27, 30–37 ; *Heb.* xiii. 3 ;
Prov. iii. 27 ; xiv. 31 ; xvii. 5 ; xxi. 13 ; xxiv. 11, 12 ,
Matt. v. 7 ; vii. 12 ; xxv. 34–45 ; *Mark* xiv. 7 ; *Deut.*
xv. 7, 8, 10, 11 ; xxiii. 15, 16 ; *Job* xxix. 11–17 ; xxxi.
15–22, 32 ; *Ps.* xli. 1–3 ; lxxxii. 4 ; *Is.* xvi. 3 ; lviii. 10 ;
Jer. xxi. 12 ; xxii. 3.   Each of these references was
followed by appropriate explanations, questions, and
remarks, which the reader must imagine for himself.

ANSWER.

City of Jefferson, Aug. 12, 1844.

BRO. THOMPSON :

As to the abstract principle of Slavery, we would
not attempt to vindicate it—but as to the measures by
which the evil is to be removed, that is quite a different
matter.   That modern abolitionism is fraught with dis-
astrous consequences both to master and slave, is a fact
too notorious to be denied.   Measures should be adopted
for the emancipation of the slaves, but without interfer-
ing with our political institutions any further than by
moral suasion.

I find slavery from the days of Abraham to the present time, and none of the sacred writers ever interfere
with it as an institution, but they enjoin obedience on
the part of servants to their masters, and never
authorize resistance on their part, or an effort to secure
their freedom.   The apostle says, " Art thou called,
being a servant, care not for it ; but if thou mayest be

free, use it rather"—that is, if the master of the slave will voluntarily free him, let him receive his freedom—but if not, let him not care about it!

As to the passages of Scripture you quoted, I deem them all irrelevant, and having nothing to do with the subject of slavery. They have general reference to acts of oppression, as practised by the rich upon the poor, and will be seen in the conduct of the rich in free States towards their hired servants, more clearly than in the conduct of the master toward the slave," and so on, a sheet full of opposition to abolitionism, of a similar character to the above.

It needs no comment. He did not give me the letter till about nine months after I wrote to him, and then just as he was leaving, so that I had no opportunity to reply to him.

As to the references, I leave the reader to judge, whether they are relevant or not.

THE MISSOURI BROTHER.

The following letter was handed to us, privately, but it is deemed not unadvisable now to make it public. It was a reviving cordial to our souls. It shows also, that even in Missouri, are some warm-hearted friends of the slave. This man was known to be anti-slavery, but being a wealthy merchant in St. Louis, he stood his ground.

THE LETTER.

Jefferson, Nov. 23, 1843.

To my dear brethren, Thompson, Burr, and Work, "Peace be multiplied from God our Father and from Jesus Christ our Lord :"

MY BELOVED BRETHREN :

Will please excuse the liberty I take in addressing this to them. The other day, when in the confines of your wretched abode, I saw you all, but was denied the privilege of speaking one single word to you, though I could scarce refrain. I wanted to tell Bro. George

Thompson to be " strong in the Lord," knowing that " all
who live godly in Christ Jesus, shall suffer persecution."
The more the God of this degenerate world exalts himself in opposition to truth, the more he disposes every
sincere heart for the reception of it.   You are, my dear
Brother T. in a trying and afflictive situation—but oh,
trust in *God*, and these afflictions that appear dark and
mysterious, will ultimately work out your eternal good
and the general good of thousands.   " I would that ye
should understand," says Paul, " that the things which
happened unto me, have fallen out rather unto the fur-
therance of the gospel," &c.   The Lord bless thee, my
dear Brother Thompson, with all his communicable fulness.   Be assured his grace shall be sufficient for thee.
Trust in Him with all thy heart, and thee shall be
enabled to say with St. Paul, " I take pleasure in infirmi-
ties, in reproaches, in necessities, in persecutions, in
distresses, for *Christ's sake*."

> " Prisoner of hope, be strong, be bold,
> Cast off thy doubts, disdain to fear,
> *Dare to believe*—on Christ lay hold.
> Wrestle with him in mighty prayer,
> Tell Him I will not let Thee go,
> Till I thy name, Thy nature know."

Farewell, my friend and brother.   Thee shall not be
forgotten at the mercy-seat.   Peace be with thy spirit.
To MY DEAR BROTHER BURR :—" Because thou hast
kept the word of his patience, the Lord, even thy *God*,
will keep thee in the time of affliction, trial, and temptation."   " He that overcometh, shall be clothed in white
raiment, and shall sit down with my Father in the kingdom."   Bear in mind the immutability of the *promises*,
and be assured they are on your side.   " Lo, I am with
you alway, even unto the END," says the blessed
Savior.

O, believe it, dear Brother Burr.   *Humble faith* claims
the blessed Jesus as the help of the helpless—the
strength of the weak—the riches of the poor,—the peace
of the disquieted—comfort of the afflicted, light of those
who sit in darkness, the companion of the desolate,

Friend of the friendless, the redemption of captives—
in a word, He is our all and in all, *now, this very moment,*
and shall be *for ever.*

Never fear, my dear Brother B.   Be not in the least
cast down.   Rather count it an honor to suffer for the
cause of Christ, and his poor, afflicted, suffering people.
The time is not far distant, when Ethiopia shall stretch
her bleeding hands to God, and this wicked nation shall
know that there is a God, who executeth judgment and
justice, and who ruleth in righteousness.   Lord, hasten
the time.   Thousands of his saints join in—Lord, hasten
the time ; Amen.

The influence by which my brethren are surrounded
is *bad*—it will, therefore, be highly essential for you to
importunately entreat the Searcher of hearts, to keep`
the candle of his grace lighted in your souls, then you
will easily discern, if the inward parts are " Holiness to
the Lord."   The Lord bless thee, by dear Brother Barr,
with every new-covenant blessing.

> " No man too largely from Heaven's love can hope,
>   If what he hopes he labors to secure."

" Man's inhumanity to man, makes countless millions mourn."—
Burns.

> " Man is to man the sorest, surest ill."—*Young.*

· I am thy affectionate friend and brother.

———

To my Dear Friend and Brother Work :
    To you as well as to the other two brethren, I am
a stranger in person, but not in spirit. ˙

I would say to Brother Work, " take courage."
God says to thee as He did to Abraham, " I am thy
shield, and exceeding great reward."   I was at Quincy,
a short time ago—went to see thy companion, and thy
dear children—they were all well.   Thou need not feel
concerned about thy family.   The Lord will raise them
up friends.   I have no doubt that many of the brethren
will esteem it an honor and a privilege, as well as their
Christian duty, to contribute to their necessities, whilst
the head and father suffers in the cause of truth and
righteousness.

The Lord thy God will bless thee and thy family. He will make thy light break forth as the morning. I understand Brother Work is a Mason. I will not fail to try what the Grand Lodge will do for his deliverance. I think perhaps something can be done in this way. Try and be patient. Trust in the Lord, and He will bring it to pass.

I know you suffer unjustly, and am persuaded in my own mind that you have been put where you are, ILLE-GALLY, according to the laws of Missouri. On the other hand, I believe the Lord overruled the affair, for the saving of your lives—for if you had been acquitted, you would all have certainly been murdered. The infuriated mob, with their faces all blacked, had prepared the gallows, and even the ropes, for your execution!

O! " tell it not in Gath, publish it not in the streets of Askelon." But never fear, Dear Brother Work, nor be in the least discouraged; it will come out right at last. But look to him on whose shoulders is laid the government of the world, and yet, astonishing humiliation! felt the infamous load of a malefactor's cross! Barbarous soldiers, followed by an enraged mob, led Him like a lamb to the slaughter, that WE might be delivered from the heavy curse of the law, and gently conveyed by the celestial powers, into Abraham's bosom. My sheet is full before I was aware—so I must subscribe myself,

Your sincere friend and brother, in the cause of God and of the oppressed.

This letter was to us almost like a voice from heaven. The Providence which gave it to us was remarkable— but the Lord will find ways enough to convey to his children all that they need.

CHANGE OF WARDENS, AGAIN.

About the ninth of December, Capt. Richmond sold out his half of the penitentiary, to a company in St. Louis, " Blaine, Tompkins, and Barret," ungodly, avaricious men.

Many regretted the change, but we committed it all to God, believing that he could guide our vessel safely through.

The new wardens were wealthy business men, and they introduced many changes, improvements in machinery, &c.

They were also slaveholders, and looked upon an abolitionist with feelings more bitter than Brown and Richmond—but, by our conduct, we commended ourselves to their consciences, so that they were obliged to treat us with respect. But Blaine's character will more fully appear as we advance. Just here, I will say for him, that he treated the sick with more humanity, and would have the prisoners fed better, than any previous officer.

NEW OVERSEER.

Our uncle Joseph (as we called our good overseer), was so kind and gentle that many would take advantage and misbehave—yet all liked him, and his kindness has often conquered the hardest, where whips would only have exasperated to desperation. But he was not cruel enough to satisfy the wardens, and he had to resign his station to a new overseer, on the 11th of December. And "then a new king arose, which knew not Joseph." He was a very unfeeling, tyrannical man, having been so long accustomed to rule over men, in other prisons, that he seemed perfectly hardened. He walked about in a very lordly manner, with a haughty scowl, giving *his* orders and regulations.

His first step was to forbid the Savior's name being acknowledged at the table, and turning us, as far as he could, into infidels or brutes. This step caused the wicked to triumph. They had been much annoyed by having a blessing sought on the food, but when they saw this new regulation, they exulted over the Christians, as if they had gained some great victory. We went to the former overseer—his power was gone, and he could do nothing. We went to Judge Brown—he would do nothing. We went to the inspectors, and they did nothing. We went to Jesus, rolled our burden on Him, and there left it.

LAMPS TAKEN AWAY.

Judge B. and uncle Joseph had granted a number of the prisoners a lamp, by which they might spend their evenings in reading. and thus improve and store their minds with useful knowledge.

Many of the converts were thus privileged, who eagerly improved it, much to their benefit and comfort. We furnished them with books, which they read with great interest and profit. But this was too much for Blaine and Mc C. (our new overseer). They could not endure to see *prisoners* take so much enjoyment and quiet satisfaction. Accordingly, their next step was to take away all the lamps—thus obliging those who desired to improve themselves, to spend their long, cold, winter nights, in darkness and solitude. While many were benefitted by the lamps, no one was injured thereby. But Mc C. must show either his authority, or his hatred to that which is good.

We were ordered to put out our light, and did so—but the next day, we went to Judge B., who readily consented to let us have it again, and we enjoyed our usual privilege, while others were deprived. Soon, another, and another, and another obtained from him the same privilege; and some took it without asking. Then again, after a while, Mc C. gave another sweeping order, and all lights were extinguished. We went to Judge B.; he readily granted the continuance of ours. The same thing was acted over again and again, but still the Lord gave us our lamp. Finally, Judge B. said, " You can have it, but you must keep it to yourselves, and not let other prisoners see you have it." So we had our steel, flint, tinder, and matches, and lit our lamp after we were locked up at night. " Behold the goodness of the Lord !"

On every occasion, when our lamp was taken away, we went to God and asked Him for it—He heard, and immediately restored it to us.

For this blessing we cannot be sufficiently thankful. I know not how I could have got along without it. Besides our devotional reading, and singing, newspaper reading, book reading, letter writing, journalizing, book writing, &c., my volume of Poems, composed at my work, has been principally written after night. I am aware that our officers and Missourians little thought of what use our lamp was to us, but our God knew what we needed, and provided it. But setting aside all our writings, our light was an invaluable blessing. By it, we read the Bible through and through, and who can compute the value of the knowledge thus obtained!

Ah! little do they who have never been deprived of their comforts realize the importance and worth of what they enjoy, and of which multitudes are deprived. Reader, may it never be necessary for God to take away your privileges, to teach you the worth of them.

THE LOAD OF SIN.

In a prayer meeting, Dec. 17th, three of the converts, in speaking of the goodness of God to them, mentioned their improved health, which they attributed to the casting off the *load* of *sin* which bore so heavily upon them; and to their loving, and obeying God. Multitudes of Christians would never have thought of such a cause; and yet it is perfectly scriptural. The Bible speaks of "length of days," "long life," freedom from disease, &c., as being a *result* of obeying God. As "envy is the *rottenness* of the bones," so a "sound heart is the *life of the flesh*"—and "godliness has promise of the life that now is." It is also a very natural result. -O! could you hear them tell of the continual sorrow, and disquietude of their minds, while in sin, you would say, it must be very wearing to the physical life—but when they turned to God, their souls were filled with peace and quietness. Solomon says, "A cheerful heart doeth good like a medicine." What active Christian does not know this?

NEW RESPONSIBILITIES, AND DUTIES.

Dec. 18. The overseer called me to the guard room,

and said, " We have agreed to place implicit confidence
in you, that you will regard the best interests of the Institution." "I have, sir, heretofore, and I shall continue so to do. I feel it to be my duty." " That's the
character given you, and now we want you to act, as
foreman of the weaver's shop (about twenty hands).
I shall hold you responsible for the conduct of the hands
—the quantity, and quality of their work, and for the
supply of *materials* wherewith to keep them busy, you
will be responsible to me, and I shall be responsible
to the wardens. And now 1 want you to report
every instance of misconduct, otherwise the blame will
come upon you," &c. I felt it to be a very undesirable
station—for I found it about as much as 1 could do, to
watch, and keep myself straight, together with all the
care, anxiety, and watchfulness, devolving upon me, respecting the many weak lambs, without the load of
twenty wild, profane, mischief-making men, being laid
upon me. But go forward, I must, claiming the promise,
" as thy day is, so shall thy strength be." They were
continually breaking the rules ; but to report, and have
them whipped, I did not desire. I coaxed and warned,
I threatened and plead, but they only took advantage of
my good nature and forbearance, which often almost
vexed my spirit to impatience, but the grace of God was
" sufficient" for me.

The station brought with it its advantages as well as
its trials.

1. I had to work but little.

2. I could talk freely with them all, on any subject.

3. I could go to any shop in the prison, and talk with
the prisoners when I pleased.

4. I could spend much of my time in reading.

5. I could go to my cell for prayer when I chose.

6. I could remain out of my cell, on the Sabbath, and
converse with whom I saw proper, and other similar
privileges. I tried to improve these advantages for the
good of my fellow prisoners—and not in vain. God
blessed my efforts.

But the station brought with it other trials. It was

customary for the hands to do overwork, for which they
were paid in flour, molasses, tobacco, &c., on Sabbath
morning.   The foreman had to go all around the prison
to find his hands, and give them their pay.   This I determined I would not do on the Sabbath.

On one morning I was called to the guard room, ignorant of what was wanted, and was offered some molasses, short cake, butter, &c., (as all foremen were allowed).   I told him, "I do not wish any, sir."   "Tel.
Work to come down, and get some if he wishes."   " He
does not wish any, sir—the greatest favor you can grant
us is, to let us have the Sabbath sacred to ourselves."
"You may, but you must conform to *prison rules*—they
must be obeyed, without distinction.   *We* keep the Sabbath sacred, and make the prisoners observe it.(!)   We
wish to see all moral. (!)   I believe in being religious
every day,(!) though I belong to no church.   You may
stay in your cell, and read, and pray, as much as you
choose," &c.   And that very day, a number of hands
had to work a great part of it, getting bagging to the
river !   And this is a specimen of how they "keep the
Sabbath sacred."   Everything that can possibly be, is
crowded into the Sabbath, to save week time, and yet
with brazen face they can say, " We keep the Sabbath
sacred !"   Abominable.

He gave me some tobacco to carry round to my hands,
which I kept till Monday, and then gave it to them, as
they came to their work.

A TRYING TIME.

On a certain week, a number of my hands did overwork.   I looked forward to the Sabbath with many anxious thoughts.   Saturday night I went to Judge B. and
begged to be excused from waiting on my hands on the
Sabbath.   "You cannot be excused, Thompson."   I
looked at both sides of the question—by refusing, I
might expect the displeasure of the officers, and their
influence *against* me—a mangled back, and scars for
life ; and what more I knew not.   On the other hand, I
should have a consciousness of " obeying God, rather

than men," remembering that "it is *thankworthy,*
if a man for conscience toward God, endure grief,
suffering wrongfully." I went to God, and my mind
fully settled on *keeping the Sabbath,* let the consequences be what they might. I threw myself on the
promises, and patiently awaited the morning of decision
—when, lo! a fellow-foreman came for my book, and
of his own accord, offered to attend to my hands, himself, that I might not be troubled on the Sabbath. The
hand of God was manifest, and my heart involuntarily
arose in thanksgiving to the "Hearer of prayer."

This prisoner was a wicked man, but knew my feelings about the Sabbath, and having hands of his own to
attend to, volunteered to attend to mine at the same time!
I was no more molested in this way. The hand of God
on the wicked officers, restrained them from ever asking
us to break the Sabbath.

THE NEW YEAR.

Jan. 1*st,* 1844, we observed as well as we could, as
a day of fasting and prayer for the conversion of the
world. We fasted, but being so occupied with labors
we could not pray, except at our work, while others
were eating, and in the evening; at which time we had
a blessed season.

In my journal I recorded "How comforting to feel
that God knows all our circumstances! If there be
first a willing mind, it is accepted," &c.

The past has been a year of great things, but its accounts are now sealed for the judgment. How has Jesus
plead our cause! While the arrows of envy, malice,
and spite have been darted at us, we have been kept
under the shadow of his wings. While death has cut
down on the right hand and left, we are spared. While
thousands have suffered with hunger, "bread has been
given us, and our water has been sure," and we have
had many comforts. While others have been filled with
fear and uneasiness, we have been kept in peace.
What scenes have we witnessed! What songs of
thanksgiving from "new-born babes?" Our cell has

been "the house of God and the gate of heaven.'
Truly it is the Lord.

We will thank God and take courage—" Praise him
for all that is past, and trust him for all that's to come."
He who has been with us thus far, will not now forsake
us—no never, *never*. Come what will, we shall " lack
no good thing."

EXTRACT OF A LETTER TO A FRIEND.

Speaking of a prayer meeting on the first Sabbath of
the year I said,

" I expect to remember that delightful season when at
the right hand of my Savior with all the blood-washed company. And do you not think it will interest the Redeemer
to listen to my simple story, of the amazing goodness
of that Savior in whose presence we shall all be assembled? And will it not heighten their joy, and increase
the sweetness of their harps, as I may be permitted to
point to one and another, and say, " This man was born
there." O, there are many trials, yet " it is good to be
here." Never did I feel more contented with my condition than now, and you will find the *reason* beautifully
expressed in Abbott's " Young Christian," chapter second, page thirty-seventh, last half—story of Howard.

Alanson says, if ever he goes as a missionary, he feels
bound to the place, " where the Ethiope dwells."
James' heart flies across the ocean to the same. We
agree as touching this thing."

GEORGE.

A GREAT BREAK.

When one or more run away, it is called " a break."
On the fourteenth of January, after preaching, as some females were going out at the gate—a plan having been
previously laid—one man knocked the gate keeper
down; another pulled the gate open, and a rush was
made for *liberty*. Seventeen went out before the
gate could be closed. They were so eager, that they
trampled one on another, each caring only for himself.
The large bell rang, and the citizens of Jefferson were

quickly in the pursuit, on horseback and on foot, with muskets, and other warlike weapons. The prisoners were surrounded, and before midnight, all but one were again within the walls. This one was shot in the side, and was unable to be brought back for months; finally he came.

All were sentenced to receive thirty-nine stripes with the raw-hide, and to have the head shaved with the razor, for six months. It being on the Sabbath, and just after preaching, it was a distressing scene. Thus the minds of all were diverted from the truth to which they had been listening. O, how many ways has Satan to "catch away the word that is sown."

In times of such disturbances, the innocent suffer with the guilty, for *all* are treated with more rigor and severity for some time. In the midst of such confusion and excitement, it was sweet to us to reflect, "Thou rulest the raging of the seas—when the waves thereof arise, Thou stillest them." "Surely the wrath of man shall praise Thee—the remainder of wrath wilt thou restrain."

THE BROKEN ARM.

On the 19th of January, as James was at work calendering bagging, his fingers caught in the machine, winding his hand and arm around an iron bar about one and a half inches in diameter. Before the machinery could be stopped it had wound his arm up about half way to the elbow, mangling and bruising the fingers and hand, and breaking into a number of pieces the two wrist bones, one of which protruded through the flesh. It was providential that his whole arm was not taken from his body, or he in a moment crushed to death. But the Lord, who is wise and good, knows just how much to afflict us, "that we may be partakers of his holiness"—how *far* to suffer the proud waves to advance, before He says, "Hitherto shalt thou come, but no further"—and he will not lay upon us more than we are able to bear, for "He knoweth our frame, He remembereth that we are dust."

He came to the cell—the doctor was soon present, and set it according to the best of his skill; which we feared at the time, was not very good, as the result proved. He bore the setting very well, scarcely uttering a groan—painful yet needful.

The weather being moderate, he chose to remain in the cell, as the hospital at that time was extremely filthy, and the company unpleasant and disgusting.

After all had left the cell, he broke out into singing—after which he said, "*It is all right.*" "Good is the word of the Lord," &c. At our evening devotions, he united with us in singing and prayer. That night and most of the next day, I was with him. The pain, of course, was constant, so that he lost much sleep. In the course of four or five days, the hospital was prepared for him, and he was removed thither, where the steward waited on him. There he had his bed, large rocking chair, books, fire, and some few things from outside—a little milk, a trifle of light bread, a few apples, &c., but his diet was principally such as the prison afforded—corn bread and bacon, mush or gruel. He was there tolerably comfortable, though much annoyed. The doctor assisted in dressing his arm two or three times, and then left it to do as it might, and probably he would have lost his hand altogether, but for the kindness of Capt. R., who was an old sea-doctor, and gave counsel respecting it.

In about eight months, he began to do a little at light work, but it became stiff, so that he can do but little of any kind of work, and it being his right hand, he is the more disabled. And there is no doubt that it is owing to Dr. Moore's ignorance, but more to his carelessness and indifference, that James has not now the free use of his arm. Dr. Davidson looked at it, and said, "It *might* have been saved if it had been *attended* to, but now it is too late." Other experienced physicians were brought in to look at it, and gave the same opinion. But "it is all for the best."

If the cause in, and for which, we are suffering, be that of Truth and Righteousness, then are all our suffer

ings here for the sake of Christ, and his "little ones."
Such being the case, James can ever after sing a song,
in which I cannot yet unite, viz. : " I bear in my body,
the *marks* of the Lord Jesus." And what Christian would
not glory in being able to say this in truth ?   What a
satisfaction to the mind of one who has been lacerated,
wounded or maimed, to look on his *scars*, and feel that
they art for the sake of Jesus!   And as they are
tokens, or evidences of his love to his Master, so are
they the means of quickening, increasing, and *cementing*
his attachments to his Lord and Savior.   " Henceforth,
let no man trouble me, for I bear in my body the marks
of the Lord Jesus."   Sweet !

TO MRS. BEARDSLEY—JOY OF FAITH.

BELOVED SISTER :
        I am full of joy and peace in believing.   It flows
into my soul like a clear, smooth, peaceful river, proceeding from the throne of God.   O, the blessedness of
believing what our heavenly Father says.   It keeps the
soul quiet in times of commotion and danger; fills it
with light in the deepest darkness—yea, as the Prophet
has inimitably expressed it, " in perfect peace."   A
little *faith* will disperse every cloud, put to flight every
lion, and scatter all the objections, and hobgoblins, that
unbelief can present.   It is a lesson that takes some a
great while to learn, but the *why* is because they want
their own way, and think they know better than God,
what will be for their good.   How else can we account
for the murmurings of so many, when God frustrates
their plans.   Why so much uneasiness when a shower
falls at a time they did not wish, or frost cuts off the
crops, or their fields are laid bare by some providence ?
Why all this weeping and dejection, when sickness pros-
trates them, or their friends or relatives are snatched
away by death, or by some rude barbarous hand, into a
hostile country, to suffer and toil ?   *Why* all these, and
ten thousand similar feelings, under afflictive dispensations of Providence ?   Either they do not really believe
that God governs the world, or that He mistakes Himself

sometïnes, with respect to *their particular case.*   Could
they in all dispensations, see and acknowledge the hand
of God, as wise, kind, faithful, mighty, O, how instan-
taneously would the troubled emotions of the soul be
quieted to peace and joy unutterable.   I sometimes am
so filled with pity for those under the influence of
unbelief, I almost wish a tongue and power I have
not, to place before them the excellencies of *faith.*   It
opens the blind eyes—it looks at things as they *are.*
See two persons in the same circumstances, under the
different influences of faith, and unbelief, and what a
contrast !

I rejoice that I *came* here—that I *am* here—that I *may
be* here.   When the Lord has done with me here, he
will give me another field.   "My meat is to do the will
of Him that sent me."   My self, circumstances, interests, friends, comforts, trials, *all,* I commit to, and leave
with my God, saying, "Father, glorify thy name."
"Here am I, do with me, as seemeth thee good."   Farewell.   GEORGE.

CUTTING HAIR, AND SHAVING HEADS.

It was the usual custom of the officers to cut the hair
close, on one half of the head—and in cases of misconduct, to shave the head.

For a year and a half or two years, our hair was cut
in the fashion.   Then it was suffered to grow naturally.
Most of the prisoners thought it a great trial to have
their heads thus disfigured—and indeed it did present a
singular appearance—but I never thought it of sufficient
consequence to ask for—if they "gave me my hair,"
well and good—if not, it was all the same.   They were
welcome, as I frequently told them, to a half, or the
whole, if they wished it.   The *character* was not affect-

ed thereby. It is done to keep prisoners from escaping, but it is all folly—for if a man is resolved to run away, he will go just as quick without, as with hair. Shortly after McC. came, he gave orders to shave one side of the heads of the prisoners. Some, by hard pleading, got excused—but to us there was nothing said about shaving heads, or cutting hair. And from that time, with a few short exceptions, when there has been great excitement, on the occasion of a " break," or some such thing, we have had our hair.

Many have been sent forth with one side of their hair cut close—and one man had his whole head shaved, a day or two before he was discharged—both of which are in direct opposition to *law*.

DR. ELY.

Jan. 28. The celebrated Dr. Ely preached to us. All that he said, was good, plain truth, but spoken in such a light manner, as to cause much laughter, and I fear, spoiled the good effect it might have had. The recollection of his past conduct, respecting Marion city, and his slave Ambrose, and slavery, so rushed upon my mind, that, I confess I could not receive that profit, I otherwise would have gained. He once was a great man, but where is he now? O! how his case should teach us to keep humble at the Savior's feet, and watchfully avoid everything that will *tend* to lead us away from God!

I spoke to him. He said he recognised me as one of the *three*—(he was present at our trial). He went in to see James, and talked with Alanson, but could not give much comfort—"If I was thus separated from my family," said he, " I should be very unhappy."

GOV. REYNOLDS—SUICIDE!

Feb. 9, 1844, was an eventful day. Gov. R. after making out his will, writing letters to several persons, &c., retired from the breakfast table to his office, and deliberately committed suicide, by discharging the con tents of a loaded rifle into his head. He had pardoned out a number of *wilful murderers*, while the cases of others were rejected; and finally has gone himself to reap a murderer's reward!

Something of the kind we had looked for. We had long prayed that if he could not be converted, but was fully bent on withstanding the Almighty, and trampling down justice and judgment, he might, by some means, be *removed*, that the cause of suffering humanity might advance. The cries and tears of many fatherless children, and desolate widows, had long been ascending to heaven against him. And as God has said He "will surely hear their cry," is it any wonder that he was cut down, in awful judgment?

"The fatherless and widow," are objects of heaven's special care, and protection. And just as certain as "in thee the fatherless findeth mercy," so surely will their "Redeemer thoroughly plead their cause," "hear their cry, and save them" from their rich and proud oppressors. Well did a noble British officer,* in the time of the Revolution, on hearing of the cruelties of some of his fellow-officers, to the widows and fatherless, remark to a widow, "Such men will ruin our cause; for the word of God assures us, that His ear is always open to the cry of the widow and orphan—and believe me, madam, I dread their cry, more than I do the shouts of an *enemy's army*."

Yes, sooner let kings and monarchs seek my life, than the orphan's or widow's cry ascend to heaven against me. Rather let me cause "the widow's heart to sing for joy;" and let "the blessing of those who are ready to perish, come upon me," and I am happy.

Remembering the danger of indulging in improper feelings at the downfall of an enemy, we called to mind the injunction, "Rejoice not, when thine enemy falleth, lest the Lord see it, and it displease Him."

As we felt it to be the hand of God, we could but say

* Major Muckleworth.

Amen, and pray that He would accomplish His own purposes, by the event.

The Lieutenant Gov. Marmaduke was sent for, and took his place.

THE CLASS ORGANIZED, AND BROKEN UP.

I had often urged the chaplain to form some kind of an organization for the converts, by which we might be regulated in receiving, disciplining, and cutting off members—that it might be known who were " of us," and who were not—but was put off from time to time, with one excuse and another, for about eleven months. Every one who went up to be prayed for, was looked upon by the wicked, as having " joined the church," and when any who had been to the anxious seat, whether converted or not, " *turned back*," they were pointed at, saying, " There is one of your professors !"   " That's your Christianity !"   " I knew they were all hypocrites !" &c.   Thus the reproach was cast upon *all*—" for whether one member suffer, all the members suffer with it."

And there being no way to deal with backsliders, they were still looked upon by the wicked, as belonging to the church, and in fellowship with those who walked uprightly.   Some of these very backsliders would sometimes attend the meeting, sing, and even pray, which grieved some honest hearts, and gave the wicked occasion to rejoice, but what could I do ?   Should I tell them that I did not wish to see them in the meeting, this would create disturbance.   Should I forbid them to sing or pray, I should be called partial, intolerant, and charged with domineering over men's consciences.   I was much tried—yet felt it my duty to give full liberty for any to speak or pray, who felt so disposed.

At length the chaplain came with a methodist " class paper"—talked with the overseer, who gave permission to have a class formed—promised to furnish a room, where we could meet every Sabbath—that I should put such names on the paper, as I thought proper, which persons should be allowed to attend the meeting—must

12*

give the guard a list of the names, that he might know
whom to leave out of their cells, to meet in class—for
now all others were locked up, and not allowed to attend
unless they belonged to the class !

I felt myself placed in peculiarly trying circumstances—dark clouds were fast gathering—the officers were
evidently working against the prayer meeting, which had
done so much good, but to *go ahead*, as long as I could
move, trusting in God, I was determined.

We met four or five times in the capacity of a class,
and were then forbidden to meet any more, to the great
grief of many ! I talked with the overseer, but he was
unyielding. I asked for a reason—he replied, " I think
there will *no good* result from it." " I know of no *evil*
that has resulted," said I, " but *much good*. Has there
been any improper conduct in any of the meetings?"
" None, but I think evil will grow out of it !" Not the
first instance of evil could he point out, but meet we
should not ! There seemed to be a settled determination to oppose everything that had good in it.

I went to judge Brown—he refused—though he had
positively promised that we should have the meeting—
that he would make all the prisoners attend, and would
attend himself. He was turned like a weathercock, by
McC., whither he would. All hope from this quarter
failed. I went to the chaplain—he could do nothing.
We went to the inspectors—they promised time and
again, that it should be established. I rehearsed its history to them—its rise, fall, and results—they saw no objections, and said they would attend to it, but they never
did anything. We carried the case to our Father, and he
seemed to say, " Let it suffice thee—speak no more to
me concerning this matter." We ceased, saying, " The
will of the Lord be done."

As numbers of the brethren were allowed to stay out
of the cells on the Sabbath, I begged the privilege of
having them come to our cell and pray with us. McC.
and Judge B. both utterly refused. We could get together in companies and talk—the most wicked men in

the prison could laugh and talk together all day, and no fault was found! but meet to *pray*, we should not!

As our cell was open on the Sabbath, we ventured to invite the brethren at all events—some were afraid, and others resolved to come, till they were obliged to stop—they came, and we had precious seasons together. The Lord richly blessed our souls. And from that time, we had occasional prayer meetings, just as we could get any of the brethren together long enough. Of some of these seasons, I shall hereafter speak.

CHAPTER VI.

CHARACTER OF THE CONVERSIONS—INCIDENTS.

INTERESTING CASES.

First.—Old J. D. was a colored man—for a misdemeanor he came here, and served three years. He once was a slave, and bought himself and family. For himself he gave five hundred and fifty dollars—for his wife, four hundred and twenty; for his daughter, four hundred, and for a child *before it was born*, thirty-five dollars! *Unborn children*, bought and sold! Was ever such a thing heard of in the most savage nation under heaven? And yet in this gospel land, it is not an uncommon thing!* O! shame, *shame*, on my country! O! slavery, where is thy blush?

J. D. was a remarkable old man—he could not read a word, but was a striking instance of the power of grace on the uneducated mind. He seemed taught by the Holy Spirit. His afflictions brought him to the Savior's feet. I could wish that those who say, " the niggers

---

* A prisoner who had long been an overseer in the South, said, "It is a common thing South, to sell unborn children. They commonly bring one hundred, and frequently one hundred and fifty dollars."

have no souls," could only hear him talk and pray—surely their mouths would be stopped. *No souls!* What blasphemy! His views of gospel truth, and Christian duty, in many respects, were very clear. He talked understandingly, and, when engaged, with great energy, eloquence, and application. He was always active and ready. From many of his sayings, take the following as specimens.

On one occasion in the prayer meeting, he said, "God has so placed me that when I kneel down to pray, the devil *runs away*, for he don't like me, and thank God there's no great loss, for *I don't like him.* They may take me how, or when they please, *I'm always ready*, and have something to say about God and his goodness to me."

What a reproof to many who can find nothing to say for Jesus, unless they are in a particular mood—who can talk about everything else but religion! "Always ready!" What a lesson!

In the same meeting a young man professed to give his heart to God, before whom J. D. took his stand, and addressed him as a young soldier, at some length in a spirited, affecting manner, concerning the difficulties, doubts, dangers, &c., of the Christian life—much to the edification of all present.

In another meeting, he said, "My heart has leaped for joy to-day. Trusting in God! There is nothing like it in all the world. I thank God for sending me here. It has been the means of saving me from everlasting torments."

After the prayer meeting was broken up, he came to our cell one Sabbath, and we sang and prayed together for some time. He arose before us to "tell us the state of his soul," and said, "It has now been a long time since we met here, but I feel the knot drawn tighter than ever, and my soul is anchored out in the cause of the Lord. I feel that God is good in sparing me. When I came here, I did not expect to live one year, but he has helped me to worry my time almost through. I hope and pray that He will spare me a little longer,

that I may meet my little family, and tell them what he
has done for my soul—to meet them, with Jesus in my
soul, and glory in my view.   And oh! brethren, when
I'm gone, I shall remember and pray for you.   If we
should meet no more on earth, we shall meet in heaven.
I shall *know* you there as I do *here*, and there, there will
be no more locking up.   Glory to God!   Press on then,
brethren, through every difficulty, that you may be re-
warded.   The prize is great, and soon the time will
come when it will be given to us.   And when I'm gone,
I want you all to pray for old gray-headed J——y, for
though I am far away, when you kneel down; *your
prayers will reach my heart.*   Sometimes when I reflect
what God has done for me, my heart leaps for joy; and
I believe if the prayer meeting had continued until now,
I should have been able to move a mountain!   It was like
going to a *school* to be instructed and strengthened.   I
sometimes get cold now, but what little I *have* they *can't
get from me.*"
    Notice his estimation of the prayer meeting.   Many
felt as he did.   He left the prison, alive in religion, and
spent most of the day going round the city, talking to
the slaves and directing them to trust in God.
    He came into the prison again, and said to James, " I
feel better than I did, the day *I bought my head.*"   He
took and gave many lessons on abolition.   He was wa-
ter-drawer the most of his time, and talked with many
slaves.
    Second.—H. B. was a father.   In the prayer meetings,
he often spoke of his family, while the tears would flow
freely, in view of his past unfaithfulness to his wife and
children.   And to hear him pray for them was affecting.
    On one occasion he said, " I would give ten thousand
worlds, if I could only hear of the conversion of my
children."   The Lord heard him.   In a few weeks news
came of the conversion of two of his daughters, which
filled him with great joy.   He wept as he related the
news, and blessed the Lord.
    At another time, his little son came to see him, with
whom he conversed.   Said he, " Tell your mother that

I am spending here the happiest days of my life. I am contented. I should like very well to come home and instruct my children, but cannot just now.''

At another time, news came, that his son, about seven years old, had died. The spirit which he manifested was so perfectly *Christian*, so sweet, so submissive, and his conduct so exemplary, that we rejoiced in happy disappointment. He felt perfectly reconciled and satisfied with what his Father had done—felt that it was right, and all for the best—that God would take care of his child better than he could, " and I cheerfully give him back to Him, who gave him to me. The Lord gave, and the Lord hath taken away, and blessed be the name of the Lord.''

But his wife came a few days afterwards, and informed him that the boy was alive, and had not even been sick. He received his son as Abraham did Isaac, " from the dead, in a figure.'' He felt that he was dead, and under this impression manifested his faith and delight in God's will, and when his faith, as it were, was proved, as Abraham's, God gave him back his son, whom he was so willing to surrender at the call of the Giver.

At two different times he was at work outside in the woods. The guard was his relative, and said to him, " Now B., if you wish to go home to your family, go, and I will not stop you. You can have my pistols and go.'' His family lived only about twelve miles distant, but religion made him unwilling to receive liberty in a dishonorable manner. He chose to trust in the Lord. Once, he, with a company of others, had determined on " liberty or death,'' but the plot was providentially discovered and broken up. See what a change the grace of God makes. His general deportment gave us great comfort in our affliction. At length a pardon came for him, and he went home, after retiring with us to our cell, to pray and commune together, probably for the last time. Anticipating his departure, I composed and gave him the following :

ON THE RELEASE OF A PRISONER.

I.

Go, Fellow Pris'ner, here so long confined,
  By iron doors, and locks, and gloomy walls;
Leave all thy tears and suff'rings now behind,
  And answer to thy little children's calls

II.

Go find your darlings—wipe away their tears—
  Cheer up their hearts—their sorrows drive away—
Bid them to banish all their former fears,
  And now rejoice to see the wished-for day.

III.

Go find that weeping, broken-hearted wife,
  Whom thou hast caused to mourn by evil ways,
Go sweeten, now, her long-embittered life,
  And in God's fear together spend your days.

IV.

Go to your friends, whom you have made to weep,
  And who have followed you with many prayers;
Go wipe the tear from off that furrowed cheek,
  And lighten life's oppressive, anxious cares.

V.

Go, tell them all that you have seen and felt—
  The evil of your former wicked ways;
That Jesus' love your hardened heart did melt,
  And filled your soul with songs of grateful praise.

VI.

Go show the world by upright, holy acts,
  And godly conversation joined with all,
That you henceforth will mark your Savior's tracks,
  And do, in earnest on his name now call.

VII.

Go, Fellow Pris'ner, go be useful. Go,
  And be to man a blessing where you dwell:
The end of sinful ways to sinners show,
  Which lead to prisons, gallows, and to hell

VIII.

Go serve Manasseh's God and your's till death,
  Nor e'er forget your lonely prison-cell;
"Remember those in bonds," with prayerful breath,
  And meet me finally in heaven.   Farewell.

He had spent many pleasant hours and Sabbaths with

us, and seemed as dear as an own brother. Our hearts were knit together like those of David and Jonathan.

Third.—W. F. P. was a young man of feeble constitution, and of rather loose habits. He was converted soon after coming here, and lived so that the wicked were obliged to confess, " I believe that he is a Christian." He was sick much of his time, and often thought he was near his end; but was always composed, and willing to die or live, just as God saw best. How has my soul been refreshed, as I have conversed and prayed with him, in view of death! O, he was so sweetly resigned to his Father's will. The spirit that he exhibited, and the testimony he bore would amply reward us for all our sufferings, had we nothing more to comfort us.

At one time he said, " I am better satisfied and more contented here, than ever I was outside. I praise God for his afflicting rod, and feel that my two years here will be the happy means of saving me from the prison-house from which none are pardoned."

Again, I called on him, when he was very sick—conversed and prayed with him. Found him in an excellent frame of mind. He said, " My pains are great, but I feel that God is my friend. He is good and does all things right, and knows best when to afflict. ' He does not afflict willingly,' nor will He afflict me more than I can bear. I am willing to lie and suffer as long as my Lord sees best. All is in love, and for my good. We should be thankful for afflictions as well as mercies, for all are blessings." He had doubt about getting well, but was not alarmed. He felt some anxiety about his old father and family; but committed them to God, and felt that by prayer in prison, he could procure for them blessings and necessaries, which he could not when at liberty, a wicked man. I fed him with some of the promises, upon which his faith seized with eagerness, and I felt that it was well worth coming to a penitentiary, to enjoy such a privilege of comforting one of Christ's " little ones."

He spent his last Sabbath in our cell, much to our satisfaction.

Fourth.—C. S. was a Russian, from St. Petersburg He gave us much comfort—was exceedingly interesting in prayer meetings or private conversation—full of life and zeal. He attributed his first serious impressions, to seeing us so frequently on our knees, and hearing us pray, when he carried around bread at night. He thought if we needed to pray, surely he vastly more. And to hear him talk and pray in his broken English, would do any one good.

Reader, I have given you some specimens of our *prison fruit.* I might multiply cases, if my limits would permit, but these must suffice for the present.

It was my habit when any who were friendly to us came in, to intercede with them to use their influence to restore Alanson to his family. As the inspectors were frequently in, I plead his cause before them. They listened, felt an interest in his case, and promised to speak to the Governor, and use their influence to get him out—but it was their opinion that when one went, we would all go. They always treated us with great respect and kindness.

At one time, a Mr. C. was inside, to whom I said— " Tell the Governor that if he will let Alanson go, he may add his remaining time to the end of mine." But they would not admit of this kind of substitution.

At another time, an honorable Judge came in, with whom I made myself somewhat free, and who seemed to feel for us, and had said to our friends that he believed we were innocent. He was a man of extended influence, and could help if he would. I asked, " cannot something be done for Work's release?" " I do not know—Work is a first rate fellow." I said, " If there is an honest, conscientious man in the world, I believe that he is one." The Judge replied—" I have no doubt of it; I have no doubt of it." He also asked many questions respecting Alanson's family, and then went up stairs and talked with him.

EXECUTIVE RESPONSIBILITY.

He promised Alanson he would go and see the Gov

ernor in his behalf, but added, "I think no Governor will take the responsibility of turning you three . out, without the co-operation of the Legislature."

Responsibility! Indeed! If a thief, a whore-monger, a robber, a "man-stealer," or a murderer, is petitioned for by his friends, the Executive can very readily take the "responsibility" of turning them loose upon the community, without any fear of public censure, or risk of losing his popularity, or election to some higher seat of honor! And this FEARFUL "RESPONSIBILITY," has often been taken without even the form of a petition! But when asked to "open the prison doors" to those who are acknowledged to be honest, conscientious men, against whom they have "no imputation," who have a "good character," and are "first rate fellows," O! they cannot endure the "responsibility!" To pardon the whole list of criminals, is no responsibility; but to release those who love and desire to benefit their fellow men, and whose lives are devoted to doing good, this is insupportable "responsibility!" For such persons, in Missouri, are execrated, and should the Executive turn them loose, a torrent of public disapprobation may be expected, which he cannot meet, since he "loves the praise of men more than the praise of God." What a notion of "responsibility!" But more:

Gov. Marmaduke came in, and had a number of the prisoners called before him—two or three murderers and Alanson were among the number. He said to Alanson, "I have received two letters from your wife, and answered one of them, informing her that I could not, consistently, let you go. I have also received a long argumentative letter on slavery from Mission Institute, signed by three individuals. I am glad to hear of your behavior here—though you are far from friends it has made friends of all who have had anything to do with the place, and it has also made friends outside! If I consulted only my own feelings as a father, I would immediately turn you out, but I cannot consistently with my executive duties. The excitement, all over the country, is the greatest it ever has been, and I do not think that I, or any other Executive would be *sustained by public opinion*, in letting you go. And further—should I let you go, it would have the appearance of GIVING UP THE POINT!" What point? Why their opposition to our principles. They hold us here, because we will not "give up the point"—and if they should let us go while we persist in our doctrines, it would have the appearance of giving up to us that we were right and they were wrong. But if *we* would only give up the point, they can let us go, and boast, "We've conquered them at last."

I have not heard of their being troubled about the "appearance of giving up the point" to thieves and murderers* who have been pardoned out, and who declared, too, they would do the same thing again!

To act in accordance with the convictions of conscience, while the frown of a few ignorant, unreasonable, feeble men, is incurred, is great responsibility—but to do wrong, and incur the displeasure of that just and Almighty Being, who holds their life and eternal destiny in his hands, is no responsibility! What a vitiated public sentiment do such things bespeak! Yet such is one of the natural consequences of slavery.

Contrasted with such principles, how noble is the conduct of him, who, with promptness and resolution, will do *right*, though the displeasure of the whole world should be incurred, or the sacrifice of his life be the consequence. The man who thus acts from a principle of duty to God and man, leaving consequences with the Lord, finds a rich reward in his own bosom, though outward sufferings and reproaches may be heaped upon him.

We are thankful that we are not in prison as State felons—but we rejoice that we are "counted worthy to suffer shame," as abolitionists—as the friends of suffering humanity. We ask no higher honor in this world.

* Gov. M., soon after this conversation with Alanson, pardoned out two murderers—one of whom wilfully shot his neighbor.

JAMES AND THE MISSOURI LAWYER.

As James was reading his Bible, in the shoe-shop, a lawyer from Boone County came in, and asked, " What book is that ?" " The Bible, sir." " Do all here have the Bible ?" " Many are without any, but would be glad to have one." " Is a Bible given to each one when he leaves here ?" " It is given to none, sir." " I think it would be an excellent plan, it might *save* them in the hour of temptation. What is your name ?" " My name is Burr, sir." " Ah, that is just what I should expect from the character I have heard of you outside, to find you with your *Bible*. Hold on to it." " I expect so to do as long as I live !" " Yes, it is the only thing worth sticking to."

Would to God that all lawyers could thus speak of the Bible. O! what an overturning would there be in our courts of *mock*-justice ! How much less fraud, lying, and extortion would be practised by them! And how many more would be willing to plead for the *poor* as well as the rich, and " open their mouths for the dumb," in the cause of humanity !

March 11. James returned to the cell—having been absent six and a half weeks. About this time, Captain Richmond was expecting to move away, and Alanson and James were permitted to go outside alone, at two different times, each, to converse with Mrs. R. Nothing prevented free conversation on any subject, and the topic of slavery and helping slaves, was discussed with kindness and good feeling. Mrs. R. had always been kind to us.

About the middle of March, a citizen was in the shoe-shop, conversing with the hands about petitions. He turned to James, and said, " Here is Burr, I will not sign a petition for him, because he will not give up his principles."

EXTRACT OF A LETTER.

I am happy to find again a few words from Alanson

and James, that they may speak for themselves. They wrote in my letter—

DEAR WIFE:

I sympathize with you in your troubles, but can only relieve you by advice and prayer. I hope you will draw your consolation from the word of God. Affliction sanctified, is better than affliction removed. God's promises are exceeding large, especially to the widow and fatherless. Will not you and the children look out all you can find, and make them your own. Then you will rejoice in tribulation. I want you should be able, with a full heart, to testify to the faithfulness of God in supporting and carrying you in triumph through all your troubles. Be not troubled about me. I am well. Be faithful to the children. Tell them to be good, and then we shall meet in heaven, if not before.

The Lord bless you, and keep you, and provide for you. Farewell,

ALANSON WORK.

FROM JAMES, WRITTEN WITH HIS LEFT HAND.

FRIENDS:

Why do I not hear from you more often? I am sure if you were in prison, " enclosed in hewn stone," and could neither see nor hear of what was going on in the world—if you were obliged to see one thing all the time—and in addition, if you had a broken arm to *cheer* the gloom, you would wish for some one, now and then, to comfort you with a word of consolation. You know but little of the worth of a letter in prison. I want you all to do what you can for the salvation of souls. Do as the " Village Blacksmith" did—" set a trap, and bait it with faith and prayer." Do all the good you can.

J. E. BURR.

THE LEGISLATURE—DOCTRINE—LAW.

April 4. One of the four legislators who came to our cell one Sabbath, mentioned in Part II, called to talk with me. He began, " I suppose you feel about as you did when I last talked with you." "I am not aware, sir, that any material change has taken place in my mind, and I do not think the people of this State, can, with reason, require us to give up our sentiments, before they will let us go." The absurdity was so plain, he had to acknowledge it, and said, "They do not, nor could they in any land of liberty."

Reader, you have been shown time and again, that they *do* require this—that our *principles*, and they alone, sent us here and keep us here. "Give them up, and you may go," is the cry from every quarter.

The man went on, "If you can promise neither to come to this State, nor aid others in coming to assist slaves, there will be no difficulty in getting your time shortened." "We have repeatedly told you we should not come to this State again, for that purpose." He had considerable to say about the law—that it was made by the people, and till repealed, should be observed—that the way to alter it, was to enlighten the people. Very good and true, but how are the people to be enlightened? They shut their eyes, and stop their ears, and make special laws to keep out the light from the State. They will neither hear nor read on the subject of Anti-slavery, and if any one dares to attempt to " enlighten the people," he is mobbed, banished, or cast into prison. How shall we *enlighten* them? Will the slave-holding statesmen tell us how?

Again the man said, " For one man to disregard the law, is to set himself up against all the people, and tends to the subversion of all government."

But what does all this amount to, so long as the law is against the Bible, and contrary to God's law? If the law is unrighteous, and tends to the subversion of the law of heaven, it must be opposed, though it should subvert every government on earth. There must be those who will cry aloud and refuse obedience, even unto death. When human and divine laws conflict, the latter are always to be regarded. " We ought to obey God rather than man," is the Christian's motto.

FEMALE PRISONERS.

In the early part of our time, a woman of vile character was sent here—staid two or three days and was pardoned. About a year afterwards another came, for killing her husband. Her sentence was five years—she staid nearly two, and was pardoned.

She worked outside, at Capt. R.'s and Judge B.'s house. Mrs. B. abused her so shamefully, she ran away, but was brought back the next day and locked up in her cell, where she had but little to eat or drink, for some days. The horrid cruelty towards her, while thus locked up, so aroused the indignation of certain wicked prisoners, that there was strong talk of a " *muti-ny*," unless Judge B. altered his course. After about three weeks she was again taken outside, where she worked about four months—coming to her cell every night. In the fall she became the mother of a daughter. The doctor refused to be present at the time of her delivery. Mrs. Brown would neither come nor let any one else attend—the overseer told one of the prisoners to assist her—who did so, and he was the only one to wait upon her for some time. Mrs. B. refused to come near her, or to furnish any materials for the child's clothing —so that she remained in her cold cell, with her child, for nearly a week before anything was done. Nor was she allowed to have any fire during the cold winter weather—but suffered in her damp and chilly cell, till she was pardoned out! The whole is a horrid, disgraceful affair, on all sides. But can anything better be expected from slavery?

The next woman was put in a cell and rivetted fast, having a stove, and everything brought to her by other prisoners, with whom she conversed much. A great many resorted to her cell to converse with her. Her conversation was very disgusting. She was sick much of the time, and often in the night have we been awakened by her groans and screams for help. After a time the door was unfastened, and the guard could go there when they chose! She staid about six months and was pardoned out.

The next was a colored woman. She arrived here in the night, and was locked in a cell with three wicked vile men! The next day she was arrayed in prison colors—half of her dress yellow, and the other half white. This was the first time that any female had been so clothed. The others wore their own clothes, which they brought with them.

She was then placed in the wash-house, to work with two wicked men—if in her cell by day, it was unlocked, so that any prisoner could visit her, or any guard by night! Now *why* is she treated in this manner? "O! she is nothing but a *nigger!*" And what respect is paid to a "*nigger's*" purity in a slave State? Many other things might be mentioned respecting the abominable treatment of these women, but I must pass along.

A PROHIBITION.

So many of the prisoners who were trusted outside alone, had run away, that the inspectors prohibited the officers from sending any men out without a guard. But as James had been sick and was quite feeble, he asked one of the inspectors, if he could go out and breathe the fresh air for his health. The reply was, "I have no objection, and I presume the other inspectors will have none. We are not at all afraid of you. There is not the *least imputation* against you!" "No imputation!" and yet will not let us go!

At different times James went out and enjoyed the liberty of recreating himself as he chose, which greatly invigorated his system.

Usually, in the morning, the guards went around and unlocked the cells, not waiting to see whether the prisoners came out. But McC. gave his order, that the guards, after they had gone round, and unlocked the doors, should go round again, and *lock up* every man who was not out of his cell. Then whoever was thus locked up, was taken to the guard room, to give an account of himself. Generally, there were two bells—one for rising—the other fifteen minutes after, for opening the cells, at which time, every man was ordered to be ready to come out, and proceed to his place of work. Frequently the guard would forget themselves, so that the two bells would ring almost immediately after each other—or there would be only one, which often deceived the prisoners, and they were unable to get out in time.

Our morning devotions were often disturbed by the unlocking and slamming of doors, but pray we would, leaving consequences with God. Some of the guard would not mind anything about us, if we were in our cell, but others wished to show their authority, and importance.

One morning, as I was on my knees, such an one came around, and saw me—stood a moment, went to the window, and waited—then came back, as I was ready to go out, and said, " I'll lock you up every morning, if you do not come out sooner." I simply replied, " I am willing, sir." He reported me to the overseer, but he knew that I understood my own business, and said nothing about it. The guard, poor man! Did he think he could frighten a Christian from prayer? We felt the *need* of it. It was our "*vital breath*." Look at this, Reader. The poor prisoners are driven to work, from before they can see in the morning, till after they can see at night—having not more than half sufficient time to eat—and yet if one is found on his knees after the door is opened, fault is found because he is not at his work, whether he has anything to do or not! This will give you an idea of the trials of the dear converts. Such circumstances teach us the value of secret retirement. Deprived of this, we could lift up our hearts, while at work. This, man could not prevent.

"MY CUP RUNNETH OVER."

About the first of May, a barrel came from our friends to Judge B. It was more than half full of crackers—of which we had not a taste. In the same, was nearly a half bushel of dried fruit, which was given to us—also a quantity of medicines, which we received—a bundle

13

of letters, on which we feasted, and a valuable addition to our library, Memoir of Elias Cornelius, and Hannah Hobbie, Pike's Young Disciple, Pilgrim's Progress, Counsels to Young Men, Infidelity, Alleine's Alarm, Baxter's Call, Bouge's Evidences, and Missionary Heralds. As we had many calls from prisoners, for books, we could now supply them more fully. We had long felt the need of more religious books—for such was the general anxiety to *read*, they would read anything, however plain and cutting it might be. A number of *novels* had also been furnished by Mrs. Brown, which were devoured with great eagerness. To counteract this influence, we needed the *truth*, and God abundantly provided it, from time to time. Beside our books, we had a good supply of tracts, magazines, papers, &c.—so that our cell was a general resort, on Saturday nights, and Sabbath mornings, for something to read on the Sabbath, which gave us again the opportunity of speaking to them about their souls. In this way, " a great and effectual door" was opened for us to do good, for which we blessed the Lord.

SEARCHING THE CELLS.

It was customary, now and then, for the guards or overseer to go around, and search all the cells, to see what could be found, that was not allowed—if any were breaking out, &c.

When guards who were acquainted with us, went around, they did not disturb our cell, and frequently, as they passed, or looked in at the door, the remark has been heard, " There is no danger here"—" Everything is right enough here," &c. But sometimes new guards were sent around, who knew no better than to take everything as they went, making no distinction. At such times there was a great rumaging, and overturning in our cell. They found many things to look at—yet such was the general appearance of the cell, that the almost irresistible impression was, " There is no danger here"— for it has more the aspect of a student's room, than of a prisoner's cell.

At one time, a very self-important guard came in, while James was unwell, and searched the cell. He took down my letter box, which before had not been disturbed—in which I kept my own letters, my journal, and various trinkets. He examined the letters, and looked at my journal, but the Lord blinded him, so that he did not know what it was. He exclaimed, "Why, what an extensive correspondence this fellow has!" He took some little articles, which the overseer and Judge B. restored to us. Thus the Lord was good to us.

At another time, some Dutchmen went around. They turned everything up-side down, and took a number of things, which Judge B. gave back, as soon as we asked him. All my writings and papers, they passed by, not knowing that there was any harm in them. This work was then partly written, besides various other writings, any of which, if they had fallen into the hands of the officers, and been read, would have brought me into *deep water*, but the Lord blinded them on every occasion. "He disappointeth the devices of the crafty."

As the overseer had been around examining the cells, I asked him, "Did you find anything amiss in my cell?" He replied, "It looks more like a *store-room*, than a prisoner's cell," and yet the Lord did not let him take away our "store" of goods. But at the last searching, we had a narrow escape—yet the "way of escape" was opened in due time, so that God, again disappointed them, and delivered his little ones, who cried unto Him.

In the cell were a number of boxes—one large chest, in which James kept his papers, and our spare clothes—another, filled with dried fruit—and another containing all my papers—journal, and writings of various kinds.

The two former were left—the latter, with all its contents taken.

They so arranged it, that no one could go to his cell, to get anything, and we could only lift our hearts to God for help, which was granted. As my box was on the way to the guard-room, I told the guard, who was standing near me, and who had always been very favorable to us, that there were some things in it, I would like to have—he stopped it, and I took out all my papers, and everything that was of any consequence. He looked at my journal, but made no objection. Had he not been present, I should not have dared to stop the box—it would have been examined, and myself probably severely punished, and my time here much extended —but God has promised to defend those who trust in Him, and He did so.

———

CHAPTER VII.

DEATH—LETTERS—VARIOUS EVENTS.

FIFTH DEATH-BED SCENE.

ABOUT the first of May, a fellow-prisoner was taken down with consumption. At different times we were called on to sit up with him. James was with him one day and night, and asked his feelings in view of death. He replied, "I know I am not prepared to die. I know it—I *know* it, but my pains are now so great, that I have just as much as I can attend to, without thinking of that."

I was with him one night, but did not talk much, as he seemed inclined to sleep most of the time.—There were three others in the hospital. I read a portion of scripture, and prayed with them, and they retired. Towards evening of the next day he sent for me. I went, and found him worse. I asked, "Are you in pain?" "I have no particular pain (of body), but I have another sort of misery, *misery*," referring to the distress of his mind, in view of his condition. He continued, "O, I have a *heap* I want to say to you, when I have opportunity." "Do you think much about your past life of sin, as you lie here?" "O yes. Have I not, to-day, been dissolved in tears, in view of it?" I urged

upon him the necessity of true repentance, and immediate submission to God, while reason was continued—and
placed before him the danger of delay—to which he as-
sented.   He felt that he should not get well, and wished
me to send the minister to him, which I did, on the Sabbath after preaching.—Poor man ! he had not only his
pains, and feeble state of body and mind to contend
with, but the sneers and " wickedness of the wicked,"
who made light of his seriousness, and tried to divert his
mind.   Alanson was with him one night, and conversed
and prayed.   The next night I was with him, but had
not much conversation—spent the most of my time writing some of the foregoing pages.

A day or two after, he called for me in the morning.
He was very glad to see me, and wished me not to leave
him.   He wished me to sing, "Eden of love," which I
did ; he said, " That is the most delightful song I ever
heard."   Then occurred the following.—" Do you feel
prepared to die?"   " No."   " Do you feel the importance of it ?"   " Certainly—certainly—but you
see how *low* I am—so weak I can do nothing, I cannot help myself to anything."   " Though you cannot
walk, you can think, and speak to God in your heart."
" O, I *do* think, day and night."   " Do you feel that you
have been a great sinner ?"   " I *know* it—but not so bad
as some—I am better than many."   " Do you think
your good works will do you any good, or be of any
avail before God ?"   " No, they will not."   " Your
good works are but '*filthy rags.*'   You must come to
God as a guilty sinner, as a rebel, as a beggar of mercy,
for Jesus' sake, and cast yourself wholly upon Him.
Do you think God is willing to forgive you ?"   " I expect so ; why not *me*, as well as others ?"   " He will, if
you come as he has directed."   " I am willing to come
so."   " Are you willing to confess your sins ?"   " Yes ?"
" Do you ?"   " I do ; but what is repentance ?"   " It is
true sorrow for all sin ; and putting it away.   Now
should you get well—go forth into the world—have
plenty of money, and the prospect of living many years,
would you not love *sin* as much as ever ?"   " No, I

would do right." "God has been very kind to you all your life." "Yes, He has." "But have you ever done anything for Him?" "No, I have done nothing, and now I am so weak, what can I do?" "You can repent, and give your heart to God. If you now fix your *affections* upon Him, and strive to please Him in your mind, it will be as acceptable, as the *actions* of those who are well. You can now sin in your heart, as well as others in their actions. And you may soon die, therefore it is the more important that you now secure the salvation of your soul, and make Jesus your Friend." "Is He not my Friend?" "I do not know. He is if you love, and try to please Him." "If I get well, I will never do wrong again."

On the evening of the next day, a wicked man called to see him, and in a light manner remarked, "O, you will be about again in a few days, and walking around—won't you?" It was with difficulty the sick man could speak, but he exclaimed with emphasis, "Go away—I am dying, go away, go away. Don't you see death hovering around me?" He felt that he was near the grave, and did not wish such persons near him. As he looked up and saw me, he asked, "Is that you, Mr. Thompson?" "Yes, how do you feel?" He could but faintly utter, "About as usual." The next morning I called to see him, but he was beyond conversation, or perception, and soon breathed his last.

He said, one night, to the man who was watching with him, "I am *murdered.* If I had been brought here (the hospital), three days before I was brought, and when I *wanted* to come, my life might have been saved—but instead of that, they made me work when I was not able, and now I must *die?*" And he is not the only case. I shall have occasion to mention others. He was buried —I was going to say "with the burial of an ass," but truly there is more solemnity at the burial of many a dumb brute, than there was in this case.

While he was yet in the hospital, some were swearing —others talking and laughing about him, as if nothing had happened. Such carelessness and indifference as was manifested around this dying and dead man, was most shocking—and bespoke a depravity of the human heart, not to be expected among savages, and probably to be found only with gospel-hardened sinners. How just the complaint of God, " Seeing many things, but thou observest not ;"—" my people doth not consider."

REFLECTION.

How uniform and united is the testimony, that " a sick bed is a poor place to prepare to die." And yet how many are acting the same foolish part, and surrounded by such a " cloud of witnesses," are " putting far off the evil day."

Reader, *our* death-bed may be attended by such burning fever, racking pains, and distraction of thought and mind, as will utterly *disqualify* us for thinking upon our latter end—for arranging our business, for meditation and prayer—for warning sinners, or inciting saints to duty. Then let us think of death, judgment, and eternity *now*—arrange now, and so keep arranged, all our business, that it will not require our thoughts upon a dying bed. Let us do our duty to our own souls, to saints and sinners, now—prepare now to meet God, and henceforth, *live* in a continual state of preparation to depart suddenly, or by a lingering disease, or in any way, time, or place God shall choose.

EXTRACT OF A LETTER.

BELOVED PARENTS AND FRIENDS:

" EBENEZER,"—God is faithful. Though the earth be in motion, and rock from centre to circumference—though the nations are moved and agitated, while war is raging, and " rumors of wars" continually fall upon our ears, yet a simple *trust in God*, will preserve us from all anxiety and apprehension of evil—from all that would disturb the sweet repose of the soul in Him.

Beloved, it is *unbelief*—a secret unwillingness that God should rule and govern as He pleases, that causes all the disquietude, fretting, murmuring, discontent, and sorrow, which is so common among professing Christians, when things do not go just as *they* had desired or planned. And this unbelief is very offensive to our kind Father. It evinces a very bad, unsubdued spirit, entirely unbecoming obedient and submissive children.

God has promised to give this world to his Son; but a great work is yet to be done before it can be brought into subjection to his holy will. Mankind are in a state of *alienation* from Him—degraded, depraved, and sunken in ignorance and vice—yet this work is TO BE DONE, and that speedily. And all opposition to the onward march of His kingdom, and the victories of His cross, will be as vain as they are unreasonable. The wicked may scoff—infidelity may spread itself abroad, and fill our land with its deadly poison—Catholicism, with all its absurdities and blasphemies, may sweep over our fair heritage like a deluge—and Satan with his combined legions may rage, and bring into exercise all his crafty devices—but *all in vain.* Immanuel's victorious chariot, shall ROLL ON—"the stone cut out of the mountain without hands," shall "*increase,* and fill the whole earth"—the "little leaven" shall work, "till the *whole* is leavened." This revolted empire shall be completely subjugated; and to JESUS "every knee shall bow," and all nations, tribes, and tongues own Him their Lord and King. But in what way is this glorious triumph to be brought about? By Christians being "*co-workers with God,*" "*laborers together with Him,*" and *co-operating with the Holy Ghost.*

The day has come when every one who bears the Christian name, must make this work the great object and business of their lives, or give up all hope of being friends of the Prince, who calls upon all his followers to fly to his assistance, and lay down their lives, if need be, for his cause. O, who can—who dare sleep, in such a day as this?

GEORGE.

THE BEATEN HORSE.

Judge B. had often beaten, very cruelly, a poor horse which was somewhat balky. As he was thus beating the poor beast one morning with a hoop-pole, he was kicked in the face, disfigured and seriously bruised, escaping narrowly with his life. The doctor was speedily called, who washed and sewed up the wound. "A merciful man is merciful to his beast," and cruelty to dumb brutes, is not overlooked, nor suffered to pass unpunished by Him, whose are "the cattle upon a thousand hills." Then how should they tremble, who can treat *human* beings, stamped with the image of God, *worse* than they treat their brutes—who inflict wounds, and stripes upon a fellow, "which mercy with a bleeding heart, weeps, when she sees inflicted on a beast." "Blessed are the merciful!"

THE SLAVE AND LIBERTY.

A slave was in on business, with whom James conversed. He expected to be free in the Spring, by means of his master's will. He said, "in the time of the war, all were for liberty. Every ball that was shot was for liberty; and I am for liberty too." The very thought seemed to give him new life and animation.

O, liberty, sweet liberty! thou gift of heaven, and dearest boon of man, on earth, for which our fathers bled and died, how art thou now by thy children, denied to three millions of our brethren, in this our boasted land of liberty. How art thou abused! How little valued, and how little understood! O, long desired day, hasten thy approach, when the inestimable blessings of "liberty, and the pursuit of happiness," shall be enjoyed, open, and free alike to *all.*

THE HOLY SPIRIT.

On the ninth of June, a Campbellite preacher "held forth" before us. He was brought by the overseer, who favors that religion, because he can have it and hold on to his wickedness. The preacher was gifted, and said many good things, but he spoke too lightly of the influence of the Blessed Spirit; and it is to be feared that they who can speak lightly of *that,* but too plainly evince their ignorance and need of his heavenly efficacy.

13*

Take away the Holy Spirit, and what can we do? We cannot know Jesus, for the "Spirit takes of Him, and shows unto us." We cannot understand the Scriptures, for the Spirit is our "Teacher." We cannot see the guilt and depravity of our own hearts and lives, for the Spirit "convinces of sin." We cannot pray, for the Spirit is our "Helper." We cannot find happiness, for the Spirit is our "Comforter." We can know nothing of the joys of Heaven, nor have any view of the things unseen and eternal, for they are "revealed unto us by the Spirit." We shall never love and obey God, shall neither speak, will, nor do good, for it is the Spirit that inclines, persuades, and draws us—speaks and works in us "to will and to do." "It is not by might nor by power, but by my *Spirit*, saith the Lord." "Uphold me by thy free Spirit." "Thy Spirit is good—lead me into the land of uprightness." "Grieve not the Holy Spirit," but "Be filled with the Spirit."

THE SLAVE AND HIS CRIME.

June 13. A slave was brought here in chains, handcuffed and barefoot. What was his crime? Why he had been torn away from his wife, whom he dearly loved, and went one hundred miles to see her! And for this was he brought here, with a special charge to our tyrant, "Work him hard, feed him lightly, and flog him for every offence," all which was eagerly fulfilled.

It was McC.'s custom to give those who did their task, a piece of meat at night. The slave did more than his task, and came among the rest for meat. McC. addressed him, "What do you want, nigger?" "Some meat, sir." "You can't have any, there's none for you." "Why, he has done more than his task," said one. "That's nothing. I'll make *him* do that, and feed him twice a-day." O, cruel slavery!

He was also flogged very severely for nothing, except that he was a poor slave. After three months he was probably sent South, for an infamous dealer in human flesh was around here buying up all he could, to take to the low countries.

With what fear and agitation, must the bosoms of the poor slaves be convulsed, when a "trader" is in the neighborhood! Christians, and ye husbands who love your wives, look at this case. Think of it, and remember there are at this moment *thousands*, whose wives and children are as dear to them as yours are to you, from whom they are rudely sundered, and sold to distant climes, to meet them no more on earth! Have you the heart of a Christian? Then let it ascend to God in their behalf. Have you a mouth and tongue? Then cry aloud against such abominations, and " open your mouth for the dumb." Have you the common feelings of humanity? Then awake and exert your every power for humanity, bleeding at every pore.

EQUALITY OF SLAVEHOLDERS' LAWS.

June 19. A man *seventy-three* years old, was brought here, for ten years, charged with *Lev.* xx. 15! Astonishing, if true. The old man could do nothing, and the officers interceded for him, so that he was pardoned in a few weeks. Why? Not because he was not guilty, but because he could do nothing for the profit of the officers. This has been the case in a number of instances.

But look here. Slaveholders will send a man to the penitentiary for ten years, for the crime referred to· while for fornication and adultery, if perchance the female be a slave, no notice is taken of it ; but high and low, black and white, bond and free, may thus indulge with impunity. O, Slavery! where is thy blush? Alas! thou art one of those " who being past feeling, have given themselves over to work all uncleanness with greediness !"

OUR " REFORMER."

As a crazy man was reading aloud the tract, " We are all here," at the same time attending faithfully to his business, Col. Price came along, and forbid his reading, took the tract, and tore it·in pieces on the spot, before our eyes! How similar is this to one of Israel's kings, who cut the Book of the Law in pieces, and threw it into the fire! He also once forbid me to read, when I had nothing to do at the time. Again, he refused to give me a letter, because it had a few words in it about the abuse of a servant girl; and there is no doubt that he destroyed a bundle of our letters, which we had written with the permission of other officers, to send by a friend. A prisoner wrote a letter to the inspectors, which every prisoner has a right to do by law. Col. P. threw it into the fire, before his eyes!

Many other such things I might mention, respecting Col. P., but will speak of only one more: he is an unreasonable, oppressive, fiery tippler.

Such is one of the men placed over criminals to reform them—such the inveterate hatred to all good, of one of our head managers? "A place of reformation!"

On the 27th of June, a small cloud of promise arose, which raised our hopes a little, that God was about to do something for this place. The chaplain was deputed by the inspectors, to ascertain how many Bibles there were in the prison, and report to them. He went into every cell, leaving tracts and searching for Bibles, and found forty! Here are eighty cells, and about one hundred and seventy prisoners, and forty Bibles among them all! In many of the cells there are two, and in some three, so that more than three-fourths of the prisoners were without any Bible, and many without a book of any kind, except as Satan sent them a novel, or as they borrowed from others. We had numerous applications for a Bible, and had to lend our own to supply the demand. We were rejoiced to see that the inspectors were waking up upon this subject; for we had frequently spoken to them, to ministers and legislators, pleading for Bibles. But look at this case. The law provides that every prisoner shall have a Bible. See the neglect. Yet it is called a "place of reformation." This term in the mouth of Satan, and applied to this place, is full of meaning—for it does, mostly, reform men from good to bad, and from bad to worse! But as the term is used by Christians, to apply it thus to this place, is a mockery of language and an insult to common sense. "But have

not many been truly reformed here ?" Yes, but no
thanks to our wicked "reformers," for the greater part
of the reformation. True, for a while they granted us
the privilege of having prayer meetings, for which we
and thousands of others will thank them eternally—for
souls were saved thereby—but a great part of the religious reformation has been carried on, *notwithstanding*
al their hatred and opposition to the work, at the risk,
many times, of bringing down upon us their displeasure
and their fury. Take out the few Christian prisoners,
and then the only influence and tendency of the whole
system, under its present officers and regulations, is to
damn the prisoner ; to harden and destroy the officers ;
to curse the community, the state, and the world. Many
come here, who either know nothing about crime, or they
are mere children in such knowledge. After studying a
few years under such willing and experienced teachers
as are the officers and many of the prisoners, they
become perfect adepts in the business. The old and
learned become chafed and exasperated, till they are
prepared for more daring deeds ; the weak become
strong, and the strong become stronger in wickedness
and vice ; and all, with a few exceptions, are made ten-
fold more the children of hell than before ! " A place
of reformation !"

THE FOURTH OF JULY.

All hands were allowed to quit work about three
hours before night, and keep *some* of the fourth—of
which day, the most of the prisoners thought much, as a
day of gambling, drinking, feasting, and carousing.

An *extra* supper was prepared, consisting of wheat
flour biscuit, unleavened, fresh pork, and coffee ! After
supper, the prisoners stood in groups, talking as much
as they chose, no officer making objections, except in
one case. As I stood conversing with a colored man,
a guard looked at him and called out, " See here, come
away from there." Had he been talking with any ex-
cep one of us, there would have been no objection.

But *he* celled with a *slave*, and was talking to an *aboli-tionist*. They dislike to have us communicate with the slave in any way—but, thank God, we did place "the salt" before them by proxy, though we could not always speak to them ourselves.

For a few days in the beginning of July, I was sick, and quit work. While thus sick, a letter was given to me, bringing the joyful news that my oldest brother was preaching—for which I had long been praying—and that m y youngest, with his wife, had devoted himself to pre-paration for the missionary work. Language failed to express my feelings. An extract from the answer is all I can give.

THE EXTRACT.

"I almost feel to say with old Simeon, 'Lord, now let-test thou thy servant depart in peace,' for thou hast heard my prayers. I can cheerfully spend my life in seclusion and toil, or with a willing heart, depart from every earth-ly field of labor, since you have arisen to fill my place. You have now a thousand times repaid me for all my anxiety respecting you. Labor to get enlarged views of the Gospel, and of the work before you. Remember, 'The field is the *world*,' and not some little 'garden spot,' here at home, where they have rejected the gospel a thousand times. The great portion of the field is yet *uncultivated*, covered with thorns and nettles, having never yet heard the 'joyful sound:' and in unbroken crowds, the inhabitants are sinking to rise no more. The gospel would have saved them if carried to them. Chris-tians might have done it, they neglected it, and millions are lost for ever! Where is the guilt?

"From every land, they *now* cry, 'Come over and help us.' If they receive the *gospel*, they may be saved. Christians can, and should, give it to 'every creature.' If they *refuse*, may the Lord deliver me from their ac-count. Do you not say, 'Here am I, send me?' A hearty missionary spirit, is the only true spirit of Chris-tianity. It is this that constitutes the very condition of discipleship. 'Whosoever he be that forsaketh not *all* that he hath, cannot be'—a deacon? a minister? a missionary? No, no, but 'he cannot be my *disciple*.' Let this spirit fill your soul. Let the gospel be given to the *present* generation of heathen, or they will perish, and rise up in the judgment to condemn all who *could* and who were urged to go, but 'would not.' O! look forward to the judgment. Will you there have thousands curse, or bless you? I pity those who can satisfy themselves with excuses, when millions are crying, when all nations are stretching their hands for the ' bread of life.' Truly the work is great and responsible, but our sufficiency is of God." Though I am ' shut up, and cannot go forth,' I do rejoice to hear of others entering the field. Though we are weak, blind, and ignorant—our foes numerous and strong, and obstacles fill our path—yet glory to God! We hear, ' My grace is sufficient for thee.'

" George."

As a few of James' letters have fallen into my hands, I delight to extract from them, that he may speak for himself. The first should have been introduced previously to his breaking his arm, but it will be interesting here.

FIRST EXTRACT.

Dear Brother:

" God is love." He desires our greatest happiness more than we or all the bowels of humanity concentrated could desire it; and his Omnipotence will surely bestow on his children everything that will be a real good, in time or eternity.

When my sickness was most alarming, I had a bright foretaste of heaven, and longed to take my departure, to unite with the bright throng before the throne.

My soul was filled with rapture at the thought of meeting good old Abraham, the prophets, apostles, and all the martyrs, who have " come up out of great tribulation." Nor do I now feel anxious to tarry long on this earth. I am only a pilgrim and a stranger, as all my fathers were. I long to join the happy company above. God has shown me the vanity of all terrestrial objects

—that " this world is poor from shore to shore," and has nothing that is worth one hour's toil, compared with the joys of heaven. I would like to leave this world for some fairer clime, and I know of no place short of heaven, worth stopping at.

SECOND EXTRACT.

DEAR BROTHER:

I am obliged to write with my left hand, as my right arm is broken. For the last four months, my health has been better than at any previous time since I came here. God has " stayed his rough wind, in the day of his East wind"—for my former poor health and a broken arm in addition, would have been both winds together. The Lord knows what we can bear. You see I have been called to "sing of mercy and of judgment."

God is ten thousand times better to me than all my earthly friends. Notwithstanding all my unworthiness, He has gone before me in all my troubles, and has been a " sun and shield" to me. He has not forgotten his " exceeding great and precious promises." He stands pledged that not a hair of our head shall perish; yet it depends on our staying where He commands us. If we forsake Him, as did the children of Israel, we must expect the rod. But what a privilege! that He who cannot err is as willing, as He is able, to lead us! To Him I will repair. He " doeth all things well."

J. E. B.

THE INCENDIARY LETTER.

She who is now my wife once wrote me a letter on an anti-slavery sheet of paper, having stamped on it a colored woman in chains, on her knees, crying " Am not I a woman and a sister?" It created considerable talk and stir, for slaveholders cannot endure to see in *picture* what they see every day in *real life*—they are very sensitive. However, they reluctantly gave me the letter.

At another time (the first of July), she wrote, giving an account of her journey to the Indians and their habits, and her return home. Among other things, was a

story of a certain servant girl, who was very much
abused, whipped, punished, and scratched by her mis-
tress, till the blood trickled down her face. It was not
stated that the servant was a slave,* or that she was
even colored ; but Col. Price, who was familiar with
such scenes, supposed of course she must be a slave,
and would not give me the letter. I ascertained from a
friend that the letter had come and was withheld. I
mentioned the case to the Chaplain, which greatly incensed McC. and Col. P. against me. I spoke to Col.
P., he declared he would not give it to me. I spoke to
Judge B. again and again, till he procured the letter and
brought it to our cell, saying, " Read it, and hand
it to me." Had the letter fallen into his hands in
the first place, there would have been no difficulty ; but
since his partners had refused, he gave it to us secretly,
lest they should turn against him.

Said Col. Price, " You have been corresponding too
freely, and it must be stopped." Judge B.—" The
Governor, inspectors and officers have agreed that no
prisoner shall be allowed to write or receive letters respecting any means for their liberation ; but I have and
shall allow you three to write freely to your friends on
that subject ; and shall give you every chance to help
yourselves, in that way, that I can."

The day after we heard of the letter, one of their
horses dropped dead. In two days another was found
dead—and they soon gave up the letter.

MY DEPOSITION.

While they were thus excited about the letter, I was
suddenly taken from the weaver's shop, and placed in
the cooper's shop, where I would have none but myself
to watch, and also could learn a new trade. But the
next week they were obliged to send for me, to fill my
old place—which I did for a few days, and then went to
weaving.

All the reason they pretended to offer for removing

* I have since learned that she was a slave—and the inhuman mis-
tress was the wife of an officer of government, among the Indians.

me from the foremanship, was, "You are too easy with the hands—too tender-hearted—too desirous of keeping peace with them all. The hands are not *afraid* of you." And who would not wish to keep peace, and to have his workmen do their duty from love, and not from a slavish fear? If I had caused three or four of my hands to be whipped every day, I should have been a first rate foreman! But because I would not exercise the spirit of a slave-holding tyrant, they are displeased —this is proven by many facts.

But more. Another very obvious reason was, because I would not break the Sabbath, honor their dignity, and sacrifice all principle to please them, as did the other foreman.

Judge B. had nothing against me. He remained calm and kind, and took my part against the other officers.

Col. P. did not speak a word to me for more than a year after that time, so that I had no further difficulty with him.

ANSWER TO THE TROUBLESOME LETTER—EXTRACT.

" Where have Christians shone brightest, and exhibited to the world the excellence, and power of religion in its greatest brilliancy? Surrounded by comforts, luxuries, friends, and everything that heart could wish —temporal and spiritual? Go to the prison—the dungeon—the stocks! Hear the persecuted saints sing, and pray, and shout, supported and comforted by a hand unseen—a power divine. Go to the rack. See the astonished multitude look on and wonder! The bones are cracking, the sinews snapping, but songs of praise and prayer for enemies, mingle and ascend to God! See them at the stake, amid circling flames, blessing their persecutors, and shouting in prospect of eternal blessedness. Witness Daniel in the den—the three children in the furnace —Joseph in the prison, and a host of others. In them religion shone forth, with charming lustre. O! give me such a religion! What gave to the world some of Bunyan's rich works? A prison. What taught Baxter the sweetness of "The Saints' Rest?" A prison—long and severe afflictions. What gave "Dodd's Prison

Thoughts" to the afflicted? A prison. What Memoirs are most spiritual, and exhibit most of the gospel? Those which give the history of *suffering saints*. Witness Payson, Page, H. Hobbie, and many others. What says the humble Christian of every age? " My most *afflictive* days have been my *best* days." Think of Job. Read the eleventh of Hebrews. What would the " afflicted, tossed with tempest, and not comforted," do, without these rich examples of patience, submission, joy, and faith?

What drew forth the overflowing, never-failing fountains of comfort, joy, and peace, in a multitude of the Psalms, to suffering saints? Sore afflictions.

Let us not then be afraid to meet any trial that our Father places before us. He will be with us. " My grace is sufficient for thee." GEORGE.

INSPECTORS' SECOND EXAMINATION.

They heard many sad tales. Some had been unjustly punished—some shamefully neglected and left to suffer when sick—others complained of their food—others, of oppressive tasks, &c.

The inspectors promised to rectify these things, but that was the last of it. They generally talked much, and did little.

When I was called before them, the officers were very uneasy and greatly agitated. They stood before the door, went away, returned, looked in, talked, and squirmed as if they were on nettles. They thought I was exposing their abominations—and so I was, and they could not help themselves. Many things were laid before them. I gave them a history of the rise, effects, and fall of the prayer meeting—spoke of the need of, and general desire for one, &c. I added, " It seems to be McChesney's object to break up every thing like religion here." They all agreed there could be no harm in having a prayer meeting, and promised to make arrangements. They said to James, " We mean to do all we can to bring things *right* here, and to have a prayer meeting."

They told Alanson, and some of the converts, that they could see no possible objection to it, and gave great encouragement that it should be re-established—but that was the last we heard about it! We informed them of the Sabbath breaking, by officers and prisoners—but things only grew worse.

CHAPTER VIII.

SICKNESS—LETTERS—SLAVES.

FALSE NAMES.

It is quite a common thing, for prisoners to come here under a false name—thinking thereby to keep their friends from knowing that they have been in the penitentiary—that they may go out into the world again, and not be known as a "convict." In the time of the prayer meetings, I told them that all such were *living lies*, and they must give up their false names, and be honest, or they could not be Christians. One of this class professed to be converted. We told him he must take his right name—and he was just ready to do it, when he asked the chaplain about it, who told him there was no harm in it, and we could do no more with him.

Others gave their right names, and were willing the world should know their characters—"converted convicts!"

After we were forbidden to meet together, a number of the brethren were in the habit of coming to our cell, on the Sabbath, to sing and pray. At one time, an old man, who had belonged to the Old School Presbyterians, in Ireland, and in Philadelphia, was present, and confessed he was here under a false name. "I have been much troubled about it. It was foolish and wicked in me to do so. It is a transgression, for which I must

humble myself before God." He confessed his true
name, and felt relieved.

We were now so hurried with work, that we had but
little opportunity to look after the lambs. Take the following for a specimen. A brother, who slept under the
same roof with ourselves, was very sick for four days,
before we knew anything about it! Other prisoners
have died before we heard they were sick.

A NOTE OF THANKS.

I have mentioned that many prisoners read our books.
The following note will show with what feeling they
were received by wicked men. It was written by one
who had read the most of our library. He was a great
thief, yet a great *reader*—an Englishman. Just before
he left he wrote :

Sunday, July 28, 1844.

To G. THOMPSON :

Please to accept my thanks, for the many favors
you have bestowed on me, in allowing me the use of
your books, from time to time. I wish it was in my
power to make you some compensation beside that of
empty thanks. You have my best wishes. While you
walk in the flowery paths of *religion*, you have nothing
to fear ; for the God whom you worship, is the same that
delivered Daniel out of the lions' den. I should be very
glad to see you, and your companions, at liberty. "Let
me die the death of the righteous, and let my last end
be like his." G. L.

How many Christians are often dejected, and fearful,
in times of trial ! Says an enemy, " You have *nothing* to
fear." Christians, cheer up.

The same person read " Christian Perfection," and
wrote on a blank leaf, " I have read this book, not with
any prejudice against the doctrine it contains, nor have
I read it with indifference, but still there is a something
—a longing disposition to hang on for the pleasures of
the world." The judgment is convinced—the will
rebels.

TASKS.

For about two years after we came, there was no task work,—except in the brick yard, where they were regulated by brickmakers' rules. When task work began, they were quite moderate. By rewards, and promises, prisoners were encouraged to do overwork, and when they had shown that they could do it easily, the task was raised. Take the case of the weaver's shop. At first, the task was thirty-five yards (bagging) a-day. It was a long time before they could get any one to do this. They coaxed, and threatened, and hired, till one did it —then *all must* do it. Next, forty-four yards, by hiring, was done. This was one piece. The task was then six pieces a week, and a reward offered for *seven* pieces. When that was done, it was given as a task—do it, or be punished—and a reward offered for eight. And so on to twelve pieces—Judge B. and McC. solemnly giving their word, from time to time, that they would not go any higher. But word, honor, and every principle of honesty, propriety, or decency, was sacrificed to feed the avaricious desire !

The weavers, trusting their veracity from time to time, continued to do overwork, till the task was raised from thirty-five to one hundred yards a day, which the most could do before night. I could do my task and have Saturday to myself, for reading and writing this book. And after I left the shop, they continued their improvements, till some would weave their six hundred yards by Wednesday and Thursday night.

This is only a specimen of the rope walk, the factory, the hackle house, the cooper's shop, &c. A *few* who were strong, and accustomed to the business, would do a great day's work—then that is the task, and all must do it or be punished—and many poor weakly men have been often punished because they could not do more than they could—or as much as some others. Thus while some can " play" at their business, others are worked far beyond their strength. Some facts would not be believed, and I will not tell them.

THE SICK, THIS SEASON.

Many were taken down with fever and ague, and
other complaints. As many as forty were on the sick
list at once, and O ! what a miserable spectacle did they
present ! Many were driven to work till they could go
no longer. Then they must go before a doctor, who has
not so much feeling for them as for a brute—who will
order them to their work, when they need their bed and
careful nursing—at other times will give them medicine
to *make* them sick—again will refuse to look at, or hear
a word from them, when they come before him, and then
go and tell the officers that there is nothing the matter
with them.

Next, the officers are impatient and fretful every hour
the prisoners are sick, almost ready to command them to
get well and go to work, yet will do nothing to make
them able. In one instance McC. gave orders to a sick
man, " J., you have been sick long enough. I shan't
put up with it any longer, now go to work and get
well !"* Many, many have been driven to work long
before they ought to go, or were able to work. The
consequence was, they had a relapse, and were worse,
perhaps, than before.

Again, they are committed to the care of a fellow prisoner, who is almost as bad as the doctor—ungodly,
hardened, selfish, lazy, having but little concern whether they live or die.

It is not of much consequence what the disease is, the
prescriptions are much alike—generally a heavy dose of
calomel and jalap, or blue mass, or oil, or quinine. A
number of men went to the doctor to have their teeth
pulled, which ached severely—he ordered an *emetic* for
them, and they had to take it ! Other cases might be
given just as absurd. And his dietetic prescriptions are
general, for all alike, whether they can eat the food or
not. For breakfast they have a piece of dry, hard, corn
bread, and a cup of bitter rye coffee ; for dinner, some
dry mush, or potatoes, or potato soup, and dry corn
bread—at times, beef broth ; for supper, the same as for

breakfast. Some extreme and favored cases get now and then a piece of dry, wheat bread, or if they are dying, a little chicken broth! The common complaint is "I can't get anything that I can eat." Generally, nothing suitable or nourishing is provided, and thus they are starved, till they are driven to work again, on their corn bread and fat bacon, which often brings a relapse. And, except in dangerous cases, they are confined to their cells where the air is impure and oppressive, with no one to fan, cheer, or help them. "O, this is exaggeration!" says one. "I speak that I do know, and testify that I have *seen*," and FELT, and yet "the half has not been told you." I cannot portray it fully.

On the 5th of August, James was taken with the chills, fever, and headache. He went to Dr. Moore, who utterly refused to do anything for him. In the course of a week, he was about again. On the 12th, I was taken with the chills. For five days, I was unable to get *any* medicine. And when it did come, I was obliged to get up every hour, for two nights, at the knock of the guard on the door, and take it alone. About this time James was taken again. We had but little to strengthen us— little that a sick man or weak stomach could bear.

On the 26th, Alanson was taken sick, and quit work for a week.

On the 3d of September I was taken again—a shake every day. To get strength on the diet we had, seemed almost impossible. Two weeks I kept still. Towards the last of September, Alanson was again brought to his bed. During this sickness, he succeeded in getting *one* small piece of light bread. Otherwise, the diet was as previously described.

While thus stretched upon our beds of pain and languishing, we had no kind, angel hand to soothe, and administer to our necessities. While one was burning with fever, the others were obliged to be at their work, leaving the sufferer alone with God.

But the Lord made all our bed in our sickness. *Ps.* xli. 1-3. He " stayed his rough wind in the day of his east wind." Whatever we lacked we were assured that we had what was *good*. While food was denied the body, our souls had food they knew not of. The promises were reviving cordials. The heavenly letter was full of consolation, vast and free.

By these trials we learned how to sympathize with the poor—we better understand the heart of a prisoner, and the condition of thousands of the slaves, who in sickness are not treated half so well as we were. We are better prepared to labor for them. O! how little do they suffer from sickness, who are surrounded by kind friends, anxious to make them as comfortable as possible, who have all they can wish or ask for, when compared with a poor prisoner or a slave, who has much to make and keep him sick, and but little to make him well! "Sick, and in prison."

I have been thus particular,

1. That the world may know these things, and if possible, that a change may be effected.

2. That Christians may pray for them.

3. That they may be thankful for the mercies they enjoy.

4. To magnify the grace of God, who stood by and comforted us in all our afflictions.

When we were sick with chills, we generally could read or write every other day; and in this manner I read much, and wrote many of the foregoing pages, when I had to bolster up in my bed. Other parts were written late at night, while others were asleep, and when I much needed to be asleep.

RECOMMITMENTS.

The majority of the prisoners came from St. Louis in gangs, from two to seventeen, with sentences from two to ninety-nine years, on charges of all kinds. Many are not satisfied with one trial, and come again. Since we have been here, four or five have served their time out, gone forth to stealing, and came back again—and some have served out their *second* term, since ours commenced. One man served two years, had the dropsy, just went out with his *life*, went to St. Louis, committed highway rob bery, and was sent back for ten years, having been absent about six weeks. He will probably die here. Many go from here, almost directly to *other* prisons, and from thence to others—thus they spend their lives in the various prisons of the world. We have, and have had them here from nearly all the penitentiaries in the Union, East, West, North, and South. And many have been in two, three, four, penitentiaries, and so on, before they came here. One man spent *twenty-two* years of his life thus, before being sentenced here for six more.

To many, there is no place so *natural* and so much like home as a prison. And I have remarked of a number of new comers, " That man has been in a Penitentiary before." Why? " He acts perfectly *at home.* He knows all about the ways and manners of convicts."

When a *new* one comes " he acts like a cat in a strange garret," as the saying is. He is awkward and confused, and frightened, and disconsolate.

A number are here from New South Wales. They escaped from there on vessels, went to New Zealand, and lived for nine months naked with the natives, till an opportunity offered to come to this country. One lived thus among the natives two years—married a chief's daughter, and had two children. He is a *polished* rogue, very affable in his manners. Thus they go from one place to another. Steal they *will*, for it is the only way they know to get a living—and thieves are *caught*—and prisons are made for thieves. Their sin finds them out, and they find " the way of transgressors is hard—here, and hereafter. Pitiable objects! Yet, this is a place for moulding such characters !

EXTRACT FROM JAMES' LETTER—SEPT. 24, 1844.

DEAR BROTHER :
This is the first I have written with my right hand, since I broke it—and as it is now so stiff that I cannot shut it, I have no hope of ever having the proper use of it again. I can do but very little of anything with it. Looking at the circumstance in a worldly point of view, many

would think it a hard matter to be a cripple all their days, but I do not have a murmuring thought about it—feeling that all that God does is *right* and *well done*. He has a special regard for all his children, and will always do what is for their best good. I feel that dying is nothing. God will do "all things well."

JAMES.

QUIETNESS—EXTRACT OF A LETTER.

" When He giveth quietness, who then *can* make trouble?" There is the quietness of the calm which presages the dreadful *storm*—and there is a quietness of the *soul*, produced by a sense of God's favor, and protection. It arises from a confidence in his goodness, power, and faithfulness to all his promises. It results from an implicit committing of ourselves to his disposal and care. It is a " *quietness*," which all the storms of earth cannot discompose, consisting of " *perfect peace*," of " joy unspeakable and full of glory." O! blessed " *quietness!* "

GEORGE.

THE CHRISTIAN SLAVE.

About the middle of September, a slave was brought here from the city. His crime was this—a suspicion on the part of his master, that he *would* run away. The slave was a Christian. He said to Alanson, " If they sell me South, *the Lord is there*. I don't care where they put me, the Lord is with me from time to time. I am happier here than I was outside. I have a house in heaven, I am bound to believe in Jesus Christ, &c."

The following occurred between him and James : " Do you know whether your master will sell you South ?" He replied, " I do not. I have lived with him fourteen years, and always tried to do well." " Wherever they send you, live for God." " That I am determined to do. Though all forsake me, God is my friend. Send me where they will, they can't take *Him* away from me. He is all the comfort I have." " Can you read ?" " Some." " You must try and improve all you can." " I will—but we have only one book" (among three). " I will lend you a Testament next Sabbath." "I wish you would. I like to read—but above all, I like to look into the holy book of God—that's the best of all." "I would be glad to help you if I could, but it is for trying to help just such a man as *you*, that I am sent here." "I know it," said he, "and there is a *great reward* laid up for you." "It don't matter much," said James, "if we are bound in this world, if we are Christians, and get to heaven, we shall then all be alike and happy—there is *no slavery* there." "I know it. I am sure of that." "I pray for you every day." "I thank you," said he. "I too pray for you all."

What a lesson many Christians may learn from this poor slave! No outward trouble or circumstances could destroy his happiness. And mark how the slaves regard our sufferings. Give me their prayers and blessings rather than the favor of their opulent masters.

On the 19th, the master came in with another man, and asked, "How much do you think you can give me for him?" Who that has human feelings is not shocked at such a question? His master is a professor of religion. See him bartering away for money, a brother in the Lord—one of Christ's "little ones!" Yea, selling CHRIST HIMSELF, according to his own declaration. How similar to Judas' question!

What multitudes are sold and abused who are true Christians, by those who profess to be the same! O! when all these things shall be published at the great, day, what scenes will be exhibited! And yet this is the system that the mass of the Church are countenancing—in which many of her members are engaged, and which many of her watchmen refuse to rebuke and oppose!

Sept. 20. Sabbath morning, the slave came to our cell, and we had a blessed season of conversation and prayer together. O! that prayer! How childlike! How submissive, and truly evangelical! It did us good.

He told his experience, which was very touching, and highly scriptural. It reminded us of some of Bunyan's figures—such as the burden, a view of the cross, and the Savior offering to help. His views of the evil and de-sert of sin were very remarkable. He was evidently taught by the Spirit. "Come life or death, I am fully determined to press on in the narrow way, and never look behind, for there is nothing to look back after. God will be with me everywhere, and if we have Christ we have all. With Him and his love in our souls, the trials and sufferings of earth are nothing. If we lose Him we lose all, and nothing can comfort us. Thank God! I can stand up before ten thousand worlds, and say—'I am born of the Spirit.' I know God hears prayer, and that the prayers of the righteous do avail much (referring to the prayers of an aged slave woman for his conversion). If I get home first, I shall be looking for you, and I hope to strike hands with you there. If you get home first, look out for me, for I am bound to meet you there. I shall be continually scratching that way."

As he shook hands with us, he said, "God bless you all." Two of the converts were present. "Pray for me. I shall remember you. Let us so live that when we get to heaven, we shall be looking for one another." We told him something of what many were doing for the slaves, which animated and cheered his heart. O, how far, *far* superior is he to his rich master. And who would not choose the slave's seat in heaven?

Should slaveholders see us outside, conversing with their slaves, they would be almost horrified, but they can send them here to us.

Sept. 22. The slave left, in chains. Farewell, brother.

Perhaps his master is described in *Zech.* xi. 5.— "Whose possessors slay them, and hold themselves not guilty ; and they that sell them say, 'Blessed be the Lord (very pious), for I am rich.'" (Very thankful.) Oh ! oh ! the abominations of our "peculiar and do-mestic institutions."

Our hearts were deeply affected by this slave's case, because it has come under our own observation ; we saw the Savior in him. But the cases of thousands of others much worse than this, never come to the light. They have no one to cheer and comfort them; no one to heal their wounds, and go with them to the mercy seat. They suffer and groan, they languish and pine, they are bought and sold, they bleed and die alone. "Remember them in bonds, as bound with them."

Oct. 1. Some kind friend sent us a quantity of sweet potatoes—we know not who, but it is evident some one thinks of us.

3. James was directed to stay with a sick man, in his cell, during the day and half the night, till he recovered. He waited on him about a week.

On the same day a master pointed me out to his slave, who stared as if he meant to know how an abolitionist appeared.

9. A company of prisoners working in the back side of the yard, succeeded in getting a hole through the stone wall. That evening was the time to make their exit, but when the leader had advanced nearly through, he saw a number of guns pointed at him, and drew back. Their plan had been discovered, and preparations were made to meet them. A number were severely punished, while the ring-leader went clear. One man received two hundred strokes with the cow-hide, because he would not say he did anything, but only knew of the plan. He was whipped and scarred from the ends of his toes to the crown of his head, and the ends of his fingers; so that when they brought him forth again, they could find no place to strike him that was not already cut! The man would not confess, and was almost killed. "For five months after that, I had running sores on my back," said he to me. For a long time he went nearly double, and could scarcely move about.

The same man was so abused and starved that he was driven to the extremity of cutting off the ears and tails of living hogs, boiling them in a cup with corn, and eating them. For this he was again punished. "How could he get these things?" Very easily. The meat was thronged with hogs, and with a little corn he could easily catch them.

"LIKE SEEKS LIKE."

In the weaver shop, the meanest and worst man of the company was appointed foreman. In the black-smith-shop, the rope-walk, cooper-shop, hackle-house, and factory, the greatest thieves—the most false, dishonest, and evil-disposed men in the prison, are foremen. So did the emperors of old—each one appointed officers according to his own character. " They that work wickedness are set up." Said one of the hands to me, " Thompson, you must be more mean ; then you will soon be foreman again."

Oct. 17. One of the hands had a fit. While with him in his cell, I saw written on the wall, "God hath delivered me to the ungodly, and turned me over into the hands of the wicked." *Job* xvi. 11. I was glad to see that he acknowledged the hand of God in his affliction.

THE UNJUST LAW.

Oct. 27. Our chaplain preached from, " Sin is a re-proach to any people." He said many good things, but did not tell how great a sin slavery is, nor what a re-proach it is to our nation. One remark pleased us much. After laying down the broad ground that any, and all sin is a reproach, he said, " The transgression of an un-just law cannot constitute a man a sinner." We trans-gressed no human law, yet suppose there had been one, as there is now, is not such a law an unjust law, in every sense of the word ? It makes a man an offender who obeys the divine law, to love, do good to, and re-lieve our fellow men. It makes it a crime to " plead for the dumb," " rebuke iniquity," to be " eyes to the blind, and feet to the lame," and ten thousand other things which God requires. What can be more unjust ? Then we are not sinners.

On the next Sabbath he preached his farewell, from " Righteousness exalteth a nation,"—a perfect Fourth o'

July harangue. He said nothing about the debasement of our nation, in consequence of its unrighteous and cruel oppression. Every other sin and iniquity but the greatest, the cherisher and protector of all others, may be rebuked, but touch not " our craft by which we have our" unrighteous " wealth."

NEW CHAPLAIN.

Nov. 10. Our new chaplain preached to us, and as he was not a singer, I was called on to lead the singing. The singers being scattered all over the room, and so many discordant voices uniting, the sound was rather distressing than pleasing. I made application to have all the singers sit together, which was granted. I chose my own singers, who took a front seat, which helped the matter a little. Till I left, I thus led the singing.

A few days after, the chaplain came to me, and said " I am a stranger, and hardly know how to proceed or what to do. I want you to advise me what steps to take." I led him to my cell, where I gave him a history of things, and told him what I thought was his duty. He is a young man, talented, but not at all calculated to preach to prisoners. He don't understand a prisoner's heart. However, he felt fettered, as he said to me one day. He knew the officers did not want him here, and he feels restraint almost as much as we do.

About the middle of November, Alanson and myself were let out, at four or five o'clock, to make a fire in our shops. This was continued all winter, which gave us an opportunity to read considerably in the morning, as well as evening.

DEATHS.

On the morning of the 10th, P. R. died. He had been sick but four or five days. I knew nothing of his sickness till after I was locked in my cell, the night he died. He had been here one year. He was very fond of his children, talked much about, and longed to see them. A short time before this, his little son sent to him, "Pa, you are gone too long." Poor boy! What will he think now? How will his little heart break, to think he can never see Pa again.

Soon another was called away, after being sick one week. He had but five months to stay, would do any-thing to gain the favor of the officers, but neglected to seek God's favor, "which is life," till death took away his spirit, and the doctors his body for dissection.

Three days after, another died, trusting in his own morality.

When I went out, early in the morning, I asked the steward, "How are the sick?" "They are all dead." James had been sitting up with them, and a guard asked him how they were. "The Doctor says they might get well, if they could only have the proper attention paid to them." The guard replied, "Ah! you know that cannot here be obtained." For the want of it, numbers have died.

THE LEGISLATOR.

Nov. 23. The man with whom I have had two con-versations (previously mentioned), called to have an "abolition argument," as he said. His principal topic again, was about the *public opinion* with regard to this or any other evil. "The only true and safe course, is to enlighten the people, and bring public sentiment against it." I answered, "I heartily believe this is the *best* way to do away slavery."

But how, *how*, HOW, is the slaveholding public to be enlightened? If they believe in "enlightening the public," why this fear of the light, and making làws against it? Ah! well do they know that their cause will not bear the light. To "enlighten the people," is just what we want.

A few days after, he came again, with two others, to my loom, and we had a long talk. They asked many questions about the treatment, clothing, work, books, &c. One was strongly in favor of a Sabbath School, and Li-brary. Newspapers, and other religious means, to make the prison a place of reformation. The need of all these

14*

things I strongly urged. Said one, " We expect that
you will tell the *truth* about the institution !"

29. A number of legislators talked with Alanson,
proposing the same old questions, " How do you feel ?"
—" Do you think it was wrong ?" They would not
sign a petition, because he would not " yield the point,
and give up to them." They urged him to " yield, and
not be such an enthusiast—yield for the sake of your
family, and for your own sake." This was touching to
the parent's tender feelings, but the grace of God ena
bled him to stand firm and unyielding.

Afterwards he asked another, " Do you think they
will let me go home to my family ?" He replied, " I am
afraid not. There is too much prejudice yet." Yes,
yes, that's it—cruel, unreasonable *prejudice !*

During the legislature, many of the members were in
to see us.

MONTHLY CONCERT.

Though in prison, we have observed the monthly concert for the oppressed, and have had some cheering seasons. At one time Alanson conversed with a slave,
who came to him to get some work done. He said that
many slaves were running away from St. Louis. Others
brought in the same news. And from other sources we
learned that many were going from other places. This
gave new life to our little concerts. We rejoiced and
took courage.

As a slave was standing by Alanson, he asked,
" Do you know my name." " No." " Do you
know what I am here for?" " I do not." " It is for
trying to help a poor slave." " O ! you are one of the
preachers ! I preaches sometimes. I have been in the
cause five years."

Dec. 1. After preaching, the chaplain came to me and
enquired about the class, and said he would attend to it,
and have it started. But he little knew the opposition
there was to encounter. " On the side of our oppressors there was power."

FIGHTING.

It is a rule, that if two prisoners fight or quarrel, they will certainly be punished. Two fought in the rope-walk. They were led into the guard-room, where were Judge B., Capt. B., and McC., to behold the sport—to witness the diabolical tragedy, which follows.

The prisoners were stripped of coat and shirt—their left hands tied together—a raw hide given to each—and the command, " Now take *satisfaction* out of each other !" It was cut and slash, over the eyes, the head, or the back, where they thought they could get the most " satisfaction," till one cried " enough,'' and they were parted.

In ancient times, they assembled to see wild beasts worry and devour each other ; but in this enlightened age, this Christian country, this place of reformation, official men, can feast themselves, in seeing their own species act the part of wild beasts, and witness with ecstatic delight, scenes which would make an angel weep and put humanity to blush. Under such instructors is it any wonder that villains are multiplied ?

OUR STOVE.

Dec. 10. Alanson obtained permission to have a small sheet-iron furnace in our cell, which made it very comfortable in the coldest weather. How great the blessing ! How agreeable were our mornings and evenings ! How pleasant our Sabbaths, compared with former and latter days ! We kept it through that winter. The next we could get none. It furnished us facilities for reading and writing, we could not have enjoyed in the cold. We praised the Lord for his mercy.

At that sitting of the Legislature, our friends had expected to be present, to intercede for us, but were providentially prevented.

Dec. 22. After sermon, I was called on to pray for the first time since I was turned out of the foremanship. During the remainder of my time, it was the chaplain's custom to call on one of us to pray. And towards the latter part, I had to pray, sing, and line his last hymns for him.

CHRISTMAS HOLIDAY.

The day was given to the prisoners. Our food was extra—light biscuit, roast meat, coffee, sausage, and apples The majority spent the day sporting and carousing as they pleased. We almost imagined ourselves in some large city, when we heard the fiddle, flute, dancing, boxing, wrestling, laughing, hooting, shouting, racing, &c., &c. Col. Price, McC., and the guard, were spectators, and encouraged the sport. The mass were all taken up with the foolishness and wickedness. But in the "hallowed cell," a company of Christians assembled, and we had a reviving prayer meeting. I also wrote a letter for a colored brother to his wife and brother, who are slaves. Increased our temperance signers—talked with the visitors, &c. A citizen came to see us, and said, "Murderers, robbers, thieves, and all villains, can get pardoned out from here before Burr and Thompson. They will stay their time out!" On that day, a man from Quincy arrived with a petition for Alanson, which he circulated among the Legislators

---

CHAPTER IX.

LEGISLATORS—ALANSON'S RELEASE, &c.

SIXTH DEATH-BED SCENE.

Early on the morning of Dec. 16th, I found W. G., our first prison brother, very sick. He was bled—fainted twice, and was taken to the hospital. The next morning James asked him how he felt in his mind. He answered, "I am so sick, I have no mind, I can't think." "Are you willing to leave all in the hands of

God ?" " Yes." " Are you willing to die now ?" " I
am."   We frequently watched with him during the
night, and comforted him with the promises.   I asked,
" Do you feel anxious about your family ?"   " No, I do
not, at all."   We often called on him during the day,
and watched the. feelings of his soul.   He was at all
times, calm and submissive, desiring the will of the
Lord.

The following letter, which I wrote his wife, will give
further particulars :

PENITENTIARY, Jan. 6, 1845.

SISTER G.,
        It devolves upon me to announce to you " heavy
tidings"—yet not of such a nature as to produce despair,
though they cause you to weep and mourn—for you will
not mourn " as those without hope."   Endeavor, then,
to be calm, while I say to you that your beloved husband, W. G., has left this troublesome world of pain and
sorrow, for his *eternal rest*, " at God's right hand, where
are pleasures for evermore."   He had been sick about
three weeks, during which time I frequently conversed
and prayed with him, much to his comfort.   A day or
two ago, we thought he was a getting better, but last
night and to-day he grew worse, and gradually failed,
till near sundown, when he breathed his last.   He
wished me to write to you and tell you his feelings—
exhort you to train the dear children for God, and meet
him in heaven.   In view of death he was composed.
During all his sickness, was willing to die, and felt that
through the cleansing blood and meritorious sacrifice of
Christ, he was prepared to " depart and be with Him."

To-day, I asked, " Do you feel that Jesus is your
Friend ?"   " Yes."   " Will he be with you in the hour
of death ?"   " Yes."   I then repeated to him the promises, and prayed with him.   A few minutes before he
died, I asked, " is the Savior near to you?"   " Yes."
" Are you afraid to die ?"   " No."   " Can you commit
your wife and children to the Lord?"   " Yes."   This
was the last word he spoke.   There can be no doubt of
his happy state.   For more than three years here, his

walk *has* been *unblamable*—so that the most wicked
were compelled to say, "I believe he is a genuine
Christian." Perhaps I knew as much of his *heart*, as
any man, having had sweet fellowship with him for
three years, and I can assure you that his spirit, dispo-
sitions, principles, aims, desires, hopes, were those of a
true, humble, devoted child of God. He was ever fond
of his Bible, and "ready for every good word and work."
I mention these things for your consolation, and the
comfort of his friends."   G. T.

The letter went on to comfort her, but I cannot copy.
A poem, which I composed on the subject of his death,
closes:

> Thus are his toilings, griefs, and sufferings o'er;
> And now, on Canaan's happy, peaceful shore
> He'll see the wisdom, goodness, love of God,
> In all the pains and smartings of the rod;
> And for them all, will praise, adore and love
> With all the blissful company above.
>
> O! happy brother! what a glorious change!
> Here, suffering prisoner—now with Jesus reigns!
> Here, cast out, scorned, disfigured, trodden down—
> Now, honored by Immanuel with a crown!
> From earthly prisons, and from cruel foes,
> To heavenly mansions, and to GOD he goes.

By the man who came from Quincy, we received a
bundle of letters, dried fruit, and clothes. We answered the letters, and wrote a number of others, to send
back by him, but they never were sent. Probably they
fell into the hands of Col. Price.

Jan. 1, 1845. "I enter upon a new year, "not
knowing the things that shall befall me here, save that
the Holy Ghost witnesseth, that bonds and afflictions
abide me." "But none of these things move me."
Let come what will, if GOD come with it, it shall be
welcome. With Him, I have *all*, without Him, *nothing.*"

The last three Sabbaths Alanson spent with us, he
went round to all the cells distributing tracts—"no
man forbidding;" he talked with the prisoners, and

found a general desire to read anything he would give them.

Jan. 15. Judge McBride, and other legislators, came in to see Alanson. The Judge said, " Some friends are making an effort to get you out, and I have come to inquire about your feelings. The Governor says he will do nothing, without a pledge, through us, that you will do so no more." Alanson said, " The act was imprudent, and done without sufficient consideration. I will not do so myself, nor will I encourage others to do the like." " Your wife pledged herself to use her entreaties to get you to go back to Connecticut—if you will do so, you will be *out of the way*, where you *can't* interfere with our rights." " As for going back I do not know about it—I don't know as it will be so that I *can*,—though the entreaties of my wife will have considerable influence. I don't know as I have any property." " I believe you have not—your wife is living on charity." Alanson did not promise to go back to the East.

18. To Capt. Carson and other members, I said— " Can't you do something for me, this winter, to get me out of this place?" " I don't know, Thompson, it is doubtful. There has been much talk about you among the members, and they generally think that the rigor of the law should have its course on you a while longer. It is generally considered that you are the ring-leader and instigator in this affair, because you are the most forward and intelligent." " It is a mistake. In the three indictments, I was only brought in as accessory. Have you heard anything against my character or conduct, since I came here?" " Not a whisper." Another —" Did you belong to those abolitionists in Illinois?" " I was a citizen there, and a member of Mission Institute." He was very fiery—spoke of the " under ground railroad," and the work of the abolitionists—was willing at once to go and fight them, and tear Illinois all to pieces. Another—" It is a pity, a pity, you got into this scrape—have your sentiments changed?" " No sir." Capt. Carson—" Well, I will have further conversation with the members about it."

ALANSON PARDONED.

Jan. 20. Alanson left us. He had been a prisoner
three years, six months, and seven days. We rejoiced
to see him go. It was a general time of rejoicing
among the prisoners, to see "old man Work" go out.

He carried out with him, in his open hand, upwards
of two hundred pages of this work, besides all my journal up to that time. Such was the "good hand of our
God upon us," the officers did not even look to see
what he had ; otherwise, we all should have found trouble a plenty.

My poem on " The Departure of Alanson" closes as
follows—

I.

O, happy Alanson! released from his chains,
  And compassed with spirits akin to his own :
His tongue will break forth in unknown, joyful strains,
  And tell with exulting what Jesus hath done.

II.

The songsters of nature his bosom will cheer,
  And earth's blooming prospects enrapture his sight :
The sound of "the church-going bell" he can hear,
  And view happy throngs with enlivening delight.

II.

Go, go, happy brother, to freedom again,
  The great boon of heaven improve and enjoy.
A little while longer, your partners remain,
  To labor, and suffer—and "count it all joy."

IV.

Farewell, now, dear brother, farewell a few days,
  Though parted in body, we're still joined as one,
For all these afflictions, our Father we'll praise,
  And adore him for ever, around the white throne.

The man who came from Quincy with the petition
was here about four weeks, and his conduct was anything but that of a gentleman. He represented Alanson to the legislators as a " poor, weak-minded man ;"
said " he was over-persuaded and duped into it by the
others, who were more crafty, and deserved their punishment." " Weak-minded !" Would that he had a quar-

ter of the mind that Alanson has.   And when he came, a year after, he told the same story about James—representing him as having no mind, and myself as the "crafty" one—telling things directly contrary to what he said a year previous.   These things I had from an ungodly legislator, who heard both stories, and who despised his wicked conduct.   He also lavishly spent hundreds of hard earned dollars, where there was no need.

THE ARTICLE OF PARDON—ALIAS, BANISHMENT.

THE STATE OE MISSOURI,

To all who shall see these presents: GREETING.

Know ye, that by virtue of authority in me vested by law, and for good and sufficient reasons appearing, I, JOHN C. EDWARDS, Governor of the State of Missouri, do hereby pardon Alanson Work, who was, on the ——— day of October, in the year of our Lord one thousand eight hundred and forty one, by judgment of the circuit court of Marion County, committed to the Penitentiary of said State, for the space of twelve years, for the crime of stealing negro slaves, in this State.   And I do hereby restore and entitle the said Alanson Work to all the rights, privileges, and immunities, which by law, attach to, and result from, the operation of these presents —*on the express condition,* however, that said Work returns to the State of Connecticut, his former residence, with his wife and children, and settles himself there.   In testimony whereof, I have hereunto set my hand and caused to be affixed the great seal of the State of Missouri.   Done at the city of Jefferson, this, twentieth day of January, in the year of our Lord one thousand eight hundred and forty five, of the independence of the United States, the sixty ninth, and of this State, the twenty-fifth.

By the Governor, JOHN C. EDWARDS.
JAMES L. MINER, Secretary of State.

This is like giving the slaves the privileges of the freemen of the United States, if they will go to Africa! And who ever heard before of a Governor having power to banish a person from States other than his own? Well, it is just like SLAVERY.

A LETTER FROM ALANSON.

When the pardon was handed to me the conditions were not pointed out or mentioned, and I came out of the prison without knowing that the condition was in it. Capt. Swartout was present when the pardon was given to me and we came out together. After we had started, he told me he had put the name of John Smith on the way bill, instead of Alanson Work. Abernethy, the State's Attorney* rode thirty miles in the stage with us. He did not know me. Where we stopped for dinner, he began—"Have you been to Jefferson city?" "I have." "Were you acquainted with Thompson, Burr, and Work?" "Yes, I had some acquaintance with them." "Did you go into the penitentiary to see them?" "Yes, I went in there." He then said, " I am sorry for them. They have staid there long enough. They ought to be turned out." He told Swartout he wanted to make some acknowledgments to me, but assured him he did no more on our trial than the law compelled him to do.†

Some months after Alanson left, a citizen, by the name of Chase, came in and said to James, " I have had a letter from Work, at Poughkeepsie. He said, ' if you ever get out, you must never think of a *nigger* again, for I am thoroughly convinced, that the course we pursued, was wrong, unconstitutional, and against God, an: man.' I think Burr, will get out before long, bu Thompson is so head-strong, I believe he will have to stay his whole time out, unless he talks differently from what he said to me. I would not sign a petition for him."

Work never said any such thing,‡ but this man tried

* Our Prosecuting Attorney.
† It is false. He did do more.
‡ Since writing the above, I have received a letter from Alanson. He says, "I have written but one letter to Mr. C., and that one was written from Mission Institute, soon after my return to my family. That I should write what Mr. C. says I did, is too inconsistent to be believed by anybody who knows as you do, that we should have been released two or three years sooner, if we had only bowed to them enough to say we had done wrong.

"Now, if I would not say that, when, by so doing, the prison doors would have been opened to me, think you I would, when I had clean escaped the lion's den, and was restored to my family? That I would, when many hundred miles from the power of slaveholders, voluntarily

his ingenuity to deceive, frighten, and get me to re
nounce my principles.

At one time, he came in, and began, " Well, Thompson, they have played the mischief with the abolitionists
in Cincinnati. They have tarred and feathered Birney,"
&c. I made some plain remarks, and he replied, " If
that is the way you talk, you will stay every day of your
time." Again, he said, " They have driven the abolitionists from Quincy—whipped some, mobbed others,
and they have all left, o: will leave soon—and if you
were there, they would hang you right up."

And again, he came to me, " Thompson, will you sign
a paper, for ever renouncing Abolitionism, and all connexion with it—never to advocate it in any way, but
assist in putting it down? On these conditions, you can
now be got out!"

I have no comments—but will only remark, he was
known as a man who regarded not the *truth*, who had an
inveterate hatred against Abolitionists, and yet *professed*
to be our *friend!*

A MAN MURDERED.

Jan. 24. A prisoner died—insensible to the last.
For a week or more, he had been crazy, having fits, and
in great pains most of the time—yet the doctor said,
" *nothing was the matter with him!*" He begged for
medicine, but could not get it! At night, he was locked
in his cell with his sickly cell-mate, without any light,
where he frequently had fits! I hesitate not to say, he
was MURDERED!

On the same day, Capt. Gorden came to be our overseer, to whom the principal management of the prisoners was committed.

A FUNERAL SERMON.

Jan. 26. The chaplain preached the funeral sermon
of W. G., mentioned in the last " death-bed scene." It

make the concession they required! No, dear brother, you will not believe it. No, I did not write to Mr. C. from P. at all, much less say
what he says I did. " ALANSON WORK."

was the first and the last thing of the kind, known in the prison, while I was there.

Jan. 29.   Another man died about the middle of the afternoon, and was buried that evening, I knew not of his sickness, till I heard of his death.

THE COLPORTEUR.

Feb. 4.   A dear brother called to get some work done —inquired us out, and left some American Messengers —a Christian Almanac, and some precious tracts, which were a rich feast to our souls.   On the 22d of December, he called again, conversed, and left tracts, almanac, &c. . On the 26th, he came in with a basket of books and tracts, distributed around to the prisoners, and gave me what books and tracts I desired—also a bundle of American Messengers.   The Lord bless and reward the brother for seeking out those who are " sick, and in pri-son"—for administering to the wants of the suffering, and despised.   We followed him with our prayers.

THE GREAT CROSS.

A slave came to me and said, " Do you pray yet ?" " Yes, I shall do that, as long as I live." He replied, " When you are praying for all others in the world, re-member poor *me*.   I want you to pray that the Lord wil' take me under His feet, and keep me there till the storm is over.   Your brother has a great cross to bear, and it is just as much as he can do to wag under it."   Truly the poor slaves have " a great cross" to bear, and all their toils, and sufferings, and reproaches, are " just as much as they can wag under."   Lord, hide them beneath thy wings, till the " storm is over."   Reader, will you help the slave bear his " great cross ?"

Feb. 24.   I was, at my request, placed in the wagon-shop, where I remained till my release—thankful for the opportunity of adding to my knowledge, preparatory to the work of a missionary.

THE TEMPERANCE LECTURER.

Feb. 27.   A man came in to collect facts respecting

intemperance.   He went round to each one with many
enquiries.   He asked me the cause of my confinement.
I replied, " My *benevolence* brought me here."   " Abolitionism ?"   " Yes sir."   James said, " My kindness to
all men, brought me here."   The man replied, " It was
unfortunate for you.   Some of the Abolitionists carry
their points a little too far.   There are Abolitionists
here (in Missouri), but they don't go so far," &c.

PRAYER WITH THE PRISONERS.

March 2.   The chaplain did not come.   I was permitted to sing and pray with all the prisoners, who had
assembled for preaching.   The same privilege, I frequently enjoyed after that time, when the chaplain failed
to come.   Sometimes Capt. G., and sometimes a guard
requested me thus to sing and pray with them.   After
preaching, either James or myself, were generally called
on, by the chaplain, to pray.
March 13.   I worked on the ware-house, at the river,
where I narrowly escaped, with my life.   The scaffold,
under which I was at work fell, and struck me on the
head.   It was very providential that I was not killed.

DID HE " LOVE LIBERTY ?"

J. A. was a slave in Virginia.   He resolved to buy
himself.   For two years he saved what he could by odd
jobs, and working Sundays, saving a little here and there,
as he could get a few cents for the object.   His master
moved to Missouri.   Here he bought his time for twelve
dollars a month—excepting that during two summers he
paid one dollar a day.   All he could earn over was his
own.   He worked *eight years*, and gave $650, for him-
self.   To this add what he paid for his time—about
$1250,00 beside the two years, yea, and all his former
life in Virginia, and what a price !   Ten years he toiled
for what he didn't love, did he ?   " Can't take care of
themselves !"   Try it.   Let a poor, ignorant pale face
beat it.   In addition he earned nearly enough to buy his
wife.   He has here been converted, and is a lovely
Christian.   I have written to his wife, and have read a

number of letters from her. She thinks she would be
"better satisfied" to belong to her husband than to
another man. Who would not? She talks like a good
Christian. I had intended to insert some of her letters,
which I have, but my space will not permit.

SABBATH WORKING.

From the time that McC. came as overseer, the Sab
bath began again to be desecrated, and its profanations
increased till he left. By officers and prisoners it was
contemned and trodden down. Capt. G. came with
great pretensions to reformation. He told one and another that it was wrong to work on the Sabbath, and pretended to disallow it saying, " We want no man to work
on the Sabbath, but to read their Bibles and Testaments.
If you had read your Bibles more, probably you would
not have been here." Read the Bible!—and one half
of the prisoners had no Bible, no Testament, or any
other good book. " Want no men to work on the Sabbath!"—and the very man to whom he spoke these
words, a short time after, was compelled to work all the
Sabbath day, time and again! For the last year the
most prominent record in my journal, is their awful Sabbath breaking. It has been amazing. I began to keep
an account of the names of those who worked on Sunday, what they did, and by whom ordered out, and continued it for a few months; but it was too tedious to record all their abominations, and too shocking for
the mind to dwell upon. It is one continued scene of
noise, pounding, hallooing, bedlam, and confusion, as
soon as the Sabbath returned!
The blacksmith's hammer was heard nearly every
Sabbath. In the carpenter's shop work was common
on the Lord's Day. The Sabbath was the day that the
guards, Mrs. Brown, and others took, to *hire* the prisoners, for a trifling sum, to work for *them*. In the brick
yard, in the hemp, in hog killing, many were hired, and
others compelled to work on the Sabbath. If any of the
machinery broke or was out of order, it was repaired
on the Sabbath. And many times when they have thus

stolen God's time, to save the time of a few hands, has He visited them with heavy judgments; yet they would not regard it. Often when we have been thus annoyed by the wickedness around us, has our prayer been, " The Lord require it," and his hand has fallen heavily upon them. We complained to the inspectors. They said, " it is a breach of their contract, and by so doing they forfeit their claim to the place." But nothing was done —Sabbath desecration continued.

, O ! how often have our souls longed for some quiet retreat, some grove or desert, the closet and the sanctuary, the stillness of a country Sabbath, and the communion of Saints. But Jesus stood by, and comforted us, taught us to prize these blessings, and to sympathize with those who are deprived of them.

April 4. For some weeks a protracted meeting in town had been in operation, and all classes were numbered among the converts—to what I shall not attempt to say.

JAMES AND A SLAVE.

James asked, " What are they doing in town ?" The slave replied, " Some are trying to pray." " Are you helping them ?" " I have to pray for myself." " Do you not pray for those who will not pray for themselves ?" " I pray for *them,* any how." " How many times a day do you pray ?" " I have not counted. How many times do you pray ?" " As often as I can get the opportunity." " Well, then, you must *pray all the time.*"

Another prisoner, " What does that mean ?—' Pray without ceasing.' " James replied, " Always be in a praying mood." " That ain't the place," said the slave, " where it says, ' Pray in season and out of season'— that means to pray when you feel like it and when you don't feel like it—when you have the Spirit, and when you don't have the Spirit."

At another time the slave said, " Seventy-five have joined the church. God knows whether they are Christians, and they may know whether they have the Spirit,

and are born of God." Shame on many gospel-en-
lightened professors, who sneer at the idea of *assurance*
in the Christian life. Let this poor, despised slave, teach
them purer theology.

CHAPTER X.

VARIOUS INCIDENTS.

THE CHAPLAIN DRIVEN AWAY.

April 6. Our chaplain had been so much engaged in
the meeting in town, that he did not come for a number
of weeks—and then, as soon as he made the last prayer,
Capt. Gorden drove him away, without suffering him to
pronounce the benediction—to prevent his speaking to
any of the prisoners, as had been his custom after
preaching? I exhorted the chaplain not to submit to it,
and he afterwards pronounced the benediction,* but was
obliged by Capt. G., to leave before the prisoners were
dismissed—so that we had no opportunity to speak to
him, except as he sometimes came in on business, and
very rarely at such times—for Capt. G. would cling to
him, till he saw him again out of the gate. At one time
James and myself were talking with him a few moments
—Captain G. saw us, came and drove James away, and
led the chaplain to the gate! Why this? They were
afraid we would expose their awful abominations, and
used all their efforts to prevent our communicating with
citizens—but they could not—we *did*, and I now *must*
bring out their wickedness to the world. The *law*
grants to the Chaplain, the privilege of talking with
prisoners as much as he desires, but what is law to

---

* He was once driven away before the benediction, after Capt. G.'s
conversion.

Captain G.? He has ruled over men, so long, he can tread it down with impunity—and such are the men placed over *outlaws*, to teach them obedience to law! Every desire or effort to reform was crushed by Captain G., but notwithstanding all his contempt and opposition, the Lord gave us souls.

THE CONVERTED SAILOR.

T. F. was from his youth a seaman, and spent many years on board an English " man of war." He had visited nearly all parts of the world, and told us many things of different nations. The last few years had been spent on the " Western waters," where he " drank freely," became intoxicated, and killed the mate of the boat. He was tried in St. Louis, and sent here for ten years—staid about seven. He was very profane, and ignorant of Bible truth. I conversed with him, and lent him many of our books—his eyes were opened, and the Lord blessed the truth. He ceased swearing and reproved the sin in others. He commenced praying, and talked with his fellows about the nreasonableness of revenge—the folly of a dishonest life, and the importance of religion.

Said he, " I pray every day, night and morning. I sit up and read sermons till the others are in bed, and asleep, then I blow out the light (which he had secretly), kneel down and pray,—confess my sins to God, and ask Him to *show* me my sins, that I may repent, and put them away—not from fear of punishment, but because they are offensive to God." I had frequent conversations with him, and we prayed together. He was very fond of the truth, and drank it in like water. The Missionary Herald he read with great eagerness, and would sit up till midnight to read one through. It was reviving to our souls to see him *grow*, and strengthen, and shine. The evidence of his conversion was cheering. Soon after the change, he was pardoned out: we prayed together in his cell, then with James, and another brother in ours, and bade him farewell.

SICKNESS—TREATMENT.

April 7. I was taken with the ague; and shortly after, James also. We had it at different periods, for more than three months—sometimes one, and then both at a time. A rehearsal of all the particulars of the sick, during this summer, would not only defile my pages, but be a disgraceful and indelible blot on humanity. At times, James and I had a little light bread, &c.; and then again, for days we have lain upon our bed, too weak and faint to walk or sit—without having a mouthful brought us to eat. When able to walk about, we sometimes, by hard begging, obtained a few potatoes, or some small article of nourishment; but when the system was once run down, it was with much difficulty that strength could be regained. When able to sit up, our time was spent in reading or writing, which added much to our comfort. During this summer, about sixty of the prisoners were sick at one time with ague and scurvy, and their treatment was inhuman. Men, with limbs swollen, stiff and blotched with scurvy, were driven to work till they could no longer walk—others were neglected till their teeth seemed ready to drop out of their mouths, and their flesh became almost putrid. The sight was awful! If they went to Judge B. with their complaints, they were turned off with " O you live so high, you are all getting the *gout*," or some other contemptuous remark. One, who was almost starved, asked him for something to eat. He replied, " I have given the Steward some flour, and you will probably get some of that ; if that won't do, *you may go sick !*" The man got one small biscuit ! many got none. The doctor gave strict orders that no sick man should have a mouthful to eat, but one third of a pint of coffee three times a day, and that I could not drink. One who had the ague, said " I have had seven shakes, and have not had *any* medicine." Another, who had been for months in the Hospital, and beheld the treatment, said, " If the Almighty *has* anything to do with human events, I should expect that he would trouble Judge B.,* for the manner in which he has treated the sick here. Some who had been sick and expected to die every hour, could not get a little nourishment, when a picayune's† worth would have saved their lives!"

Doubtless this is true, in a number of instances. On one occasion, the Doctor said, " I do not care much if they (the sick), do starve to death." He probably spoke the truth—for his actions corresponded.

Said the Steward, "I am not allowed to give the sick any thing to eat; and yet the officers are mad and complaining because we do not get strong and go to work! As I spoke to Judge B., he said, " O you can shake any time—I suppose you intend to have another shake to-day!" One who was dying said to me, " They have treated me outrageously and inhumanly." Every word is true, One man complained to Captain G., that he was sick, and could not weave—he took him into the guard-room, gave him twenty lashes, and made him work. Such is the medicine some get. These are a few specimens—I might fill a volume with accounts of these abominations, but the Judgment will reveal them.

SLAVEHOLDERS CONVERTED.

April 19. The chaplain came to my cell and talked sometime—gave me an account of the revival in town— said that Captain *Gorden* was one of the converts, and would shout as loud as any one! About ninety were converted, embracing the oldest and most influential men in the place—our *Doctor* (*!*) and some desperate tyrants among the number. The news filled us with joy, but we watched for the *fruits* of a slaveholder's revival. For a time Captain G. did seem a little different, but he soon became as bad, and worse than before—exhibiting more of his contrariness, cruelty, and opposition to all good, than when he was Warden !

The Doctor, if anything, was more hard-hearted than

* His little boy, a favorite, sickened and died very suddenly.
† 6 1-4 cents.

ever! And slave-holders continued to crush their
bleeding victims! Before Capt. G. was *converted*, he
manifested respect for us, but it was after his pretensions
to *religion*, that he treated us with contempt, and seemed
to delight in vexing and crossing us, all he could.

And it was after the conversion of some of the " influential" men, that they could come and labor to have
me renounce my sentiments!

May 12. A. G. B. died—a young boy, sent here for
life, for killing his father—had been here two and a
half years—belonged to my "class," before it was
broken up, and was very exemplary in his conduct.

SEVENTH DEATH-BED SCENE.

J. H. M. had long been sickly, and unable to work.
He was greatly abused and so starved because he could
not work, that he was reduced to a skeleton, and became
unable to move about. Upon his sick and death bed, I
conversed with him—gave him dried apples, and tried
to do him good. " Can you forgive them for their ill
treatment of you?" said I. "I have no hard feelings
towards any one, for any thing done to me. Once I
used to take it to heart, but now I do not care anything
about it." " Do you think you shall live?" "I can't
without a great change. I do not dread the sting of
death at all." " The best of us have no merits of heaven.
All have sinned and need the merits and mercy of
Christ, before they can enter there." "Yes, George, I
have been sensible of that for two or three days." I
gave him such counsel as he needed, when the bell rang,
and I had to leave. Taking him by the hand, I said,
" Farewell, perhaps we shall next meet in eternity."
He replied, " Farewell, George. I hope to meet you in
a better world." He soon died.

April 30. J. J., who had long been sick, died. His
whole mind was taken up with thoughts of liberty, and
plans for the future. Thoughts of death and judgment,
ne put far away, even while the monster stood before the
door. He had but eight days of his time to stay, when

it was suddenly cut short, and he was called to exchange
this, for the prison of eternal gloom!

THE EIGHTH DEATH BED.

L. was from Connecticut—and one who had often re-
sisted the grace of God. He died with consumption. I
frequently conversed with him. At one time he said,
" God is just, and justice is all I want. In his hands I
am safe." We were called to sit up with him. Just
before his death, I asked, " Do you feel willing to die ?"
" If I could, I would rather see my family again—but if
I must die, why I must. I have no control over such
matters." " Do you feel prepared to die ?" He looked
up with an expression of wonder, that I should ask such
a question, and with a sneer said, " Why, I can't do
anything to prepare for death. You know what my
sentiments are." As he was willing to stand or fall, on
the ground of justice, God took him at his word—but on
such terms can no flesh be justified. Poor man ! How
little did he understand of the guilt of sin, and the purity
and extent of God's laws ! And here is the delusion of
many souls. Sin is supposed to be but a little thing, and
God's law of but little account—similar to the laws of
mortals !

BIBLES ! BIBLES !

For more than two years we plead with ministers, inspectors, and legislators, to have the place supplied with
Bibles. In May the chaplain was deputed to purchase
a quantity in St. Louis, and on the 3d of June a box of
one hundred and fifty was brought in, and distributed to
all who wished for one. They were received with great
eagerness, by those who had been so long without any
book. To us it was a joyful sight, and our sinking
hopes were a little revived. We blessed the Lord for
this new token of his love.

June. 8. Two strangers preached and exhorted—a
large company of spectators in. While I prayed, one
of the ministers wept aloud. To hear a despised convict pray, was a new thing to him and to many others,

who came in on the Sabbath, apparently on purpose to see and hear us pray.

10. While we were at breakfast, two men were found attempting to scale the wall by means of a rope. They were severely punished. Numbers have dug through the wall, out of their cells, at night, but before they could get over the wall, have been observed by the guard and suffered the consequences.

15. The chaplain formed a Bible class, which took the place of preaching for some months. It was then given up, but few engaging in it.

TEMPERANCE PLEDGE.

While sitting up with James, one night, in the hospital, I drew up a temperance pledge, describing the effects of intoxicating drinks, and promising to " touch not, taste not, handle not." As we had opportunity, we obtained signatures, to the number of seventy-six—of whom thirty-four confessed that liquor was the cause of their trouble. An opportunity to circulate the pledge would have added many names. The object was to secure them against future temptation. Of their drinking in the prison there was not much danger. One man, who ran away, and was brought back after about two years, said to me, " Had I not signed the pledge, here, I should have been drunk fifty times, but I thought how I had promised before God and the holy angels, not to touch it, and I stuck to it and drank none."

I also drew up an anti-tobacco pledge, but it did not thrive much—yet it saved some from the vortex of pollution. In the pledge, I spoke of looking to Jesus, to subdue the desire for it. One said, " I never knew before that I was such a slave to it. I have often tried to quit, but never till now sought the help of Jesus, and it is no wonder that I failed. I feel assured that he will give me the victory." In one week the desire was all gone.

In two months he gave me the following. " For two years I used snuff. My nose became a trumpet and I quit it. began to smoke. I thought it made me look big, and was soon a slave. To appease the craving desire, I took to chewing. I knew it was injurious, but persisted in the use of it for eight years. By the grace of God, I was enabled lately to abandon it; and can now be a judge of its baneful effects. In two months since I quit, I have increased in weight twelve pounds, and in strength twenty per cent. I am not now molested with heart burn as formerly, nor troubled with drowsiness and unaccountable dullness of spirits. My nerves are not continually fluttering as formerly, my stomach is now always in good order, my mind clear and vigorous. In short I am now better and happier than I ever was, with my longest pipe, or my best ' honey dew.' "

June 28. Said a man to-day, " If I had my cell full of gold, I would give it for liberty again !" Ah! what has the ungodly man here to comfort him? They " are like the troubled sea."

July 4. The afternoon was given to us as a holiday. While the most of the prisoners were carousing, wrestling, boxing, and racing, we collected the Christians in our cell, and had a precious prayer meeting. All prayed and expressed their determination to cleave to God. It was a very sweet, refreshing season. The Lord blessed us abundantly.

CAPT. GORDEN'S HUMANITY !

The wife of a prisoner came nearly twenty-one hundred miles, with two children, to see her husband. Capt. G. said to him, " What do you want to see your wife for? You can have *ten minutes*, by the watch, to talk with her. You must not say one word about what brought you here, or about getting out." He sent a guard with a watch to hear the conversation. For more than three years they had not seen each other, and at first meeting were so overcome, that they could say but little in ten minutes. She went to the Governor, who sent her back, with orders to let them talk together, as much as they desired, and they did so.

At another time a wife came to see her husband, and Capt. G. said to him, " Your wife has come to see you,

—she is foolish for so doing, and you can have *five minutes*, to talk with her."

Why such inhumanity! These two men had been faithful, and worked hard. I assign but one reason. Capt. G. is a slaveholder, and by familiarity with scenes and acts of cruelty, his heart has become steeled, and unfeeling—a natural tendency of slavery.

Judge Brown, in general, was more humane, in this respect. He would let friends who came a long distance to see a father, husband, son, or brother in prison, see and converse with them.

EXTRACT OF A LETTER.

July 15, 1845.

DEAR BROTHER E.:

I have scarcely seen the day since early in the Spring that I could say, "I am well" (in body.) And now I have to lie upon my bed to write. However, I feel happy in committing myself to God; crying at all times, "Father, glorify Thy name." Those who are surrounded by health, wealth, liberty, friends, honors, &c., can know but little of what they realize, who are poor, forsaken, insulted, in prison, sick, languid, faint, and surrounded by all that is vile and odious. The former find no difficulty in trusting God, for what they already abundantly enjoy—the latter know and experience from day to day the blessedness of trusting in God, and to the world they can unhesitatingly testify to the power of Religion, to support and cheer, when all earthly supports fail and wither away.

Those in adversity drink immediately from the *fountain-head* of all comfort and joy—while those in prosperity, drink of the *streams* which are generally mingled with numerous earthly ingredients. Hence, the benefit of affliction. O, let us not "despise the chastening of the Lord," nor be "weary of his correction."

GEORGE.

"ABOLITION NIGGERS."

July 21. James was appointed servant-general of

the prison. His business was to wait on the officers,
keep the guard-room in order, light lamps in the halls
and around the yard, &c. He served two weeks, was
taken sick again, and another took his place. What
little he did the rest of his time, was winding bobbins
for the weavers.

While he was " servant," three runaway slaves, were
brought here in chains, for safe-keeping. Said Capt. G.
to James, "These are *abolition* niggers." "What!
were they trying to 'abolition' themselves?" "Yes, that's
it." These slaves were waited on, by James, who talked and prayed with them. He asked one, " Well, you
were running away, were you?" "O, no, I was only
going to see my wife in Kentucky." Again he asked,
" Can you read?" One replied, " I can. I had a testament with me in the *woods*, but a white man took it
away from me, and I've not seen it since!" He then
talked some time with them, and gave them a testament.
They frequently came to our cell, to talk through the little door, while we " enlightened their minds." Many
other prisoners encouraged them to try again; and
they said they were determined to keep trying, till they
had " liberty or death." When they left, in chains, to
to go south, they were furnished, by a blacksmith, with
instruments to cut their irons.

The sight of the " slave trader," filled my soul with
feelings which I cannot, in words, express. Heaven !
in mercy stay thy judgments !

THE UNFORTUNATE FAMILY.

A young man came for stealing—staid till his brother
came, and ran away. After a time two other brothers
came—soon, the old gray headed father, who acknowledged he had killed men, came and shortly after, the
younger, a lad of fifteen, joined them. The old lady
was in jail, and expected to come, but was liberated
again.

Aug. 13. Talked with a prisoner about studying the
Bible. He said, " I want no more to do with the Bible.
I have read it through twenty-two times, and it never
15*

did me any good." He confessed it was his own fau.t.
How many professing Christians have read it as much?

We talked with them a long time about many things
—a little must suffice. Stringfellow said to James, "I
have no sympathy for abolitionists. They are worse
than thieves, robbers, or murderers; and doing more
evil than all united." Gen. Monroe—"The slaves
running away, is but little. Those who help them off
are not the men who do the mischief—they are only the
tools of the great men. But those who *write* and *speak*
much on the subject, are the ones who do the mischief
They even endanger the Union. No one wants to hold
you here, but there is a *principle* concerned in it—if
you are pardoned out it will take off the restraint which
we wish to lay on others, and encourage them to do the
same."

Stringfellow —"Well, Burr, you are charged with
helping your neighbor—would you not think it as bad
for a man to persuade your apprentice away, as to steal
your money? James—"It would be wrong, but I do
not consider the slave as property, or bound." "Well,
if we let you go, you will do so again." "I will leave
the State, and not trouble you again." "It is a mighty
few abolitionists, that will be reformed in so short a
time." (four years.)

Many of the prisoners interceded with them to use
their influence for their liberation—and upon their recommendation, without any petitions, six were pardoned at once—three of them, murderers—one an old coun-
terfeiter—one an incendiary, and the other a horse racer.

" NOT THIS MAN BUT BARRABAS."

Soon after we came here, an old man, a murderer,
was pardoned, because of his money, by Gov. Reynolds.

A petition came for Alanson—in answering which
Gov. Reynolds came out strongly against the too free
use of the *pardoning power*. Then soon after, A. G.
who had wilfully and deliberately shot a man, and was
sent here for ten years, was pardoned after staying about
six months.

Next, E. H. who wilfully shot a man, and declared to me he would do the same thing again, was pardoned. He was first sentenced to be hung—then for twenty years in this place—then for ten—staid five and half and left, again engaging in drinking and gambling.

A. H. was accessory to a wilful murder—first sentenced to be hung—then to this place for life—then his time reduced to ten years—then pardoned at the expiration of five and a half years.

D., a Dutchman, killed a man—was sent here for two years—staid a few months and was pardoned by Gov. Reynolds.

S. H. deliberately shot a man, and declared to me he would do it again—was sent here for forty-nine years—staid two and a half and was released by Gov. Marmaduke.

J. G. charged with murdering his wife—sent here for ten years—staid five, and was pardoned by Gov. Marmaduke.

M., a woman, killed her husband with an axe—was sent here for five years—staid about half of it and was pardoned by Governor Edwards.

U., an old man, killed his neighbor—staid here a few weeks and was turned out.

J. P. shot a man for calling him a liar (and a greater one can scarcely walk the earth), staid about two years, and was set at liberty, declaring he would do the same thing again.

R. stabbed and then shot a man—came here for seven years—staid four years and three months, and was released.

T. shot his neighbor without a cause, in cool blood—sent here for fifteen years—staid nearly five and was pardoned.

W. G. stabbed his neighbor to death—sent here for fifteen years—staid five, and was pardoned.

T . F. stabbed a man in a fit of intoxication—came for ten years—staid seven, and was pardoned.

W. J. engaged in house breaking and shooting a woman, was sent here for ninety-four years—has the promise of being, and expects soon to be turned out (after staying about five years), by Gov. Edwards! Besides a host of thieves, gamblers, whoremongers, burglers, &c., who have been pardoned by the forementioned Governors! So partial did the Executives manifest themselves to murderers, that it passed into a proverb among the prisoners, " A murderer can get pardoned out soon er and easier than those charged with any other crime, though they may be innocent!" " If you wish to get pardoned out quick, commit murder," &c. Such a pub lic sentiment does slavery foster!

Sept. 2. Pope G. was in, with whom I talked. " Do you hear anything said about letting me go from this place?" "O yes, Thompson, I hear a good deal said about you." " Anything about letting me go soon?" " Why, people outside think you do *not wish* to get out." " Well I shall not fret about it either way, and if I could see that I was doing good to my fellows, I should not care for my release." " I think they should let Burr go at least, as he is a cripple, has a broken constitution, and can't do much. I suppose he can't earn his salt now."

Sept. 21. Capt. G. and prisoners at work (Sabbath). We were also annoyed by pounding, bawling from cell to cell, and dancing. I complained to Capt. G. He paid no attention to it. In the afternoon, James and myself were singing, when a new, ignorant guard came along, looked in, his face flushed with anger, and said, " Do you know you are breaking the rules?" " We do not know it." " Well, I'll help you to know it. I'll have no fuss or loud talking here. What are your names?" " Burr and Thompson." He shut both doors in a great rage. We continued our singing; knowing what we were about, and had no " fuss."

25. I asked a slave, " When are you going to be free?" " After I am dead." This is the poor slave's hope.

THE SLAVE'S HOPE.

I.

From this sore bondage I then shall be *free*,
 After I'm dead—after I'm dead.
Rest in the *grave*, there remains yet for me,
 After I'm dead—after I'm dead.
Here, I expect still to suffer and toil,
And with my heart's blood to fatten the soil ·
But oh ! I shall *rest*, from this world of turmoil
 After I'm dead—after I'm dead.

II.

ı shall be free from the tyrant's strong hand,
 After I'm dead—after I'm dead.
Nor trembling hear his loud threat'ning command,
 After I'm dead—after I'm dead.
Now, they may bind me, and beat when they please,
Press me with burdens which give me no ease;
No more, as their victim, on me shall they seize,
 After I'm dead—after I'm dead.

III.

I shall be free from their scorn and contempt,
 After I'm dead—after I'm dead.
They to their malice may give a free vent,
 After I'm dead—after I'm dead.
Far from their power, I then shall abide,
Safe from their envy—secure from their pride ;
And soon, in the dust, they will lie by my side,
 After I'm dead—after I'm dead.

IV.

I shall be FREE ! O, the rapturous name !
 After I'm dead—after I'm dead.
Free from my shackles, and all mortals' claim,
 After I'm dead—after I'm dead.
And my dear Savior I hope soon to see,
Who gave His life as a ransom for me,
That I, in his kingdom, might ever be FREE,
 After I'm dead—after I'm dead.

Penitentiary, Sept, 25, 1845.

Toward the last of September, James was sick again with ague—took much medicine.

At that time, I composed an address to the Governor in poetry, which he received kindly, and showed to numbers who came to see him. I have not room, or the reader should have the address. Here follows a short extract—

O, may I go? Can'st you my pardon grant?
Ten thousand thousand will your kindness thank.
Others have been released—O! why not I
Or must I here remain and droop and die? ·
A brother and companion on my charge
Has been restored to liberty at large,
For which a thousand thanks to heaven ascend,
And shall in blessings on your head descend;
And thousands more, with prayers for you shall rise
As sweet and grateful incense to the skies,
If a poor captive's prayer shall reach your heart,
And draw the word from you, "In peace depart."

I am a Christian, Sir, and Christ my Lord,
Will bless with vast and infinite reward,
The man, who to his suffering subject shows
Compassion, and relief from heavy woes.

In view of our relationship as *men*,
Which should all sinful prejudice condemn;
In view of prayers, and tears, and many sighs,
Which daily to Jehovah's throne arise;
In view of millions sinking down to hell,
Whose suff'rings mortal lips can never tell;
In view of time, which soon will be no more,
But waft us to a distant, unknown shore;
In view of Death, which hastens on apace,
To usher us before the Judge's face;
In view of that great, final, reckoning day,
When we shall hear him to his children say—
"Come near, ye blessed, and sit down with me
On thrones prepared from all eternity"—
But to the wicked, "Hence, accursed, depart!—
With Satan and his angels have your part;"
In view of heaven, where angels prostrate fall,
With saints confessing Jesus Lord of all,
Where endless pleasures do for ever roll,
And full fruition fills up every soul;
In view of vast eternity to come,
Which fixes our unchanging, future doom;
In view of all; I ask once more the same,
And plead for mercy in my Savior's name;
Commending you to his all gracious care,
That you may hear and grant my earnest prayer

Sept. 29. The Methodist minister from St. Louis preached for us. The next day he went, in company with our chaplain and others, to see the Governor in our behalf. Towards evening they called to see us— spoke very kindly—felt much—saw my address—said, " You will get out after a while, be patient. The *weather is setting that way !*"

Oct. 1. Two more were pardoned out, and I was appointed to supply the place of one of them, in carrying around bread at night, to one quarter of the prisoners. By this arrangement, we had better suppers. I continued so to do for nine months, till I left.

15. A young man was pardoned, who went to the Governor to plead for us. The Governor said, " I will attend to their case, and turn them out just as soon as I can consistently." Public opinion was his guide. During this month, James was sick much of the time, with bilious complaints. I began to gain strength to labor.

A CASE OF CRUELTY.

Two prisoners dug through the cell wall, unlocked another cell, and let out two others, intending to scale the outside wall. They were discovered, and terribly punished immediately. Some who celled near by, said, they " never heard such hot times in the guard-room before." Others said they heard " much whipping and loud cries," and while they were whipping one, they heard Bradbury say, " Now get up." " I can't Mr. B." He then whipped him again, " Now get up, or I'll kill you." " Judge Brown, do stop Mr. B. I can't get up." " Then *drag* him to his cell." And as he was crawling to a cell near by, he was heard, " Do stop, Mr. Davis. I am going as fast as I can." He probably was kicking him along. In the morning, Capt. G. came to me and said, " Go there into the hall, pick up S., and carry him to his cell, he has the *backache.*" Backache! O, what hard-heartedness! But this is slavery! He was lying on the bricks, in great pain, and almost as helpless as a man with his back broken. We carried him to his cell, where he remained a considerable time before he could get out.

Nov. 8. One who has lived South, said to James, "I have seen planters sit down, each *bet a nigger*, and gamble for them!" Can the history of heathenism furnish its equal? And yet who can doubt it? Is it not "just like" slavery, thus to *demonize* the master, while it *brutalizes* the slave !

On the same day, J. F., a former overseer, was in, with whom I spoke, He said, "I have heard nothing against you—nothing against your conduct here. I know no reason why you should not go out as well as Work. If one, all—for all are equally guilty. I don't think they can require any more than that you shall not do so again. I should rather have seen you go out, than some who have been pardoned, who will be curses to society."

21. James went to the quarry, with the hands, for his health. A rock burst from the effects of the fire. A guard said to James, "I am glad you came out here with us. You have the Bible, and therefore good Providence protected us from being hurt.

For a number of days he went outside, and was greatly benefited.

VISIT FROM FRIENDS.

On the 22d, W. M. and M. C. arrived at our mansion. It was Saturday evening, and we talked with them, before a guard-room full.

On Sabbath afternoon, they came to our cell, where we conversed, and prayed, and sang, till night, without restraint. From them we learned much about the state of the anti-slavery cause, and of the world. It was unspeakably sweet, thus to fellowship together once more. Why were we so favored above other prisoners, when their friends come to see them? My only answer is, "It was the good hand of God upon us," constraining 'the enemy to entreat us well in the day of evil.' "

On Monday they conversed with the Governor, who promised that he would turn us out, if they would send a petition from Marion county, from whence we were sent. He said, " They have been punished enough, and if I should act according to my own feelings, I would turn them out; but I am the servant of the people." In the evening, they came to the cell, and brought dried fruit, crackers, dried beef, sugar, honey, apples, Missionary Heralds, Union Missionaries, writing paper, &c.

That night, I spent mostly writing and preparing things to send home by them. In the morning, again talked and prayed with them, and gave them *just what I pleased*—no officer asking, "What have you there ?" They saw the *box* and the *bundle*, but said nothing. Who can deny the *restraining* hand of God? This treatment is to be attributed, under God, to Judge Brown —as also all the kind treatment of all our friends when they came. "Give God the glory." In every instance, where we were *fearful*, the Lord in great mercy rebuked our unbelief, not with the rod, as we deserved, but by far exceeding our expectations and granting us unexpected privileges. O! "how great is his goodness!" As is his power, so is his mercy to his little ones.

But the best wine was reserved till after they were gone. In reading the Missionary Heralds, but especially the Union Missionaries, our souls feasted. My journal says, "Such emotions as fill my soul, I cannot express. We both have to shout glory ! glory ! glory to God! read and rejoice—read and shout—read and thank the Lord for such a new era in the history of missions—for such a noble coming out from the abominations of slavery. O! how we have prayed here in prison, for a *purging* of the church in this thing. Glory to God for such intelligence."

In the Heralds we visited nearly all parts of the world, rejoiced, and wept with the missionaries—heard the converts sing—saw the idols destroyed—the darkness flee, and the light spread abroad. Like John Baptist, though we were in prison, we heard of the wonderful works of God. We quickly pass from Mendi to Guinea, Gaboon, Natal, Ceylon, Bombay, Madura, Siam, China, Palestine, Turkey, The Islands, the Rocky Mountains,

Red Lake, from tribe to tribe—from nation to nation—
from continent to continent, and round the world we go
—hasten back to our "hallowed cell," and lift up our
prayer for the Holy Spirit to be poured upon them.

SLAVEHOLDERS' CHRISTIANITY.

Nov. 30. Our Chaplain, before all the prisoners,
called Captain G., "Brother Gorden!!" The most
abased prisoner among us, saw the inconsistency of such
an appellation, and many made their remarks upon it.

But I suppose the chaplain did not know as much
about his "*Brother*" as we did—for on that very Sab
bath, he had been at work all day, with a number of
hands. However, perhaps this is as much as can be
expected fiom a slaveholding religion. It does not
require them to give up their sins—their *greatest* sins.
They can hold slaves, break the Sabbath, oppress, be
covetous, commit adultery, lie, steal, murder, and still
be good members of the church! *I know it to be so.*

ENOUGH TO EAT—DUCKING.

Dec. 3. Captain G. whipped a man for cooking a
little, which was very common. At the table he forbid
any man's cooking, and said, "If any one does not get
enough to eat, come to me, and he shall have it." The
next day, one went to him, and asked for more—he
took him into the guard-room and *ducked* him for it—
and that is the "enough to eat," he got!

The ducking apparatus is a large armed chair, in
which the sufferer is tied, hand and foot, so that he cannot move. Then there is a box which fits close round
the neck below, and open at the top, into which they
pour a bason or pail full of water, directly into the man's
face. Not being able to avoid the water, he is strangled,
choked, and almost killed. It is said to be very severe.
It was an invention of McChesney, our former overseer,
v to was a perfect inquisitor.

THE NEW PREACHER.

Jan. 7. A fellow prisoner, who served two years

here, preached to us. He had been to the Pacific—was converted, turned preacher, came back, and solicited his fellows to make their peace with God. He was ignorant, but zealous, and his sermon produced more effect on officers and prisoners, than all the sermons we had heard for years. Hard hearts melted, and eyes which had not wept for twenty years, were then moistened.

Such a shake of the hand as he gave us, we had not received in Missouri. He knew not how to let us go; and as he left, he said, " We'll soon be released from earth—we'll soon meet in heaven."

THE NEW PRISONER.

Jan. 9. A new prisoner came, with whom I conversed. His feelings were tender, and he wept freely. He said, " I hope it will be for my good. My old mother is a widow, and she has prayed for me, thousands and thousands of times [weeping]. I will never do so again. I am resolved to serve the Lord the rest of my days." " Do you pray?" " Yes, I have prayed, day and night, [weeping], ever since I was convicted, and am determined to continue. I wish to know my duty. I desire that all here may come to Jesus," &c. I told him of his trials, and gave him counsel. He *did* continue to pray.

Many when they first come are very tender, and open to the truth. Proper officers and treatment, would save them, but they are neglected, mingle with the desperate, become hardened and prepared for all evil.

CHAPTER X.

PETITION—STATE SECRETARY—JAMES PARDONED.

ANOTHER INTERESTING CASE.

Dec. 12. I conversed with a man who said " I believe my coming here is the best thing that ever happened to me. I have been a very bad man, for twelve or

fifteen years back--not hurting others, but myself--I
have been my worst enemy. I am now determined it
shall be my whole effort, desire, and study to serve God.
There is no other object worthy of man. It is what he
was created and placed here for. As for the riches and
honors of the world, I care no more about them than
about the dust on which I tread." He left in ten days
after.

Such cases were very reviving to our hearts, amid the
dense darkness.

Jan. 18. We took to our cell, the tinner's furnace,
with coals. As I sat looking in my atlas, James complained of his heart beating very hard, fainted, and fell
into my lap. With my foot I knocked on the door, and
called a guard; he came with the steward, and brought
medicine. After they left, he had another spasm,
and fell back on the bed—soon vomited profusely—I
had the headache all the night. Such being the effect
of our fire, we concluded to go without, and endure the
cold.

Towards the last of December, I worked evenings,
packing pork. Thousands of hogs were here killed, the
most of the feet of which we had to eat.

Jan. 4, 1846, we observed as a day of fasting and
prayer, for our own benefit, and the conversion of the
world. In the forenoon, we " remembered" Jesus in
his own ordinance, and sang hymns which I prepared
for the occasion. The afternoon was devoted to singing
and praying for the church, the boards, the missionaries,
and the world—and we longed to be in the field.

THE CATHOLIC CHRISTIAN.

A man sent here for ninety-nine years, for murder,
said to me, as I was questioning him, " I learnt all my
prayers when I was a little boy, and keep them yet. I
have not learned any new ones. I was born in the
Catholic Church, and I will *die* in it. I don't swear
much—a little sometimes, and I pray every Sunday,"
&c. Poor man!

There are many Catholics here, and generally they

are very strict to pray—every day, or at least, on Sundays—but they will get angry, swear, break the Sabbath, &c. The priest came to see them, brought books, went through his ceremonies, and *they* could have the sacrament administered to them, while *protestants* plead in vain for a minister to come, and break unto them the sacred emblems!

During the winter, when we could not keep warm by wrapping our blankets around us, we covered up in bed, so that we could read. I fixed our lamp, so that we could go to bed, and read evenings.

20. We obtained permission to have a young man cell with us, that we might do him good. Said Judge B., " If you can make him any better, I have no objection." He was with us one night—prayed, and talked well. But the next day Capt. G. took him away, and put a small boy with us, who had just come, saying, " Take this boy and teach him better morals." He remained with us about a week, when I hurt my back, and not having room in our bed, he left.

About this time, we lived in considerable suspense, having heard that Swartout had been here a month, with a large petition from Marion Co. We expected the Governor would do as he promised, but he did not. Numbers spoke to us, saying, " You will go out in a few days." We endeavored to be prepared, and then left it all with the Lord.

This was the time Chase came, and wished me to sign a renunciation of my principles, for my liberty! I talked with Judge B. " Can you do it ?" " I cannot." " Well, do not make any such pledge, unless you feel it, and can live up to it. If you should renounce, Chase, probably, would turn right round, and call you a *hypocrite*, &c. I am willing you should go out. As to your conduct and Burr's, it is known outside, as well as it is in here. I think they can make no such requirement," &c.

Penitentiary, Jan. 21, 1846·

Dear Sir :

Is an American citizen, in this day of light and liberty, to be imprisoned, because he *thinks* differently from others?　And has he not the lawful right to *express* those thoughts, without fear of incarceration?　Then is it in accordance with the spirit of our free government, to continue to *hold* a man in prison, till he shall renounce his peculiar sentiments?

Suppose, sir, the Whig party should gain the ascendency, and put you in prison, for advocating Democracy —and at the end of four and a half years, should gravely ask you if you would renounce those principles for your freedom!　Would you not reject such a proposition with disdain, and rather choose your dungeon?　Are such arguments calculated to change a man's sentiments?　But have my private sentiments anything to do with the matter of releasement?

If, in this free country, and under laws which secure to every man, the freedom of thought and speech, a man is to be imprisoned, or held in prison, because he does not think as some others do, we may as well, at once, adopt the ancient, Papal mode—incarcerate, torture, and burn all who differ from the party in ascendency!　If I have broken the laws of a state, can more be required of me, as a condition of pardon, than that I should keep, and honor those laws in future?　Or, if I could not conscientiously *comply* with them, that I leave the State, and no more interfere with them?　Such I will do.

Can more be required of me?　Should not every man of reason and humanity be satisfied?

GEORGE THOMPSON.

THE SECRETARY OF STATE—COL. MARTIN.

Jan. 26.　The above named person came to see us. " I came to have a free, candid talk with you, and I want you to answer as in the presence of the Deity. I am very much prejudiced against abolitionists.　I am a southerner—live in a slave State, and hold slaves. I came of my own accord to know your feelings.　What is the object of the Abolition Society—general emancipation?"　" Yes sir—by moral suasion, light, and arguments.　They disapprove of carnal means, except some "*hot-heads*," who are for fighting—there is a great difference between them." "What are your views?" "Slavery is wrong, and all lawful means should be used to put it away, as soon as possible." "If you were released, and, in a meeting, should be called upon for an expression of your feelings, what would you tell them?" "I would tell them honestly, and *correct their prejudices.*"

Other conversation occurred, not important to be mentioned. He asked James nearly the same questions, and others in addition. "If you were free now, what could you do?" "I would get into a free State as quick as possible, and stay there." "But that is not enough—we don't care so much about the *locomotive*, as we do the *influence*. It is the *principle* that does the mischief." "What I did, was in kindness to the black man—he plead so hard." "I don't doubt that there are a great many abolitionists who are actuated by the purest motives." "I will leave the State, and will persuade my friends not to do as I did." *

What right had they thus to pry into our private sentiments, and lead us to break the laws of Missouri, which forbid the expression of such principles? The right was the *might*, in order to find some pretence for detaining us still longer! If, then, our enemies were at any time deceived by ambiguous answers (we always spoke the *truth*), we say to them as Paul said on a certain occasion, "*Ye have compelled us.*" We told as little as they would let us tell, till our tongues should be loosed and unfettered.

If they considered us *thieves*, would they care nothing about the *locomotive?* So long as a thief keeps away from them, they have nothing to fear. The reader can carry out the reflections, and make the application.

JAMES PARDONED.

Jan. 30. In the forenoon James was suddenly snatched from me, leaving me alone—and yet not alone, for

* That is, not to go into a slave State for slaves.

Jesus was with me. He was ready—took out with him all his papers, but expecting to go myself, I had made no arrangement for him to take mine, though I had but little, having sent them away from time to time.

His pardon is similar to Alanson's, except that it is without conditions. I rejoiced to see him go. All the prisoners were glad to see "old Burr," as they called him, go out to enjoy liberty again.

DEPARTURE OF JAMES—EXTRACT.

I.

First one, now the other has left
My partners in gladness and woe:
Of all kindred spirits bereft,
For comfort to whom shall I go ?
There's none here my burdens can share,
To whom I can open my heart—
They pity, and wonder, and stare,
But none understandeth my smart.

II.

But glory to God and the Lamb !
With freedom to Him I can go :
My case He doth well understand,
And each secret feeling doth know.
To Him I'll unburthen my soul,
For He will sweet comfort afford ;
And while the high waves o'er me roll,
I humbly will trust in the Lord.

III

A pris'ner, they long may retain—
With locks, bolts, and bars, keep secure
This body—in torturing pain,
While reason, or life shall endure.
They cannot, no *cannot* they bind,
What God has created so *free*—
The spirit immortal—*the mind*—
A slave it disdaineth to be.

IV.

From dungeons it sallies abroad,
And visits earth's far distant shores,
Surveys the creation of God,
And earth, seas, and planets, explores--

From Arctic to Antarctic flies,
Where mortals did never yet tread—
From West, to behold the sun rise,
And view the life-giving beams spread

V

It enters the churches so fair,
Where saints in devotion are bow'd.
And joins in importunate prayer,
Or harmonic praises aloud.
It hastes to the lovely fireside,
Where kindred and friends gather round;
Or far where the heathen abides,
And Heralds in labors abound.

VI.

It soars to the heavenly throne,
Where angels and saints join in praise;
Views pleasures to mortals unknown,
And glory that never decays—
Holds converse with Jesus the King,
And infinite blessings receives—
Returns to the *dungeon* to bring
Sweet comfort to him that believes.

VII.

Then bind me with chains, hand and foot —
My body with burdens crush down—
Or deep in foul dungeons be put,
And all men with enmity frown—
Yet let it to all men be told—
To all who with sorrows are bow'd,
In *every condition*, I hold,
In spirit, *communion with God.*

Penitentiary, January 31, 1846.

The Lord showed me that an arm of flesh was short,
and I sank into his arms, submissive to his will. I had
some inexpressibly sweet seasons, alone in my cell,
pouring out my whole heart before the Lord. He quieted my soul in himself; I believed and was happy. I
felt that he had wise reasons for detaining me, and very
soon he showed me those reasons, and I blessed Him
that I did not go out. I soon found that my work was
not done in the penitentiary—but more of this shortly.
I am not certain that the officers did not use their influ-

ence to keep me, for the day after James left, two valua
ble hands ran away.

NEW CELL MATE.

Feb. 1. A very wicked man was put in with me—
one who had run away many times, and caused them
much trouble. I went to Captain G., and requested an
exchange, but he would not listen, saying, "I put him
there to keep him from giving me trouble."

This was the first time I had been locked up with one
who had no fear of God before him, and I sought wisdom
and grace from above. But I soon found him a very
quiet man, willing that I should go on as usual with my
devotions. He listened while I read, and kneeled in
time of prayer. Being very anxious to learn to read, I
gave him instruction. And as he was one who would
keep a secret till he died, and despised a traitor, I went
on without fear, with my writings and plans, as when
James was with me. The change in his feelings was
wonderful and rapid. He had been a thief for seven
years, and before he came to my cell, was studying and
dreaming day and night about getting away and being
taken. But these feelings soon left him, and he could
sleep soundly all night. He frequently expressed himself as fully determined to live an honest life—became
reconciled to his lot—was very much engaged in his
book—and said he despised nothing so much as thieves
—to his mind they had become loathsome. He had
many questions to ask about religion. I have hope for
him.

THE SLAVE'S REQUEST.

Soon after James left, a slave, with whom I had long
been acquainted, came to me, and was very urgent that
I should write him a free paper. "I am about to leave
this place, and want a favor." I told him that I could
not do such a thing. He entreated. Said I, "Try
without." "I shall be caught." I told him where he
would find friends. And when I made his case known
to a wicked fellow prisoner, he said, "Do you have

nothing to do with it. I'll attend to him." He wrote for the slave a " pass," and gave him all needful instruction. Whether he succeeded I cannot tell.

HOGS OUT.

Feb. 10. By order of the inspectors, the hogs were all turned out of the yard. For nearly four and a half years, we have lived in a hog-pen, disagreeable, filthy, and abominable. We made complaints to the inspectors, but till now, our requests had been unheeded ! From twenty to forty, and even to two, four, and five hundred of these filthy, condemned, and abominable creatures have associated, fed, and slept, in the same pen and building, which one hundred and fifty prisoners occupied. Well, it is just like slavery.

TALK WITH MR. STRINGFELLOW, THE STATE'S ATTORNEY.

" I am very much prejudiced against abolitionists, and have no sympathy for you. If you had done it *out of rascality, I would have felt for you,* but you had no personal interest in view, and such meddling I despise. Or if it had been some poor, ignorant, foolish fellow, I could have sympathy ; but you are a sensible man, and I have no sympathy for you. Work and Burr were represented by Swartout as weak men, having little mind, and led into it by you. I would not believe you if you said you gave up your principles. You feel as you did before, and if free, would you not turn round and say that such laws (as make men property, and imprison men for helping slaves), are not laws ? Do you not feel towards the niggers as always?" " I feel that they are men." " And have as good a right to be free as any body ?" " Yes, by all lawful means. But I would leave the continent." " Yes, and go right among the niggers, which shows that your feelings towards them are not changed. I saw one of your letters." " But I would go to instruct them, as any other heathen." " They are good for nothing but slaves—they never could, and never can take care of themselves. I cannot promise to do anything for you," &c.

No comment is needed. In addition, I heard from him more oaths and profanity than I had heard in a long time from the most depraved convict.

Again, to prove the truth of his assertion, he used his influence, and plead one hour for the release of one who "did it out of rascality"—who stole two slaves, sold them, and pocketed the money. For him, he had sympathy. Reader, put this down as a fair specimen of Missouri justice.

14. Judge B. said to me, "I think you will have to stay till next Legislature. I don't think the Governor will take the responsibility (!) without a heavy petition.* I told him, as to my part, I was perfectly willing you should go, and can do no more. Take it patiently—the time will soon run round." A prisoner who came about this time, and knew something about public sentiment, said, "All they are keeping Thompson here for, is because he will not give up his sentiments."

I have mentioned that one of Lovejoy's murderers is here—I have also had two other prisoners confess to me, that they were engaged in destroying Pennsylvania Hall—one of them was a ring-leader,—here for seven years.

TWO MORE CONVERTS.

After preaching, Feb. 22, two persons came forward and professed to give their hearts to God. Here, again, was work for me in which I rejoiced. Both talked well, and expressed themselves as strongly determined to serve the Lord. With one of them I frequently prayed. The evidence of a genuine change was cheering. They met with many sneers, but bore them patiently. I endeavored to instruct and strengthen them.

CRUELTY.

A man was whipped by Capt. G., first with a stick, then with a cow-hide, and then with the strap, because

---

* The petition which took James out, was for both of us, and was a "heavy petition," as Judge B., the inspectors, and others testified.

he would not do what he could not—beam a chain in fifteen minutes. It cannot be done with such chains as we generally get. I know something about it. " Will you do it ?" " I can't, if you should kill me." " Well, I'll kill you if you don't," &c. A slaveholding Christian !

THE LAST CONVERT.

After James left, I become acquainted with a young Scotchman, who seemed very steady, industrious, and quite intelligent. As I was always looking out for *singers*, he was recommended to me by some who sat near him in meeting, and heard him, as a good singer. I sought opportunities to converse with him—found him open and frank, and desirous of Christian instruction. Learning the state of his mind, I selected books suitable to his case, and lent to him—which he read with attention and earnestness. The Lord blessed the truth, and soon he was " sitting at the feet of Jesus, clothed and in his right mind." He adopted the words of Harlan Page, " Resolved, that I will, the Lord being my helper, think, speak, and act, as an individual—for as such I must live—as such I must die, stand before God and be damned, or saved for ever. I have been waiting for others. I must act, as if I was the only one to act, and wait no longer." He said, " Although I feel for you, being here, yet I am glad to have such a one to whom I can unbosom my feelings. I hate sin. I long to cease from sin." " The profanity of my cell-mates, often breaks in like an intruder on my best thoughts," &c. I should be glad to give the correspondence that took place between us, on blank leaves, sand-paper, and boards, but my limits forbid.

I asked the Lord to let him cell with me—he went to Captain G., trembling lest he should be refused, but the Lord touched his heart. The Scotchman was not familiar with many of our tunes, and this he urged as one reason why he desired to cell with me—that he might learn my tunes, and be able to sing in meeting. Capt. G. consented, on one condition, namely, that I should furnish bed clothing ! (which I gladly did). But how mean and unjust! By law, they are bound to provide these things, and yet it is not enough that I furnish my own,—I must also furnish for others, and for those, too, who are *forced* upon me! (my wicked cell-mate). But I was thankful that I was able, by the blessing of God, to furnish a bed for myself and others too, in a penitentiary. As J. A. came into the cell, he said "I feel as if I had been set at liberty." I found him truly converted—humble, teachable, prayerful, studious, conscientious, faithful, and desirous of knowing his whole duty. Again I enjoyed the luxury of social reading, singing, and prayer.

Our Sabbaths were delightful. His heart entered right into all my feelings, and circumstances, and principles, so that we were one. We took great comfort in singing. He was anxious to learn all the tunes he could, before I should be snatched away.

Many of our evenings were spent, in composing poetic dialogues—each composing his part. Much of our conversation was in poetry. His outward deportment commended him to the consciences of officers and prisoners—being faithful in all that was appointed him.

Our hearts became united, like those of David and Jonathan—and now, he seems as near to me as an own brother. Having "begotten him in my bonds," my soul yearns over him.

O! how often has my whole being blessed the Lord that he did not let me go with James! What would have become of these precious souls? Soon after J. A. came to cell with me, he remarked "I am bound to acknowledge the hand of God, in my affliction, and in coming into this cell. I remember the words you spoke to me, when I was sawing—to consider why God contended with me—I thought of it all night, reviewed my life, and saw my state. I had entirely forgotten God, and it is for my good that I am here." He renounced all sin—liquor, tobacco, &c., and was a happy man.

March 3. I urged the chaplain to stay, after preaching, converse and do good. Said he, "Yes, but there are so many *gag-laws*, here, I know not when I should run foul of them." He lacked courage.

March 16. Said a slave to a prisoner, in my hearing, "I have a much harder master than you have, and I would not stay here five minutes, if I had any way to escape." How "contented and happy!" Poor fellow.

March 18. A prisoner who had been an overseer in the South, told me the following. A tyrannical overseer took his place and undertook to whip Harry, an old slave preacher. Harry ran, and went to C., about two hundred miles, and told him his circumstances. He took two horses and carried Harry to a tribe of Indians. Some years after he went there and saw Harry, who was preaching to the Indians. They thought every thing of their preacher, and would not part with him on any account.

May such fugitives be greatly multiplied. Amen.

March 21. Talked with the new inspector. He is very kind—said, "As for my part I wish you was out—you have been here long enough. I believe you are an honest, virtuous man, and have a large circle of virtuous friends. I wish you was out. I will speak for you to the Governor," &c. Such language was not common.

March 24. The southern overseer told me that selling *unborn children* was common in the South! Price from one hundred, to one hundred and fifty dollars!!!

March 29. A slave said to a prisoner, "I would be mighty willing to serve seven years here, and work hard for my liberty, and so would the most of all that ever I knew." Another slave made the same remark to one of my cell-mates. O! what a horrid insult to human nature, is it to say that the "slaves are contented and happy!" Lord, spare such blasphemers!

April 12. At the table on Sabbath morning, Capt. G. gave out, "I now give from eight to ten o'clock for all who wish to wash or clean their cells!" And O! what confusion and noise—bu some sweet was mingled with the bitter. In this time I collected the lambs with some of the impenitent, and had a precious prayer meeting.. The Lord blessed our souls.

April 15.   A slave came to me for directions to liberty—said " One word from you is better than gold." I value the " blessing of those ready to perish."

April 20. A petition was presented to Judge B. with eighty-five names, that I might preach to them when no minister was here.   Nothing was heard from it.

About this time Capt. G. for some cause, very earnestly desired to glut his cruelty by punishing me—as he had never enjoyed that sweet privilege. He watched my steps, as a wolf would watch for a lamb, but God encircled and shielded me from all his devices, cast back upon him all his false charges, and brought me through the battle unhurt.

April 27.   At the table, Capt. G. said, " I have requested—I have advised you not to talk, and now I say you *shan't* talk, in your cell or out. I'll punish for every offence. There shall be no *singing* or whistling in the cells."   We sang and prayed as usual—no man daring " to molest, or make us afraid." And as to talking, they may as well try to roll back the Niagara, as to stop talking, while the prisoners work and cell together as they do.

THE LAST COMMUNION SEASON.

May 3.   I broke the sacred emblems to my beloved " son, in the Lord."   It was sweet to feed the lamb— and cheering to see him renew his strength, and burn with more ardent love.   It was a precious season to him. We desired others to be present, but Capt. G. sneeringly refused.   Said J. A., " I now feel doubly united to you as a brother in Christ."

After dinner, others came, and we had a melting season of prayer and praise.

MISS DIX.

15. The modern Howard, in feminine gender, made us a visit.   She first went round with the officers, but she had been in prisons enough to know that the truth could

not be obtained from *them*, and she talked with the prisoners, who opened the abominations before her.   I had a long, familiar, and very interesting talk with her.   She was bold, affable, and sympathizing.   She asked a great many questions, to which I gave answers.   An officer came to me, and said, "There is a lady here, who has been visiting all the prisons in the United States, and trying to alleviate the sufferings of prisoners.   She wishes to talk with you."   We talked as much as we desired.   I addressed a short poem to her, but saw her not, afterwards.

18.   The guard forgot to lock our cell, at night.   I waited till bed time, and, as I had a wicked man with me, for " safe-keeping," I went down, in the dark, and called a guard to perform his duty.

About this time, Capt. G., on two Sabbath mornings made all the prisoners go into the new building, for one hour, where they ran, jumped, scuffled, and carried on as if it were a fourth of July—the guards joining with them, and Capt. G. looking on !   A *reformer !*   He will meet all these things at the solemn judgment.

23.   Talked with a sick convert.   He said, "I feel just as I wished to feel."   "How?"   "Perfectly resigned to the will of my Maker.   Heretofore, death was a terror to me.   I prayed that God would give me to view it in its true light ; and as I was reading "Saints' Rest," (eightieth page), and thinking on death, I found *peace*, and now I am willing to die here, or where my Maker sees best.   I felt as if I wanted to tell you.   Tell J. ' &c.

24.   We were much annoyed, by the ringing shouts of warriors, and their friends, cheering them to the work of murder !   Strange Sabbath work ! !

26.   Saw an account of Torrey's death—composed some verses on the subject.   I insert two verses.

I.

Our brother died—'ut 'twas the victor's death,
  Who in his fall, his greatest conquest won ;
And more accomplished with his dying breath,
  Than he in all his life before had done.
The shock was felt throughout the oppressor's camp—
It cooled their zeal, and did their courage damp.

II.

Rage on ye haughty tyrants of our land—
  Crush down the poor and needy, in the dust—
But know the day of vengeance is at hand,
  When you shall feel th' Almighty's withering thrust
In untold depths of woe to sink you down,
While bright shall shine the objects of your frown.

CHAPTER XII.

RELEASE—PARTING REFLECTIONS, &c.

THE AGED FATHER'S VISIT TO HIS SON IN PRISON.

May. 28. My old father came to see me, and labor
for my release. When I was first brought into his presence, the *father* overcame him, and he wept, unable to
speak. I said, " Weep not, father, ' it is the Lord, let
Him do what seemeth Him good.' " His mind became
composed, and we conversed together, some time. The
next day, we again conversed alone, and in the presence
of Judge B. Speaking of giving up my principles, the
judge said, " It is like requiring a man not to eat," &c.
He talked well. At that time, I learned that it was my
letter to the Governor, and my talk with the Secretary,
that kept me here. For such a cause, I glory to stay.
A number, speaking to father of the letter said, " If
those are his sentiments still, I will *oppose* him—but if
he renounces them, I will *help* him." I did *not* renounce a particle. For nearly a week, I talked with my
father every day—each saying what we desired. He
was allowed, during his whole stay, of four weeks, to
come and talk alone with me, just when he chose. On
the Sabbath, he was with me, in my cell—where we
once more united our voices in prayer and praise. O!
delightful moments!

I learned that great numbers of petitions, from free
States, had been sent here for us, couched in denuncia-

tory language, calculated to exasperate the minds of slaveholders—and in addition, that the Governor had been obliged to pay postage on them, to the amount of *three hundred dollars !* Now, while I am confident that the Lord will overrule the whole for the advancement of His cause, I must say, that in this thing—burdening the Governor with the postage on *business* communications —my abolition friends acted very unwisely, and contrary to all acknowledged rules of propriety. And, while there can be no doubt that such petitions delayed my liberation, I bless the Lord that they were sent. If we were *thieves*, the Missourians must have seen we had a large company of warm allies—and that what *they* considered a *crime*, was, by a large part of the nation, looked upon as a *virtuous act.*

June 7. Learned that people outside are afraid of my pen, if I should be liberated; and that it is possible I may be required to give a *pledge* not to use it against them. No such pledge was required—and sooner than give it, I would lay down my life.

The chaplain said to father, "I don't know how I could get along without George." But I left one to fill my place—a worthy Christian.

June 10. Said a prisoner to Judge B., "Judge, I wish you would permit George to preach once before I go away?" "Before you go away?" "Yes." " I would if I thought it would do any good." "I think it would." "Well I'll let him." He said, and did not.

Said father, "They look upon you as a *Christian*— though in error." And for this " error," they have long kept a "Christian" in prison!

June 11. Father came in with the chaplain and Tho. Miller—Judge B. present. "George," said father, "tell these men how you feel respecting the act that brought you here." " I would not do the same thing again; and I would try and deter others from doing as I did. The step was rash and imprudent."

Chaplain—"You unqualifiedly *regret* it, and will never do so again?" "I will never do so again."

Miller—" You will deter others from it ?" " Rest assured of that, if I have any influence."*

I promised to deter others from so doing. I have done so in public and in private—and I now again warn every reader against doing *as we did.* They now have laws against it—not that it is wrong to break those laws —they are not worth a straw—they are *not laws*, nor is there the least obligation to observe them—but—keep on. *free* soil.

June 13. The inspectors came, and introduced to me the Lieutenant Governor, who was acting in Gov. Edwards absence. He asked some questions similar to those already given—was kind, and threw his influence in my favor.

June 14. For the last time, I collected the lambs, and had another prayer meeting. It was a blessed, reviving season. Beloved, sweet, " hallowed cell !" Just before I left, numbers of the influential men of Jefferson, said, " It is inconsistent and absurd to require him, or any man, to give up private sentiments in such a case—it is something we have nothing to do with." When they found they could not keep me any longer, I suppose they desired to smooth the matter over as well as possible. But it came too late. The contrary fact is too notorious, and cannot be denied.

June 18. I was taken with ague again, and continued sick till I left on the twenty-fourth.

The Governor returned, after a long absence—found most of the people in favor of turning me out—and he sent my " *diploma*," which is similar to Alanson's. except

---

* Let it be remembered, that when I said I would not do so again— that I would deter others, &c., I did not confess to them that I did morally *wrong*. This I never acknowledged, though they tried hard to have me do so. The only reason, then, why I would not do so again, and why I would deter others from going to a slave State, *as we did*, is the same that would keep me from running into a lion's mouth, with my eyes open— the same that would keep you from thrusting yourself into the midst of a pack of wolves to rescue a poor lamb—the same that kept Christ from casting Himself down from the pinnacle of the temple. He who acts *presumptuously*, need not expect the protection of heaven. Before my capture, I knew nothing of the danger—now I know it, and knowing it, it would be wrong to do the same again. Am I right ?

that there are no conditions expressed. My father was
treated very kindly by all. The Secretary Martin, and
State's Attorney Stringfellow, refused to favor, though
they promised not to oppose. The *father's grey hairs*
excited sympathy, and his presence touched hearts, that
other means had failed to move.

Our library, bedding, under clothes, &c., I left for the
good of my fellow sufferers, who were rejoiced to see
me restored again to liberty.

After I had faithfully labored so long, I was turned
away with some old clothing, which scarcely covered
my nakedness till I got home. I believe this was the
case with Alanson and James. And it has been so with
many.

That evening the Governor came to see me, and
clasped me as would a father his long lost son. He
talked very kindly. Said he, " I have no doubt that all
the States will by and by see it to be for their *interest* to
do away slavery—for a *free* man will work faster, strike
truer, bring it down harder, and work with more spirit
and zeal, than a slave who *gets nothing* for his toils.
One man in the East, will do as much as ten of our men
(slaves) here," &c. He spoke very beautifully.

Again, speaking of their contentedness and good treatment, he added, with emphasis, " But they are not *free*,
and every man who has a soul, ought to be free," &c.

The next day, we took boat and bade farewell to the
prison, and the land of cruelty and oppression.

TIME OF IMPRISONMENT.

	Years.	Months.	Days.
Alanson was a prisoner,	3	6	7
James, " "	4	6	17
George, ". "	4	11	12
Total,	13	0	5

All this amount of time, labor, and suffering, stands
entered in high heaven's ledger against Missouri.—For
it she must account, and it she must repay—she cannot
cast off the bill.

What we have given, suffered, and done, we regret not. We gave it to the slave and to God, and He will make a wise and proper use of it. Yet Missouri must meet it all, at the solemn reckoning day.

FAREWELL REFLECTIONS, ON THE BOAT WAPOOLA.

The time I have spent in Jefferson seems like a dream of yesterday. How quickly the years have fled away! The good Lord forgive my misimprovement of them—that I have been so dull to learn his lessons, and have reaped so little profit from the kind dispensations of his hand, which has meted out to us the whole in love.

Farewell! rugged hills, over which I have so often carried my heavy chain; up and down which I have dragged my weary limbs along, and whose blooming herbage and refreshing groves have so long mocked my seclusion; farewell.

Farewell! ye huge walls, iron grates, doors, locks, bars, dungeons, cells. Long did ye trifle with my misery, and deride my wishful looks, and ardent desires, for sweet liberty. Long, long, ye held me fast, and would not let me go, but now your power is broken; your prisoner is free.

Farewell! excessive toils which crushed me to the earth. Farewell! oppressors, cruel masters, tyrants: farewell.

Ye fellow prisoners, farewell. With you I have long toiled, suffered, groaned, bled. Many of you I have warned, invited, counselled. Some of you I have comforted, encouraged, cheered, strengthened, and led to Jesus. Together we prayed, together sang. The Lord has called us to part, perhaps to meet no more in time; farewell. But, though I say farewell, I cannot forget you. O no, I shall think, talk, and pray for you. I love you. I know the heart of a prisoner. But be patient; farewell.

Farewell! ye who looked and pitied, but could not help; who thought and wept, but could not relieve: who loved and sympathized, but could not rescue; who talked and prayed and urged; who gave a willing shoulder with my aged father, and to your great joy saw me come forth a *free man ;* who tendered me the hearty shake, the open doors, and the liberal supply of my wants. The Lord reward you according to your " will-ing mind," for all you have done, or would have done for a " little one."

" The Lord hath done great things for us, whereof we are glad." " It is the Lord's doing, and it is marvellous in our eyes,"—to Him be glory. " O magnify the Lord with me, and let us exalt his name together." " The young lions may lack, and suffer hunger, but they who seek the Lord, shall want no good thing." " There shall no evil happen to the just."

O! blessed promise ! to the righteous given,
While up and down this cruel world they're driven.
It cheers their hearts, supports them in distress.
And as for me, let others curse or bless,
Believe this soul-reviving word, *I must,*
" There shall no evil happen to the Just.'

CONCLUSION.

Reader, I have written a book and told you many things—but yet, " the half has not been told you." You will learn the rest at the judgment, when all things shall be revealed.

Now are you in prosperity? Will you be thankful, and improve your privileges and opportunities, before they are taken from you, and you learn the worth, by the want of them?

" Work while it is day," and " walk while you have the light."

Are you in affliction? From what you have read, be encouraged to put your whole trust in God, and earth and hell united, cannot harm you.

Had I a voice so strong and loud,
To reach from east and west,
I'd say to all with sorrows bow'd,
" The will of Christ is best."

Whatever your affliction, submit to God, and He won't

hurt you. Friends may forsake—foes gather round, the
elements combine against you, and all nature threaten
your destruction—" Have faith in God," and you shall
stand unmoved. " Be not afraid, only believe."

Are you in a state of impenitency? " Prepare to
meet your God."

Are you a slaveholder? " Break every yoke, and let
the oppressed go free."

Are you an apologist for slavery? " When thou saw-
est a thief, then thou consentedst with him, and hast
been partaker with adulterers."

Are you one who refuses to take an active part against
oppression in all its forms? " Open thy mouth for the
dumb, in the cause of all such as are appointed to
destruction. *Open thy mouth*, and plead the cause
of the poor and needy," or God will hold you as an
enemy.

Are you a Christian? " Thou shalt *in any wise* rebuke thy neighbor, and not suffer sin upon him." " Be
not partakers of other men's sins." " Keep thyself
pure." See that the blood of the souls of " the poor
innocents" is not on your garments. " Love thy neighbor as thyself." " As ye would that men should do to
you, do ye even so to them." And remember, that
" whosoever stoppeth his ears at the cry of the *poor*,
shall also cry himself, and shall not be heard."

Are you a minister of the covenant? " Lift up thy
voice like a trumpet—cry aloud, and spare not—show
my people their sins." If thou refuse to warn the
wicked of this way, he shall die, but his blood will I
require at thy hands."

Wo to him who holds his peace, in such a day as
this!

Wo to him who pleads for wickedness, in this day
of light!

Wo to him who calls good, evil—and evil, good, in
the nineteenth century!

Wo to him who opposes the onward march of liberty
and righteousness!

Wo to him who will not " cease to do evil, and learn to do well."

Wo, wo, to him who will not " *remember them in bonds as bound with them !*"

Finally, whosoever has an ear, let it be open to the *truth*—an eye, let it search for the *truth*—a heart, let it receive and obey the TRUTH. Whosoever has a pen, let him use it—and a tongue, let him employ it in opposing Slavery—the " Mother of Abominations" in our land.

Reader, farewell, till we meet at the Judgment.

CPSIA information can be obtained at www.ICGtesting.com
Printed in the USA
BVOW04s2311270714

360674BV00024B/424/P